Trafficking Trajectories

PENNSYLVANIA STUDIES IN HUMAN RIGHTS

Series editor: Bert B. Lockwood

A complete list of books in the series is available from the publisher.

Trafficking Trajectories

Vulnerability, Failed Systems, and the Case for Prevention

Alicia W. Peters

PENN

UNIVERSITY OF PENNSYLVANIA PRESS

PHILADELPHIA

Published by
University of Pennsylvania Press
Philadelphia, Pennsylvania 19104-4112
www.pennpress.org

Printed in the United States of America on acid-free paper

10 9 8 7 6 5 4 3 2 1

A Cataloging-in-Publication record is available from the Library of Congress.

Hardcover ISBN 9781512827835
Ebook ISBN 9781512827880

To all the survivors who shared a bit of themselves
with me in hopes of something better

In memory of my father, James W. Peters

CONTENTS

PREFACE

When I began the ethnographic fieldwork for this project in 2016, the book I imagined would result was very different from the book I now have written. The research began as a follow-up project to my first book, *Responding to Human Trafficking: Sex, Gender, and Culture in the Law*, an ethnographic account of the early implementation of the U.S. Trafficking Victims Protection Act and its effects on survivors.[1] The fieldwork behind that book had been conducted in New York City and Washington, D.C., between 2006 and 2008. After relocation for a faculty position at the University of New England, the data gathering for the current book took place three hundred miles away—in Maine and New Hampshire—and exactly a decade later. With that timing and those locations, I was able to examine how the U.S. response to trafficking had evolved and expanded from major urban areas and agricultural centers to more peripheral parts of the country.

When my fieldwork began in 2016, the goal was to investigate how law enforcement officials understood human trafficking and to see how their conceptions of gender and commercial sex work affected their identification of victims, especially in areas with low numbers of documented cases. I wanted to know, did law enforcement's level of understanding have any ramifications for trafficked persons? Accessing survivors had been a challenge during my original research, so at first I reluctantly limited interviews to frontline workers in the human trafficking response, including law enforcement officials, service providers, and advocates. As I began the research, however, people kept asking me whether I planned to talk to survivors. They offered to make introductions and connections, and it quickly became clear that the access issues I had faced a decade earlier would not be a problem. Survivor perspectives are so important for understanding the successes and challenges of the official response to trafficking. Ethnography is always an iterative process, and so my research focus evolved to put survivors firmly at the center.

As I spoke to frontline workers and survivors about the challenges they faced, I increasingly drew on my background in medical anthropology and public health to complement the critical feminist lens I was already using. Along with other colleagues in the trafficking field, I began to scrutinize further the lack of prevention in the U.S. human trafficking response. And so I revised my plans to focus on two interrelated research questions: (1) When localities attempt to address trafficking through criminal law, what are the implications for trafficked persons? And (2) how do survivors experience vulnerability before, during, and after trafficking?

I am a native Mainer, and conducting this research close to home forced me to consider my positionality in new ways and to revisit engaged anthropology's attention to critical reflexivity.[2] In my previous work I wrote about the harm caused by groups trying to shift the U.S. human response from one focused on all victims of trafficking (regardless of their citizenship status or the labor sector in which trafficking took place) to a more dedicated focus on "domestic trafficking" of U.S. citizen girls and women into forced commercial sex by embracing racist, anti-immigrant narratives and a "not in my backyard" mentality.[3] Anti-prostitution feminists have long attempted to conflate consensual commercial sex with human trafficking, and their strategies have contributed to an overwhelming focus on sex trafficking to the exclusion of other types of forced labor in the U.S. In part a result of these efforts, the primary population being identified in New England is cisgender women with substance use disorder who are domestically trafficked for commercial sex work. That reality forced me to confront my own biases around domestic trafficking and to consider the nuances involved.

The foreign-born survivors living in New York City who participated in my previous research endured truly horrific experiences, and many faced immense challenges in accessing the benefits they were entitled to under the U.S. Trafficking Victims Protection Act, or TVPA.[4] Despite the close connections I had formed with some of those survivors, there was still a chasm between their experiences and my own. The small-town feel of Maine and New Hampshire was a real contrast to the anonymity afforded by New York City. Conducting my fieldwork in New York, my informants were only a train ride away, but in most cases our connection began and ended with geography.

Unlike my earlier work, which progressed through professional networks, this research grew from my initial connections through personal networks. A friend I met during a birthing class worked in the field. I received a referral to a key figure in the social service world through my acupuncturist. My neighbor is a retired Homeland Security investigator and referred me to several of his former colleagues who investigated trafficking cases. Having lived in Maine for twenty-five years, my parents connected me with a high-ranking government official whom they knew socially and who was committed to the trafficking issue. These small-world connections emerged over and over, usually with much closer proximity than the fabled six degrees of separation. Once I began interviewing survivors, I realized that I frequented a bakery where one of my informants had worked during her escalating drug use and that we had likely crossed paths during that time. A good friend's divorce attorney I learned, was also the attorney for another one of the survivors I interviewed.

A community of 68,000 can feel incredibly small. After speaking with a caseworker in my home city of Portland, Maine, I connected the dots and realized that one of the survivors I was meant to interview was the aunt of one of my daughter's closest preschool friends. I felt crushed—not out of fear for my own family or even my daughter's friend, who I knew to be quite safe, but for the trauma faced by those in my community. The abuses I was studying were no longer something completely outside of my own experience. They were actually part of my social world. Maine was the state I grew up in and New Hampshire was a short drive up I-95. The survivors I encountered could have been my high school classmates a couple of decades earlier. Indeed, several frontline workers whom I interviewed had encountered their own former schoolmates in the work they did. Almost all of them were victims of the opioid crisis. We were all cognizant that the combination of the lack of a social safety net and inadequate systems have made trafficking part of our community's reality.

My mindset shifted in another way early on, when I conducted two interviews just a few hours apart. The first was with a survivor advocate who bemoaned the federal definition of trafficking that determines who is entitled to comprehensive case management and other benefits, and who is not. Many of the women she worked with who identified as survivors of exploitation were excluded because they had not experienced the force, fraud, or coercion that federal law requires. She expressed frustration that the local agency designated by the federal government to provide those services was not able to help these women. They were not technically trafficked but certainly were vulnerable to trafficking due to their circumstances, and they did not qualify for any other services. My next interviewee that day was the director of a federally funded social service program for survivors of trafficking who offered a different perspective. She acknowledged the gap in coverage but told me that a number of organizations around the country provided services to individuals who were not qualified based on the federal human trafficking definition. At the same time, recipients who did meet the federal standard and had immense needs but perhaps did not fit the "typical victim" mold of the young, white, sex trafficking victim were unable to receive the services they so desperately required.

The juxtaposition of these two perspectives struck me. I have always agreed with the second position. Indeed, my previous research showed the ways that an overwhelming focus on sex trafficking, as well as noncoercive commercial sex, within the U.S. human trafficking response led to many authentic trafficking survivors, who had experienced some of the worst forms of abuse, being overlooked and unable to access the protections they were entitled to under the law.[5] At the same time, I started to see more clearly the perspective of my first interviewee and to internalize the needs of those on the margins who occupy the spaces where prevention is most needed.

The current threshold for survivor assistance is important in the face of limited resources. Theoretically, it ensures those experiencing the worst forms of harm have access to much-needed services. As medical anthropologist Paul Farmer asserted, "all suffering isn't equal" and there are varying degrees of "hose-edness."[6] But what became clear to me as I did the research for this book was that the survivors I interviewed were all in dire straits *before* they met the definition of survivors of severe forms of trafficking—*before* they would qualify for federally funded services. Economic insecurity combined with lack of access to safe and affordable housing, health care, substance use disorder treatment, and other essential services made them vulnerable to trafficking in the first place, and then prevented them from leaving the situation once they were in it.

At the same time, interventionist criminal legal and victim assistance approaches often failed to adequately address the cycle of vulnerability impacting the lives of those trafficked and those not-quite-trafficked. For this reason, in the pages that follow, I make the case for shifting the U.S. human trafficking response from an interventionist to a prevention-centered framework that belies the need for a system of services conditioned on meeting a definition that is itself inherently flawed.[7] The prevention-oriented approach this book advocates is centered around providing resources and strengthening systems. By addressing structural vulnerability in areas including housing, health care, and drug treatment, as well as in all labor sectors—that is in both sex and non-sex-related sectors—individuals will be positioned to live stable and secure lives, and workers can achieve greater choice and control over their labor.

CHAPTER 1

A Call for Change

> Human trafficking . . . disproportionately impacts people that are already marginalized by structural and institutional violence and marginalization. . . . It is the absolute direct result of poverty, of capitalism, of globalization. . . . Ultimately the challenge of how we approach it is that we've codified it as a crime first and a social justice problem second. . . . If you're looking at it as a problem of poverty that disproportionately impacts poor people, you would never say, "This is a law enforcement based problem, and we should send law enforcement in to solve it."
>
> —May, Policy Advocate

On a yearly basis, the U.S. Department of Justice puts out more than a hundred press releases related to the conviction or sentencing of individuals for federal crimes related to sex trafficking across the United States.[1] The 2019 press release dated March 25 (see Figure 1) applauds a conviction for the sex trafficking of a minor in New Hampshire.[2] While the setting is particular, the document follows a common script, reflecting key characteristics of the U.S. response to human trafficking.

The press release illustrates the centrality of the criminal legal system in the U.S. response.[3] It quotes Assistant Attorney General Eric Dreiband stating, "The Civil Rights Division and its Human Trafficking Prosecution Unit will continue its vigorous efforts to work with our federal and state

Department of Justice

Office of Public Affairs

FOR IMMEDIATE RELEASE Monday, March 25, 2019

Defendant Who Exploited Opioid Addictions of Young Women Convicted of Crimes Related to Drug Trafficking and Prostitution

After a three-day trial, a federal jury in Concord, New Hampshire, found Steven Tucker, 33, of Manchester, New Hampshire, guilty on March 22 of one count of sex trafficking of a minor and of using interstate facilities to promote a prostitution business enterprise and maintaining a drug-involved premise. The verdict was announced by Assistant Attorney General Eric Dreiband for the Department of Justice's Civil Rights Division, U.S. Attorney Scott W. Murray for the District of New Hampshire, and Peter C. Fitzhugh, Special Agent in Charge, U.S. Immigration and Customs Enforcement's Homeland Security Investigations, Boston.

Evidence presented at trial established that, between October 2013 and June 2014, the defendant operated drug and prostitution businesses in the Manchester area. He sold heroin to numerous individuals, including young women and a minor. Witnesses described how the defendant used their addictions to cause them to prostitute for his profit. The defendant would often front heroin to the women and then arrange prostitution "dates" for them. The women were required to give the defendant half of the proceeds and then purchase heroin from him with the remainder.

On other occasions, the defendant withheld heroin from the women, causing them to suffer painful withdrawal symptoms, and then instructed them to prostitute to earn money to purchase heroin from him. The defendant's scheme guaranteed that he had a steady source of drug customers and money. Some of the women were required to help the defendant sell his heroin and received heroin in exchange. The defendant used violence and threats to maintain control of the women. The investigation began in 2014, when the mother of one of the women called the Manchester Police Department after the defendant beat her daughter.

"Motivated by greed, the defendant preyed on young, vulnerable women, selling them heroin, exploiting their addictions, and prostituting them for his own profit," said Assistant Attorney General Eric Dreiband. "The Civil Rights Division and its Human Trafficking Prosecution Unit will continue its vigorous efforts to work with our federal and state partners to hold human traffickers accountable, vindicate the rights of their victims, and eradicate this despicable and inhumane exploitation from our country."

"This case demonstrates the power of opioids to support criminal activity," said U.S. Attorney Scott W. Murray. "This defendant took advantage of young women, using heroin and violence to induce them to commit acts of prostitution for his personal profit. His conduct was even more disturbing because he victimized a minor. We will continue to work closely with the New Hampshire Human Trafficking Collaborative Task Force and all of our law enforcement partners to identify, arrest and prosecute those who engage in this type of unlawful and exploitive activity."

Figure 1. U.S. Department of Justice press release (excerpt). "Defendant Who Exploited Opioid Addictions of Young Women Convicted of Crimes Related to Drug Trafficking and Prostitution," March 25, 2003, https://www.justice.gov/opa/pr/defendant-who-exploited-opioid-addictions-young-women-convicted-crimes-related-drug.

partners to hold human traffickers accountable, vindicate the rights of their victims, and eradicate this despicable and inhumane exploitation from our country." The statement goes on to invoke U.S. Attorney Scott W. Murray, who praises the continued role of law enforcement partners "to identify, arrest and prosecute those who engage in this type of unlawful and exploitative activity."[4]

The press release strongly upholds the dominant, triangular human trafficking narrative, which political scientist Erin O'Brien distills to "A trafficking victim. A villain. A hero."[5] The story introduces a trafficker "motivated by greed" (the villain) who "preyed on young, vulnerable women" (the victims) who have been freed by the "vigorous efforts" of law enforcement investigators (the heroes). The primary victim fits the ideal mold: she is a young, vulnerable, cisgender female.[6] Despite the fact that under U.S. law human trafficking victims can be of any age and that the press release refers to multiple women, the only human trafficking conviction in this case involved a single count of sex trafficking of a minor.[7] The older women involved presumably did not make good victim witnesses: they lacked the innocence of youth and were addicted to heroin. They were likely viewed as victim-offenders rather than as "ideal" victims. Something the press release does not mention is that the perpetrator is Black, and his victims presumably are white, replicating a commonly racialized component of the human trafficking narrative. The omission obscures the racial inequalities that are built into the human trafficking response.

This public announcement suggests that the criminal legal approach will ultimately prevent and "eradicate" trafficking. A second press release related to the perpetrator's sentencing (see Figure 2) suggests that prosecution of traffickers will deter others and eventually serve to eliminate trafficking, failing to acknowledge the need for prevention at the level of root causes before human trafficking actually occurs. Acting U.S. Attorney John Farley of the District of New Hampshire is quoted as saying, "The substantial sentence imposed today finally holds Mr. Tucker [the trafficker] responsible for his actions and sends a clear message to the community that this conduct will not be tolerated." On the one hand, the sentencing press release makes a nod to the role of structural vulnerability in the lives of survivors, including a reference by Assistant Attorney General Kristen Clarke of the Justice Department's Civil Rights Division to the victims as "young women and teenage girls living in the shadows and on the margins."[8] At the same time, however, the broader language puts human trafficking in simplistic terms, as an interpersonal crime committed by an evil trafficker against innocent victims. This framing ignores the more complex and nuanced reality and fails to address the role of structural violence and inadequate systems as fundamental causes. Trafficking survivors rarely see the prosecution and punishment of their traffickers as a path to justice and, instead, prioritize prevention and healing—none of this broader context is reflected in either press release.[9]

While it is no surprise that the U.S. Department of Justice would emphasize the criminal legal approach given its mission to uphold the rule of law, the construal of trafficking within these two documents tells us that the nation prioritizes prosecution and punishment of traffickers over victim protection and prevention. In name at least, prevention is part of the federal government's 3P's paradigm to address human trafficking through prosecution, protection, and prevention.[10] While the name would suggest the 3P's are equally important methods in the fight against trafficking, in reality the order reflects implicit levels of prioritization. Since the passage of the Trafficking Victims Protection Act in 2000, the U.S. response has focused overwhelmingly on the first P (prosecution) through a criminal legal response centered on investigation and prosecution of the crime of trafficking.[11] Victim protection has

"The Civil Rights Division is committed to pursuing justice on behalf of vulnerable members of our society," said Assistant Attorney General Kristen Clarke of the Justice Department's Civil Rights Division. "This defendant preyed on young women and teenage girls living in the shadows and on the margins. He cruelly exploited their drug addictions for his own profit. This sentence sends a clear message that the United States will not tolerate human trafficking and will work tirelessly to restore the rights and dignity of its victims."

"By exploiting and trafficking multiple victims, including a minor, this defendant committed egregious and reprehensible crimes," said Acting U.S. Attorney John Farley of the District of New Hampshire. "The substantial sentence imposed today finally holds Mr. Tucker responsible for his actions and sends a clear message to the community that this conduct will not be tolerated. We will continue to work with our law enforcement partners and members of the New Hampshire Human Trafficking Collaborative Task Force to combat the human trafficking in the Granite State."

"Today's sentence brings to a conclusion one of the most disturbing cases of exploitative treatment of human trafficking victims that we have seen," said William S. Walker, acting Special Agent in Charge, Homeland Security Investigations, Boston. "Mr. Tucker's trial of harm and pain will unfortunately live within his victims for years to come, but, hopefully, they will take solace in knowing that the sentence imposed upon Mr. Tucker today effectively prevents him from causing more physical and psychological trauma to future victims. HSI was pleased to partner in this case with the New Hampshire Human Trafficking Collaborative Task Force, the U.S. Attorney's Office for the District of New Hampshire, the Department of Justice Civil Rights Division's Human Trafficking Prosecution Unit, the Manchester Police Department and the Hillsborough County Attorney's Office. Without the tireless work of these partners, Mr. Tucker's victims would never have had even the opportunity to achieve any measure of justice while continuing the healing process."

Figure 2. U.S. Department of Justice press release (excerpt). "New Hampshire Man Sentenced to 21 Years in Prison for Sex Trafficking of a Minor and Other Crimes." June 25, 2021, https://www.justice.gov/opa/pr/new-hampshire-man-sentenced-21-years-prison-sex-trafficking-minor-and-other-crimes.

played a secondary role in the government's strategy; prevention has never been a funding priority or a central pillar in the response.[12]

As policy advocate May states, the U.S. (along with the larger international community) has established human trafficking as a crime issue first and foremost, to be addressed through the criminal legal system.[13] But after more than twenty years of this approach, why has nothing been done to address the root causes of trafficking? Human trafficking is the result of vulnerabilities that go unaddressed, including poverty and income inequality; the lack of safe, secure, and affordable housing; inequitable access to quality health and mental health care; insufficient availability of accessible and low barrier treatment for substance use disorder; lack of supports for LGBTQIA+ youth; and a flawed immigration system, among others.[14] Trafficking is a symptom of larger social challenges—the conditions that make people vulnerable to trafficking in the first place and that motivate individuals to view exploiting the labor of others for their own profit as a legitimate form of moneymaking. The problem is that it is not as compelling to address structural poverty as it is to claim to be fighting human trafficking. What gets forgotten is that addressing inequality and all the issues that come along with it is what prevents trafficking. You can't arrest, prosecute, rescue, or raid your way out of trafficking—the contributing factors will persist.

The Book's Focus

As an entry into the scholarly and more public conversations around trafficking, this book has two main goals. First, it aims to center the experiences of domestic sex trafficking survivors in the U.S. and to highlight the role of structural violence and vulnerability before, during, and after trafficking. The dominant trafficking narrative of victims and villains decontextualizes and isolates the period of victimization and rescue from broader experiences of vulnerability. To upend that narrative, I focus on *trafficking trajectories*—the ways that structural vulnerability affects and constrains survivor experiences in complex ways over time—not only during, but also prior to and following trafficking. As I will describe, the period of trafficking is sometimes not the worst chapter in a survivor's life, but rather one among many traumatic experiences resulting from a series of ongoing injustices.

Second, drawing on ethnographic interviews with survivors, advocates, and frontline workers engaged in the human trafficking response, the book illustrates how the current, primarily criminal legal, approach fails to adequately address trafficking.[15] The U.S. response is overwhelmingly interventionist, meaning it does not address root causes and therefore does not prevent trafficking. Using critical medical anthropology and public health frameworks to examine structural inequality, the book highlights the specific areas where inadequate systems create vulnerability and presents opportunities to disrupt patterns of harm. Reframing trafficking as structural violence instead of as interpersonal violence requiring criminal legal intervention recognizes the compounding factors that contribute to trafficking over time. That's why I make the case for moving beyond addressing only the proximal causes of trafficking—traffickers exploiting the addictions of young women in order to coerce them into commercial sex work for their own profit. Prioritizing prevention means addressing the fundamental root causes that often remain long after trafficking: economic insecurity; inequitable access to education; lack of safe and affordable housing; inadequate health care, including mental health care and drug treatment, among others.[16]

The U.S. human trafficking response includes strategies and funding to prosecute traffickers and protect survivors, but there is no substantive plan to actually prevent trafficking in the first place.[17] Criminal legal, victim services, and outreach strategies all focus on intervention—arresting traffickers and sex buyers, removing survivors from coercive living conditions, and providing victim services for survivors—as opposed to prevention. However important, reactionary approaches like these identify people after trafficking has already occurred, leaving the structural factors that promote exploitation in place. Both law enforcement investigators and victim service providers struggle to address the needs of survivors and to provide meaningful solutions to the vulnerabilities they face. In contrast to the reactive interventionist approach, a proactive public health approach to trafficking would move "upstream" to identify and intervene at the level of root causes.[18] That is where this book comes in—shining a light on the structural violence that harms marginalized individuals and identifying where prevention is most needed and would be most effective at decreasing the vulnerabilities that contribute to trafficking.

International human rights legal scholar Ann Jordan argues that it is essential to focus more resources on participatory research "with persons whose lives are affected in order to understand (a) the root causes that push people to make decisions involving dangerous migration and/or risky employment and (b) structural impediments to safe migration and safe working conditions" and to use this evidence to develop programs, policies, and laws to address the conditions and systems that make people vulnerable to trafficking.[19] With this approach in mind, the narratives in this book spotlight the trajectories of survivors of human trafficking before, during, and after trafficking. Cisgender women with substance use disorder constitute the primary population that is being identified and receiving services in the northern New England region of the United States, though certainly they are not the only group being trafficked in the area.[20] Accounts of trafficking often focus on the crime itself and the point of identification or intervention, and they often end there. By sharing these women's stories, this book seeks to broaden the lens and shed light on survivor experiences prior to trafficking—that is, everything that made these individuals vulnerable to trafficking in the first place. Those vulnerabilities often continue during trafficking and remain long after the trafficking has ended, increasing the chances of re-trafficking.

Early in my research, I presented at an event alongside a trafficking services provider who said, "Human trafficking is the result of failed systems." That insight has guided my understanding of the dynamics of trafficking ever since. All the survivors I interviewed ended up in the trafficking situation because of an unmet need and a lack of resources to address that need, and this became abundantly clear as I spoke with survivors themselves, as well as with the caseworkers and law enforcement investigators who were witnessing the effects firsthand. The biggest unmet needs that survivors, caseworkers, and criminal legal officials cited were housing and treatment for substance use disorder, and the two were often intertwined. Over and over again, I heard examples of these unmet needs arising before, during, and after trafficking. It became clear that while these unmet needs prevented people from leaving the trafficking situation, interventionist criminal legal and victim assistance approaches also often failed to address these vulnerabilities. The rich, nuanced accounts of survivors combined with the observations and quandaries faced by frontline workers reveal opportunities for rethinking and broadening the response to trafficking to make it more effective and prevention focused.

Contextualizing the Project

The Human Trafficking Narrative

This book builds on more than two decades of critical feminist and social science scholarship on human trafficking and sex work, including analysis of U.S. anti-trafficking legislative history,[21] the prioritizing of criminal legal goals over protecting victim rights,[22] challenges surrounding implementation of human trafficking law,[23] the social construction of trafficking,[24] the racialized history of trafficking,[25] the conflation of sex work and trafficking,[26] and the disproportionate focus on trafficking for forced commercial sex.[27]

As I seek to center survivor experiences and examine the effects of the human trafficking response on those it is intended to protect, I am indebted to anthropologists and sociologists who have provided ethnographic accounts of individuals affected by the anti-trafficking apparatus,[28] working in and exiting commercial sex work,[29] living with substance use disorder,[30] and moving in and out of incarceration.[31] Denise Brennan's account of survivors' post-trafficking experiences, *Life Interrupted: Trafficking into Forced Labor in the United States*, is especially poignant in its examination of the state policies that put people at risk for trafficking and the challenges of navigating systems after their abuse.[32] Brennan's book powerfully contests the dominant human trafficking discourse and unmasks the structural factors contributing to the trafficking of migrant laborers in the United States.

Over the past two decades a human trafficking narrative has taken hold that constructs the issue narrowly and runs counter to the realities on the ground.[33] "The dominant antitrafficking discourse is not evidence-based," Gozdziak and Bump write, "but [rather] grounded in the construction of a particular mythology of trafficking."[34] This mythology tells the story of cisgender women being trafficked for commercial sex work, often conflated with movement into prostitution regardless of the presence of force or coercion.[35] The narrative depends on an ideal victim who is portrayed as young, innocent, and sexually naive who is lured into the sex trade against her will.[36] This ideal victim often comes to be understood as the typical victim through media representations and our cultural views about sex, gender, and victimization.[37] This ideal victim stands in paradox to actual victims who may be youth, but often are adults of any gender who have been coerced or compelled into a variety of labor sectors. Even the cisgender women forced into commercial sex work make for imperfect victims in that many initially enter sex work uncoerced, or as a way to meet the needs of an addiction, and only later become trafficked.[38]

The innocent ideal victim is one of a larger cast of characters on which the myth relies. An evil trafficker serves as the villain and a valiant rescuer, usually a member of law enforcement, is the hero.[39] The narrative is also gendered and racialized.[40] Much like late-nineteenth and early twentieth-century constructions of so-called white slavery, the current victims of domestic trafficking are assumed to be white, heterosexual, cisgender women or girls, while the trafficker is always a foreign, Black, or brown male.[41] The narrative dominates media coverage and public awareness campaigns and shapes government responses to the issue. "Stories of human trafficking are powerful and compelling," Erin O'Brien notes, "not just because of the horrors of exploitation they describe, but because they employ a narrative code to convey information in a simple, and immediately understandable, format."[42] Melodramatic narratives of trafficking compete with broader definitions of trafficking under the law and gain ascendency.[43] The effect is that understandings of trafficking among the general public, and also among policymakers and law enforcement investigators, often lack the nuance and complexity of what trafficking really looks like and the ways it affects the actual human beings who get caught up in it.[44] The idea that there is one type of typical or ideal victim leads to individuals who do not fit this profile being overlooked, including men, LGBTQIA+ individuals, BIPOC survivors, and those trafficked in other labor sectors, as well as those who don't appear totally innocent or don't present as "deserving."[45] Misguided and ineffective prevention and intervention strategies result—training flight attendants to racially profile passengers as a way to identify trafficking, for example.[46]

A growing body of empirical work has emerged to challenge this overly simplistic narrative. For example, Alexandra Lutnick's *Domestic Minor Sex Trafficking: Beyond Victims and Villains* sheds light on the complex realities of minors involved in the sex trades. Lutnick finds that their experiences contest the victim/villain binary and that broader systems contribute to their vulnerability.[47] The matrix of agency and vulnerability offered in Carissa Showden and Samantha Majic's *Youth Who Trade Sex in the U.S.: Intersec-*

tionality, Agency, and Vulnerability counters the three-character drama as well.[48] Nonetheless, the human trafficking narrative persists. It remains the primary lens through which the phenomenon is viewed, and it often shapes the ways in which the human trafficking response is implemented.[49] Framing the trafficking issue as one of interpersonal violence sets the stage for a criminal legal response that punishes individual evil traffickers rather than questioning the structural factors and the failure of policies and systems.[50] As a result, other solutions remain invisible. By adding to efforts to scrutinize the dominant narrative, this book is designed to refocus attention on the structural contributors to trafficking.

Gender, Race, and Intersectional Oppression

The power and endurance of the human trafficking narrative is evident both in the ways that it has persisted over time and in how it has generated resistance to alternative ways of understanding and responding to the issue. Neither the phenomenon of trafficking nor the narrative is new. The term *trafficking* alludes to the late-nineteenth and early twentieth-century "traffic in women," also known as "white slavery," and that history informs the current framing of the issue. In an analysis of one of the very first instances of the human trafficking narrative, historian Judith Walkowitz details how W. T. Stead, editor of the *Pall Mall Gażette*, published a sensational series of exposés of young women being abducted, drugged, and exploited via prostitution in Victorian London. While, or perhaps on account of, many of the details being exaggerated around the role of children in the sex trade and the recruitment tactics used, the series gripped readers and generated a frenzy of attention among "a loose network of campaigning groups, populist, feminist, and nationalist in their political zeal . . . dedicated to eradicating vice and imposing a single standard of chastity on men and women."[51] Reforms and changes to criminal law resulted, including increasing the age of consent and targeting brothel owners and sex workers. A resulting "massive political initiative against nonmarital, nonreproductive sexuality was mobilized, whose initial victims were working-class prostitutes, precisely those women who had been the original objects of concern for Stead."[52] The newspaper's account obscured the fact that most of the young women involved in prostitution had chosen that line of work and had not been drugged or physically coerced, yet Stead's writing style, as Greta Wendelin notes, "isolated sexuality from the material and economic structures that shaped the lives of the young British maidens that he was so intent on saving."[53] Stead's melodramatic narrative of passive, innocent female victims and evil male aggressors set the stage for an ongoing series of decontextualized tales of trafficking.

The narrative made its way across the Atlantic as a similar panic arose around white slavery in the U.S. context. Here too white slavery campaigns depicted young, naïve, innocent women lured and kidnapped by evil foreign traffickers into inescapable circumstances. White slavery took on a variety of meanings—from any involvement in the sex trades, to crossing international borders for the purpose of sex work, to the forceful abduction and transport of women for commercial sex—and reflected deeper fears and anxieties about women's sexuality and independence, the breakdown of the family, migration, and racial and national purity. Jo Doezema argues that so-called white slavery was largely mythical and very few actual cases were reported. Rather, stories of white slavery were triggered by the increasing number of women, including prostitutes, migrating from Europe to find work in the U.S.[54] Once again, a series of criminal laws emerged, including the White Slave Traffic Act of 1910 (also known as the Mann Act), which, though aimed at protecting women, actually largely targeted and prosecuted consenting sex workers, many of them immigrant women.[55]

At the turn of the twenty-first century as reports of both sexual and nonsexual forced labor grew, a gendered and racialized narrative resurfaced, and the same framings that dominated concerns about white slavery infuse current approaches to human trafficking. Within the U.S., the Trafficking Victims Protection Act (TVPA) was passed in 2000 to address the very real abuses of people of all ages, races, ethnicities, and genders doing work in all labor sectors, though in practice U.S. anti-trafficking policy has focused on the "typical victim" with criminal legal responses as the only imagined solution. This has resulted in the exclusion of other types of victims and in an inability to consider addressing the structural contributors to trafficking. As anthropologist Carole Vance argues, the current melodramatic human trafficking narrative, "virtually unchanged from its nineteenth-century versions," reduces trafficking to prostitution (forced or voluntary) involving a woman or female minor whose experience is one of sexual danger and injury. This compelling narrative Vance asserts, "displaces modern concepts of extreme labor exploitation and rights violations, replacing them with scripts of male lust endangering innocent women. It also replaces the trafficked person's claim to multiple rights with a single remedy, the right to be rescued."[56]

While well-intentioned, the vast majority of anti-trafficking initiatives remain highly gendered and racialized, ignoring the actual problems facing those who are most vulnerable to trafficking—migrants, BIPOC and LGBTQIA+ individuals, the unhoused, drug users, sex workers, and other marginalized groups—and resulting in ineffective and often harmful interventions as will be shown in the pages to follow.[57] The focus on sex and sex trafficking diverts attention away from larger issues within the capitalist labor system and obscures the need for safe working conditions, fair wages, and systems to report abuse. Current responses to trafficking also fail to recognize how historical context shapes social inequities. Vestiges of colonialism and slavery can still be seen in U.S. labor laws, such as the National Labor Relations Act that explicitly excluded agricultural and domestic workers in order to ensure that African American and migrant workers would not receive labor protections.[58] Migrant farmworkers and domestic workers, the vast majority of whom are Black, Hispanic, or Asian American and Pacific Islander, continue to lack the protections guaranteed to other types of workers, with women being especially vulnerable to workplace abuses on account of multiple forms of intersecting oppression rooted in systemic sexism, racism, and other systems of inequality.[59]

Human trafficking affects people in complicated ways and it is essential to consider how race, ethnicity, class, gender, sexual identity, ability, citizenship status, and other social characteristics intersect and compound experiences of discrimination and marginalization.[60] For example, Cassandra Mary Frances Gonzales notes that "Because of the construction of their bodies and sexuality, Black women and girls are not believable as victims but are easily believable as traffickers or prostitutes."[61] Ironically, the Mann Act, the law passed to address white slavery in 1910, is frequently used to charge survivors of trafficking, especially those who don't fit the typical victim profile, for crimes they are forced to commit while being trafficked.[62] The systemic failure of law enforcement to recognize Black women and girls as victims of human trafficking on account of racialization and hyper-sexualization means that fewer people of color receive the victim-centered services and resources that they are entitled to under the law.[63]

It is challenging to gather accurate estimates of trafficking due to the underground nature of the crime and the fact that punitive policies dissuade many victims from coming forward out of fear of arrest, deportation, and other harmful consequences, though data about who is identified, charged, and prosecuted for trafficking related crimes give some insight into the demographics of those affected. Black women are overrepresented as victims of sex trafficking (many likely identified through pathways outside of the criminal legal system) with Blacks representing 40 percent of victims compared to 26 percent being white.[64] The same holds true for prostitution arrests. In 2019, Black adults (primarily women, presumably) accounted for 42 percent and Black youth 51 percent of prostitution arrests in the U.S., though Blacks only make up about 12 percent of the U.S. population overall.[65] Similarly, LGBTQIA+ individuals who are also Black, Indigenous, or belong to other communities of color (BIPOC) face even higher levels of vulnerability on account of their oppression for being members of two marginalized communities. In addition to a higher risk of victimization, they face barriers to accessing services and resources to exit trafficking situations due to deeply engrained societal biases.[66]

An intersectional approach to trafficking problematizes the human trafficking narrative and considers how factors such as gender, race, citizenship status, and other systems of marginalization intersect and intensify oppression and invisibility. It also examines how other vulnerabilities such as being economically disadvantaged, disabled, or unhoused intersect with trafficking and compound both the needs of survivors and the barriers they face to achieving stability. Responses to trafficking must move beyond the sensational, decontextualized, and monolithic human trafficking narrative and approaches that primarily benefit white, cis, heterosexual, U.S. citizen, middle and upper-class women and girls.[67]

Problematizing the Criminal Legal Approach to Trafficking

Prioritizing the arrest, prosecution, and punishment of traffickers, the U.S. response to trafficking developed as a result of the passage of the Trafficking

Victims Protection Act, or TVPA, in 2000.[68] The carceral approach to trafficking emerged based on an alliance between anti-trafficking feminists, evangelical Christians, and neoconservative policymakers who worked collaboratively to advocate for harsher criminal penalties for human trafficking crimes, especially sex trafficking. Sociologist Elizabeth Bernstein's pioneering work has been essential in the critique of the criminal legal dimensions of the human trafficking response.[69] She coined the term *carceral feminism*, which she describes as "the commitment of abolitionist feminist activists to a law and order agenda and . . . a drift from the welfare state to the carceral state as the enforcement apparatus for feminist goals."[70] One of the primary successes of carceral feminists and other members of their coalition was the use of increased punitive state power—putting perpetrators in prison and imposing harsher sentences—as the primary means for addressing trafficking and other forms of violence against women.[71]

The carceral approach to human trafficking in its current form is multipronged and its goals include apprehending and punishing traffickers, as well as ending demand for prostitution by arresting customers, usually in the form of "John stings," and also arresting sex workers and potential victims of trafficking as a form of "rescue." Given the complexity of charging and prosecuting traffickers, more resources often are devoted to the second and third goals—stings and "rescue" operations. Partnerships between law enforcement investigators and social service providers often cause additional harm to potential victims. In *Control and Protect: Collaboration, Carceral Protection, and Domestic Minor Sex Trafficking in the United States*, gender studies scholar Jennifer Musto documents this and argues that the pattern of arresting potential victims as a form of "rescue" falls under what she terms carceral protectionism, an orientation to anti-trafficking efforts that blends the boundaries between punishment and protection. Musto explains that this process "can be understood as enforcement with a protective bent or carcerality inflicted with care." Noting that potential domestic trafficking victims are often viewed as victim-offenders, she argues that the strategies developed to assist them reflect this bifurcation.[72] I found many of the same policies that Musto describes as being used to "assist" youth, including arrest in the name of protection, are also used for adults, who are viewed as childlike and incapable of making informed choices in the trafficking context. Law enforcement investigators reported arresting women whom they believed to be in danger of overdosing and whom they suspected of engaging in commercial sex work, for example. Survivors in turn described how this pattern contributed to their distrust of law enforcement and unwillingness to report abuse.

An important consequence of addressing trafficking through a primarily criminal legal approach has been a tendency to focus on sexual harm and sex trafficking in isolation, with little attention to abuse in other labor sectors or to precipitating factors.[73] It has also resulted in deprioritizing human rights frameworks, including efforts to boost and protect migrant, labor, and sex worker rights. While trafficking can happen anywhere, it most often occurs in sectors that are unregulated or where worker protections are lacking, such as in agriculture, domestic work, and the sex trades. When efforts focus solely on identifying bad actors and on particular sectors like sex work, opportunities are missed to strengthen rights for all, decrease marginalization and exploitation, and prevent trafficking. For example, removing criminal penalties for sex work, and protecting rather than infringing on sex workers' rights, means that sex workers can report abuse of themselves and others and feel safer seeking help from law enforcement when needed. The same premise holds true in the agricultural context—disentangling migrant H2-A visas from a single employer would allow migrant farmworkers to seek alternative employment when abusive conditions arise.[74]

It is also important to note that the carceral approach to trafficking makes sense only within the context of mass incarceration and the effects it has on women and on Black, brown, LGBTQIA+, and other marginalized communities across the U.S. As Elizabeth Bernstein notes, increased law enforcement attention on trafficking has resulted in "an unprecedented police crackdown on people of color who are involved in the street-based sexual economy—including pimps, clients, and sex workers."[75] The arrest-as-protection strategy in particular correlates with the drastic increase of incarcerated women and girls over the last forty years. Between 1980 and 2021, the number of incarcerated women increased by more than 525 percent, and women are now more likely than men to be imprisoned for drug-related offenses.[76] Much like the War on Drugs, the War on Trafficking has shifted a social problem rooted in inequality into a criminal one that disproportionately punishes the most marginalized members of society while doing nothing to eliminate the problem (trafficking) itself.[77] Arrest and incarceration are used both as deterrents to trafficking and as rescue strategies for survivors, with little acknowledgement that these approaches contribute to vulnerability and, in fact, perpetuate the cycle of trafficking.

The goals of the so-called abolitionist feminists who advocated for the carceral approach to trafficking are quite at odds with those of feminists engaged in the prison abolition movement. Abolitionists equate the prison system to slavery and advocate for the end of the carceral state.[78] Activist Marlihan Lopez asserts that carceral feminism "ignores and leaves unchallenged the ways patriarchal and racialized violence is exercised through policing and prisons."[79] The rationale behind the carceral approach to trafficking is that the threat of punishment will dissuade perpetrators and stop trafficking, but more often it extends the reach of the criminal legal system and has the effect of harming trafficking survivors and those involved in the sex trade more broadly. For their part, prison abolitionists within the feminist movement advocate for nonpunitive, transformative, community-based responses rooted in care, such as investing in life-affirming social services. These same approaches are also vital to ending trafficking, but it has been difficult to gain traction for these types of strategies among policymakers. Oversimplified narratives dominate the media, and the misguided focus on individual bad actors as the source of the problem—as opposed to structural inequality and broken systems—stands in the way.

Nearly all government policy and much of the academic literature on trafficking construes the issue as one of interpersonal violence between trafficker and victim. This simplistic framing results in correspondingly simplistic solutions: arrest the Black/brown/foreign male perpetrator and save the innocent/white/young/cisgender female victim of sex trafficking. Effective prosecution of trafficking depends on selectively pursuing cases with ideal victims capable of serving as reliable witnesses.[80] In past research, I discovered that such cases are rare and perpetuate the narrative of the innocent victim and evil trafficker. Men of color may be convenient villains in the human trafficking melodrama, but this narrative obscures the true causes of trafficking and the state's role in perpetuating the violence of trafficking and inflicting structural violence upon marginalized communities.[81]

Millions of dollars have been spent to develop laws, train law enforcement, create task forces, and provide services to victims. The problem is that stricter laws and harsher sentencing of traffickers do nothing to improve economic conditions or to address the types of marginalization that create vulnerability. While the U.S. government's focus on criminal legal solutions to human trafficking has been successful in increasing the number of prosecutions, it has not been effective at stopping trafficking.[82] In actuality, the interventionist model has resulted in a stratified and inconsistent response from law enforcement.[83] Those from BIPOC, immigrant, and LGBTQIA+ communities or trafficked into other labor sectors are often overlooked—or worse, harmed—by anti-trafficking policies, as is often the case for sex workers who are targeted and arrested as part of sex trafficking investigations.[84] As I oft heard repeated by advocates and law enforcement officers alike over the course of conducting research for this project—"You can't arrest your way out of trafficking." The intersectional inequities of racism, gender inequality, economic insecurity, and other forms of marginalization create vulnerability for both the perpetrators of trafficking and those who are trafficked by them.[85]

The question becomes, if current criminal legal strategies are not stopping trafficking, why is the U.S. investing such vast resources in prosecution and corrections? What alternatives might we envision where those funds were reallocated toward safe and affordable housing, equitable access to education and medical care, community building, and developing policies that ensure rights and contribute to stability and well-being? In no way do I intend to downplay the effects of violence on individuals. Rather, I want to point to the power of prevention and the role of addressing root causes in order to eliminate trafficking. Complex problems like human trafficking require complex solutions. As Michelle Alexander asserts in her groundbreaking *The New Jim Crow*, "If we want to reduce violence in our communities, we need to hold people accountable in ways that aim to repair and prevent harm rather than simply inflicting more harm and trauma and calling it justice."[86]

Vulnerability, Structural Violence, and Prevention

Critical public health and medical anthropology have developed and embraced a number of frameworks to describe the effects of social inequality and structural vulnerability. These include the socioecological model,[87] social determinants of health,[88] social conditions as fundamental causes,[89] zones of abandonment,[90] hierarchies of embodied suffering,[91] and politically structured suffering.[92] The concept of social determinants of health has roots in the work of nineteenth-century German physician, pathologist, and anthropologist Rudolf Virchow who maintained that the most important causes of disease were the material conditions of people's lives. Based on his observations of the 1848 typhus epidemic, Virchow developed a theory of epidemics that emphasized the social contributors to disease and argued that prevention of similar outbreaks would require improvements in living conditions and the elimination of social inequality.[93] These ideas resurfaced in 1960s–1970s England with the efforts of epidemiologist Sir Michael Marmot and physician Sir Douglas Black. In particular, Marmot's famous Whitehall Studies demonstrated a steep inverse gradient between social class and mortality from a range of diseases. Understandings of social determinants of health have since expanded to include factors such as housing, access to healthcare, education, stigma, discrimination, and environmental conditions, among others, and have become central to public health prevention efforts.[94]

Drawing a distinction between proximal and fundamental causes of disease, medical sociologists and public health experts Bruce Link and Jo Phelan provide a model that contextualizes individual risk within a larger system of social factors. Their conception of proximal causes refers to individual-based risk factors, such as cholesterol level and history of smoking, that directly contribute to an individual's risk of developing a particular health condition. In contrast, fundamental causes are the social factors such as socioeconomic status and social support that embody access to resources and affect multiple disease outcomes. Having access to resources, Link and Phelan argue, helps individuals avoid risks and minimize the consequences of disease. Policies and interventions must address the social factors that contribute to the more commonly understood proximal causes in order to alter outcomes.[95] These same principles apply in the trafficking context in that an individual's social position either enables or constrains their ability to mitigate risk.

Similarly, the field of critical medical anthropology scrutinizes how political and economic factors influence health and the interconnections between structural forces and individual experience. For example, in *Fresh Fruit, Broken Bodies: Migrant Farmworkers in the United States* Seth Holmes documents how asymmetries in society around race, class, and citizenship contribute to unequal suffering with those at the bottom of these hierarchies in the agricultural industry (Indigenous, LatinX, non-citizen immigrants) suffering the most severe bodily harm. These inequalities are naturalized and remain unquestioned through the process of symbolic violence.[96] In Holmes' work this process shows up in the ways migrant laborers are viewed as destined for backbreaking labor in the fields and deserving of the associated dangers and lack of adequate healthcare. Within the realm of trafficking, we see this in the ways white women in the sex trades are viewed as victims while BIPOC individuals are criminalized and assumed to be there by choice.

Not to be confused with symbolic violence, the concept of structural violence, generally attributed to sociologist Johan Galtung, is useful in framing the ways social inequalities come to be embodied by vulnerable communities and calls attention to the ways social arrangements or institutions perpetuate inequality.[97] Medical anthropologist Paul Farmer describes how these structures "are embedded in the political and economic organization of our social world; they are violent because they cause injury to people (typically, not those responsible for perpetuating such inequalities)."[98] Philippe Bourgois calls attention to structural violence, or what he terms "politically structured suffering," through an examination of the effects of the war on drugs, the disappearance of the unionized industrial labor market, and the dismantling of the welfare safety net as a result of neoliberal policies on homeless heroin injectors in San Francisco, including their experiences of pain and self-inflicted abuse. This lens can similarly be applied to opioid-dependent trafficking survivors in Maine and New Hampshire in the ways that their actions and circumstances are intricately linked to systems of inequality and institutional responses to drug use, sex work, and trafficking.[99]

Trafficked persons have intersectional positionalities, and these theoretical approaches are useful for understanding their experiences of structural vulnerability and violence before, during, and after trafficking. The survivors I encountered experienced multiple co-occurring vulnerabilities. The vast majority were poor and had experienced generational trauma; many were medically uninsured and sexually stigmatized on account of participation in commercial sex; and more than half had histories of incarceration. Almost all lived with substance use disorder. At the same time, experiences of vulnerability were shaped unevenly by specific status attributes such as gender identity, age, race and ethnicity, and disability, as well as by conditions like immigration status and economic and living conditions.[100] These types of structural conditions also increase the likelihood of perpetrating trafficking, as those charged with the crime often come from the same communities as the survivors they exploit and abuse.[101] Reducing structural vulnerability at large lessens the tendency to see exploiting others as a path to success.[102]

Conceptualizing structural vulnerability as a positionality, Quesada, Hart, and Bourgois note, "The vulnerability of an individual is produced by his or her location in a hierarchical social order and its diverse networks of power relationships and effects."[103] Different types of marginalization, including racism, sexism, ableism, ageism, homophobia, and poverty, disproportionately disadvantage certain groups and communities. Vulnerability also functions as both a condition and a process. Zarowsky and colleagues describe it as "a condition of heightened fragility of a population or specific group, and a process that is potentially reversible or avoidable through appropriate interventions."[104] Social conditions can increase an individual's chances of being trafficked, therefore, addressing those conditions can mitigate those chances. Inequality may exacerbate or increase exposure to conditions of vulnerability and also may impact the capacity to cope with risks and their consequences over time.[105]

This temporal element is key to developing effective prevention measures that address vulnerability before, during, and after trafficking occurs. Corinne Schwarz frames trafficking as slow violence, or "the accumulation and accretion of the consequences of systemic oppression over time."[106] Vulnerability can become a downward spiral of successive losses after successive shocks, which coincides with the ways trafficking survivors describe the cycle of trafficking. For many of the survivors I interviewed, an addiction and lack of safe housing made them vulnerable in the first place, and then their ongoing addiction and lack of alternatives made it difficult to leave the trafficking situation. Even once they achieved a means of exit, a continued lack of affordable housing options made it extremely challenging to achieve stability and avoid re-trafficking. Intervention, too, can exacerbate pre-existing vulnerabilities with unintended consequences emerging from institutional responses.[107] For example, although intended to assist trafficking survivors in accessing services, the arrest-as-protection strategy used by many law enforcement investigators often leaves lasting criminal records that make securing housing and meaningful work difficult for survivors.

In recognition of the role that social determinants and other structural factors play in creating vulnerability, momentum has been building to recognize trafficking as a public health issue.[108] The idea of approaching it through a violence prevention framework has gained particular traction.[109] A public health prevention approach to trafficking could broaden the response beyond criminal legal intervention, make it more equitable, and address root causes. Most public health literature, however, focuses on identification, mitigation, and prevention of interpersonal violence; structural violence is usually not the direct target.[110] Framing the issue through the lens of structural vulnerability and structural violence accounts for forms of inequality and marginalization that are embodied at the individual and community levels. Further, centering vulnerability as a factor moves the discussion away from individual risk, bad decision making, and blame-the-victim approaches to the structural causes of trafficking.[111] The survivors that this book spotlights are emphatically not responsible for their own trafficking. They also are not powerless victims, but rather strong and resilient individuals who have been constrained in their choices and opportunities as a result of their social positions and inadequate systems.

Public health generally classifies prevention on three levels—primary, secondary, and tertiary. The goal of primary prevention is complete prevention of a phenomenon before it occurs by addressing root causes. Secondary prevention focuses on early intervention, identification, mitigation of risk factors, and meeting short-term needs after an event has occurred. Tertiary prevention is a long-term approach that relates to intervention and recovery. At present, nearly all human trafficking prevention occurs at the secondary and tertiary levels and includes programs like education campaigns to raise awareness among at-risk groups and services for survivors to prevent re-exploitation.[112] In particular, campaigns directed at educating young people about avoiding individual "risky" behaviors fail to acknowledge that social structures can constrain the choices facing those from marginalized groups. Knowing full well the potential consequences, people make risky choices all the time as a result of the limited options available based on their social position.[113] Telling youth to watch out for smooth-talking pimps who may promise them a way out of poverty is certainly important, but it does nothing to address the underlying deprivation and isolation that makes that kind of offer appealing. Human trafficking is not just about conscious choices made by the individuals directly involved. This is why it is so important to develop structural approaches to prevention.[114]

While most would agree it is better to prevent an adverse outcome before it occurs than to intervene after it has caused harm, devoting resources to primary prevention of trafficking is still a tough sell. Primary prevention can seem to be quite removed from the crime of trafficking, and it is usually not immediately clear to those in positions of power how structural interventions work to prevent trafficking because they occur so far upstream from the problem they seek to solve. Primary prevention is about strengthening housing systems and expanding access to health care and drug treatment—investments that do not fit into the dominant trafficking narrative of ideal victims in need of rescue. It turns out that building resilience and community supports does not provide the sensational melodramatic satisfaction that "rescue" does and is, thus, far less appealing to policymakers and those making appropriations decisions. These figures want easily digestible success stories with quick turnarounds to tout before their constituents.

This book is not the first to point out that the current approach to trafficking ignores structural factors.[115] What it adds is in-depth documentation of the structural vulnerability and violence that human trafficking survivors experience. Drawing on survivor narratives and ethnographically rich accounts from frontline workers, this book seeks to contextualize how structural vulnerability is embodied by trafficking survivors over time in order to point to where upstream responses are most needed. Expanding social welfare support, ensuring access to safe and affordable housing, reducing violence in families and the foster care system, and advancing safe migration would all decrease structural vulnerability and result in fewer instances of trafficking. To eliminate barriers to survivor stability, a combination of decriminalizing commercial sex work, prohibiting carceral protection strategies, and providing accessible pathways to access drug treatment and exit sex work would further strengthen the response. Whereas specific proposals for primary prevention are usually lacking, this book will provide concrete policy solutions based on the lived experiences of trafficking survivors.

The Setting, the Study, and the Participants

Maine and New Hampshire

Ethnography offers an especially useful approach to uncovering the complexities of trafficking experiences and the effects of macro-level policies on individuals and communities. Between September 2016 and August 2018, I conducted multisited ethnographic research in the northern New England states of Maine and New Hampshire.[116] The two states are similar demographically, though the region is decidedly different from the site of my previous research—New York City—and other large metropolitan and agricultural areas where trafficking cases have been identified in significant numbers. First, both states have relatively small populations of approximately 1.4 million and are predominantly white. According to the 2020 census, Maine is the whitest state and New Hampshire the fourth whitest state in the nation.[117] Racial diversity is limited, though Hispanic and Black populations are on the rise. Maine in particular has seen a growing number of African asylum seekers over the last decade. While often invisible, both states also rely on seasonal migrant farmworkers. Still, an overwhelmingly white demographic reinforces expectations among investigators about the racial background of victims.

Additionally, the region is mostly rural with urban pockets, though Maine's population density is much lower than New Hampshire's. According to the 2020 U.S. Census, Maine ranks as the second most rural state in the U.S., and this contributes to what many refer to as the "two Maines" in reference to the split between the more populous and developed southern coastal part of the state and the much less inhabited and less affluent region of the northern interior.[118] Maine also has a higher poverty rate (10.8 percent versus 7.2 percent) and a significantly lower median household income than New Hampshire ($69,543 versus $89,992).[119] While striking at first, New Hampshire's relative prosperity is attributable in large part to its proximity to Boston and the growing number of commuter communities in the state's southern section, obscuring the fact that poverty rates in New Hampshire range from 4.7 percent in the southeast to 12.8 percent in the state's northernmost county.[120]

Like other parts of New England, both states boasted numerous thriving mill towns devoted to paper, shoe, and textile manufacturing in the mid-nineteenth and early twentieth centuries. Starting in the 1950s, however, many of the mills closed, resulting in economic hardship for formerly thriving communities. Maine and New Hampshire are now headquarters to a handful of large corporations including L.L.Bean, Timberland, and Wex, and the healthcare, retail, and educational sectors are the primary employers in both states. Nonetheless, economic security remains a challenge for many households. For example, Maine's economy is grounded in heritage industries including fishing, logging, shipbuilding, farming, and tourism, many of which are seasonal and lead people to rely on multiple forms of formal and informal employment, which leads to economic precarity. Due to abundant natural resources and their status as desirable vacation destinations, it is easy to observe inequality in both locales with the intermingling of immense wealth and poverty often within the same stretch of roadside. It is not uncommon to see a crumbling farmhouse or a mobile home in need of repairs with lobster traps stacked across the yard a short distance from an extravagant vacation residence.

The research that informs this book took place in the years following the economic downturn of 2008–2009, when the economy was still in a state of recovery and job opportunities were limited. While demand for workers was rising in healthcare, information technology, and social and business services, positions in those industries require workers with college degrees and specialized training. Jobs in service occupations that were more widely available and open to unskilled workers offered lower-than-average earnings and resulted in limited opportunities for a living wage.[121]

Both Maine and New Hampshire continue to face a housing shortage and an affordability crisis, especially for rental homes available to extremely low income households.[122] And as in other parts of the country, due to underfunding and provider shortages there are insufficient mental health and substance use treatment options available, especially for the uninsured.[123] The states are somewhat quirky with New Hampshire's libertarian leaning tendencies and a majority of Mainers identifying as independent.[124] This has resulted in inconsistent support of social services. For example, Maine's governor during the period of this research, republican Paul LePage, steadfastly resisted Medicaid expansion and opposed using government funds for the treatment of substance use disorder, though his democratic successor implemented the latter program on her first day in office.[125] As will be seen in the pages that follow, lack of accessible treatment for opioid addiction was one of the biggest obstacles to stability for the survivors I interviewed.

In terms of addressing trafficking, the two states have unique funding structures, but during the time of my fieldwork both were recipients of federal funds to investigate trafficking and deliver services to survivors.[126] Frontline workers reported similar trends related to the types of trafficking being observed and identified; however, it is important to recognize that "cases identified" do not represent the true number, or any personal and situational characteristics (gender, age, sexual orientation, or type of trafficking). This is in part due to the social construction of trafficking that centers ideal victims who are young, white, cisgender females as more vulnerable to trafficking and, relatedly, worthy of investigative efforts and assistance.[127]

Estimates of human trafficking are notoriously unreliable due both to the covert nature of the problem and the challenges of documenting a hard-to-reach population, though data are often available on the number of cases being investigated and the number of survivors receiving services.[128] A 2015 report estimated the prevalence of sex trafficking in Maine ranging between 200 and 300 incidents annually, but did not provide any estimate for cases of labor trafficking.[129] For the year 2018, the New Hampshire Collaborative Human Trafficking Task Force reported fifty-six active human trafficking investigations, including forty-six involving sex trafficking, six involving labor trafficking and four involving a combination of sex and labor trafficking (see Table 1 for additional data reported by the Task Force). Between 2017 and 2018, thirty-five individuals received federally funded services for victims of trafficking, 53 percent of whom were trafficked for forced commercial sex work and 47 percent trafficked for a combination of sex and labor trafficking, including commercial sex work, drug dealing, domestic servitude, panhandling, and transportation services. Data indicate that at least one male survivor and one minor survivor were served during that time period.[130] Maine does not publicly release data on human trafficking, but I observed similar patterns in the distribution of clients based on gender, age, and type of trafficking in unpublished data I reviewed and conversations I had with frontline workers. The one exception was that several clients in Maine identified as transgender.

Table 1. Human Trafficking Cases by Year and Type of Trafficking as Documented by the New Hampshire Human Trafficking Collaborative Task Force

	Confirmed Human Trafficking Victims Identified by the Task Force	*New Human Trafficking Investigations by the Task Force*	*Individuals Arrested for Human Trafficking-Related Incidents*	*Individuals Indicted for Any Offense*
2017				
Sex	23	24	6	4
Labor	3	3	3	2
Sex and Labor	1	5	0	0
Total	27	32	9	6
2018				
Sex	25	23	2	2
Labor	4	5	0	0
Sex and Labor	0	1	0	1
Total	29	29	2	3

Source: Stephanie Halter, *New Hampshire Human Trafficking Collaborative Task Force End of the Year Report, 2017,* 2018; Stephanie Halter and Scott Meyer, *New Hampshire Human Trafficking Collaborative Task Force 2018 Annual Report,* 2019.

Ethnographic Approach

Immersing myself in as many aspects of the anti-trafficking responses in each state as I could, I attended statewide awareness days, brown bag lunches, conferences, task force and coalition meetings, as well as court proceedings related to ongoing cases, all with the goal of gaining an insider perspective of the anti-trafficking work taking place across the two regions. In addition to ethnographic observation, I conducted sixty in-depth interviews, which included eighteen law enforcement investigators—from the Department of Homeland Security (DHS), the Federal Bureau of Investigation (FBI), and multiple local police departments—three local prosecutors, four government officials, eleven victim service providers (including program directors, caseworkers, social workers, and others), four advocates, seventeen survivors of trafficking, and three individuals who identified as having experienced commercial sexual exploitation but not trafficking.[131] I also spoke with many people involved in the response informally, reviewed case management files of survivors who granted me permission, tracked local criminal cases, followed local media coverage of human trafficking, and analyzed archival material related to the development of local human trafficking responses. Additionally, between 2019 and 2021 I served as lead action researcher for two federal grants awarded to a local victim services program, and data collected as part of those projects also informs the book.

With this combination of research methods, I developed a multidimensional understanding of the human trafficking response and the various ways individuals interpreted its goals and experienced its effects depending on the roles they occupied within it. Seeing the response in action over time and collecting accounts from those involved in its implementation as well as from the survivors most impacted by it revealed the tensions between the intent of anti-trafficking law and policy—to aid survivors and stop trafficking—and its actual effects, which often were much more muted than expected and at times even harmful to survivors.

Survivors of Trafficking

All the survivors I interviewed were current or former clients of a victim services program for survivors of trafficking or current or former residents of a residential program for survivors. Survivors were recruited through their programs after receiving a description of the research study and an explanation of what their participation would entail. When asked why they chose to participate in an interview some survivors responded that they viewed it as part of their healing process while others alluded to wanting to contribute to knowledge on the issue and the hope to help others. One survivor named Leslie shared, "I hope myself one day to be able to help the human trafficking cause somehow. That's why I did this." I relied on a combination of life history and semi-structured interviewing techniques and asked all survivors to take the lead in terms of the topics they wished to share or avoid. In this way I sought to give them control over their stories, and the type and amount of information they shared.

The majority of research involving trafficking survivors in the United States has focused on those who have officially been recognized as victims and have been connected to services, and the present research is no exception.[132] There are likely categorizable differences between assisted and unassisted victims, and it is important to recognize which victims are systematically included and omitted from research studies.[133] Research on domestic trafficking has focused overwhelmingly on cisgender women and girls, with little attention paid to transgender survivors and cisgender boys and men or LGBTQIA+ individuals.[134] Entering into the research, I was well aware of these deficiencies yet struggled to overcome them, given the project's geographic locale.

Looking at Maine and New Hampshire, you see the same kinds of vulnerable populations that are present in other parts of the country, including individuals living in poverty, individuals in low-wage, low-skill industries, runaway/homeless/LGBTQIA+ youth, migrant laborers, and those with substance use disorders. As in other areas, individuals are trafficked into all labor sectors, but limited efforts and resources are put into identifying individuals trafficked outside of commercial sex work. Many of the service providers and law enforcement officials I interviewed had worked with survivors who were male, trans, LGBTQIA+, BIPOC, or trafficked for types of labor beyond commercial sex (and I met a small number of those individuals), but they simply were not the norm. Maine and New Hampshire's demographics as two of the whitest states in the country—combined with the ways that law enforcement investigators overlook certain survivors, who subsequently have difficulty accessing benefits legally afforded them—pose real challenges to expanding knowledge on the full range of individuals affected by trafficking.[135] Indeed, these challenges further speak to the need for new identification strategies and stronger efforts to reach survivors from the most marginalized groups who often remain invisible, or worse, are viewed as criminals rather than victims. Foreign-born labor trafficking survivors, in particular, are failed by the immigration system and often remain hidden on account of their immigration status.

None of the survivors I interviewed fit the "ideal victim" profile, but some possessed certain overlapping characteristics with those highlighted in the press release at the start of this chapter—the majority were white, cisgender women trafficked for commercial sex, and viewed as vulnerable by law enforcement investigators. However, in other ways the survivors were anything but ideal. They were all adults with substance use disorder. Most had histories of law enforcement involvement or incarceration. Many had entered commercial sex work prior to trafficking, and several continued in it after leaving the trafficking situation. All of the accounts provided by survivors complicate the human trafficking narrative by adding the nuance and complexity of lived experience.

Given the sensitive nature of the material and the fact that much of the information revealed in interviews was potentially related to ongoing criminal cases, I have assigned all interviewees pseudonyms and have changed or omitted details in instances where readers may easily be able to decipher the identity of participants. Some individuals participated in interviews without formal approval from their agencies, while others faced ongoing safety concerns from their traffickers. In all cases I have attempted to convey key elements of their identity and role without revealing specific attributes.

A Note on Style and Language

Throughout the book I draw heavily on the words of trafficking survivors and frontline workers to illuminate the ways in which structural vulnerability and inadequate systems affect the individual and collective experience of trafficking. My perspective as an ethnographic participant observer allows me to weave together their stories and commentary in a digestible format, but they are the experts, and the accounts I relay are their everyday experiences. Survivor accounts, in particular, are too often presented in sensational and voyeuristic formats for media audiences to consume. All the survivors I encountered were smart, thoughtful, and resilient with complex stories and important insights to provide. They are all so much more than the horror stories usually presented to reflect trafficking.

In an effort to avoid misrepresenting trafficking survivors, I privilege their voices, in some cases providing only limited connective tissue to accentuate their interpretations.[136] My intent is to lay bare the ways in which structural vulnerability shapes these survivors' trafficking trajectories. I take this approach not to reify their suffering but rather to provide evidence that prevention is critical and to point to the locations where it will be most beneficial and effective. Likewise, the frontline workers who inform this book bear witness to the structural violence inflicted upon survivors on a daily basis and have much to convey about the challenges of the current response. I rely on their words to directly convey those injustices.

Neither the phenomenon nor the term *human trafficking* is new, but the modern definition of the crime was only codified under international and U.S. law in the year 2000.[137] Despite the establishment of a legal definition in the U.S. more than twenty years ago, there continues to be confusion about what the term *trafficking* encompasses, as evidenced by frequent misspeaks by politicians and inaccurate reporting in the media that conflates human trafficking with illegal smuggling and commercial sex work. When I use the term, I am referring to the legal definition of "severe forms of trafficking in persons" as defined in U.S. law in the Trafficking Victims Protection Act of 2000 (TVPA), as amended (22 U.S.C. § 7102):

- (A) The recruitment, harboring, transportation, provision, obtaining, patronizing, or soliciting of a person for the purpose of a commercial sex act, in which the commercial sex act is induced by force, fraud, or coercion, or in which the person induced to perform such act has not attained 18 years of age; (or)
- (B) The recruitment, harboring, transportation, provision, or obtaining of a person for labor or services, through the use of force, fraud, or coercion for the purpose of subjection to involuntary servitude, peonage, debt bondage, or slavery.[138]

This definition includes three elements that must always be present for a situation to constitute trafficking—what are referred to as the process, means, and purpose (see Figure 3). Human trafficking affects people of all races, nationalities, ages, genders, sexual orientations, and backgrounds. While the dominant narrative focuses on trafficking of cisgender women and girls for commercial sex, anyone can be trafficked into any labor sector, whether that is commercial sex work, drug selling, agricultural labor, domestic work, landscaping, factory work, construction, hair braiding, hospitality, or any other.

Any interviewee I identify as a survivor in the book meets the legal definition of a victim of a severe form of trafficking under the law. That said, while

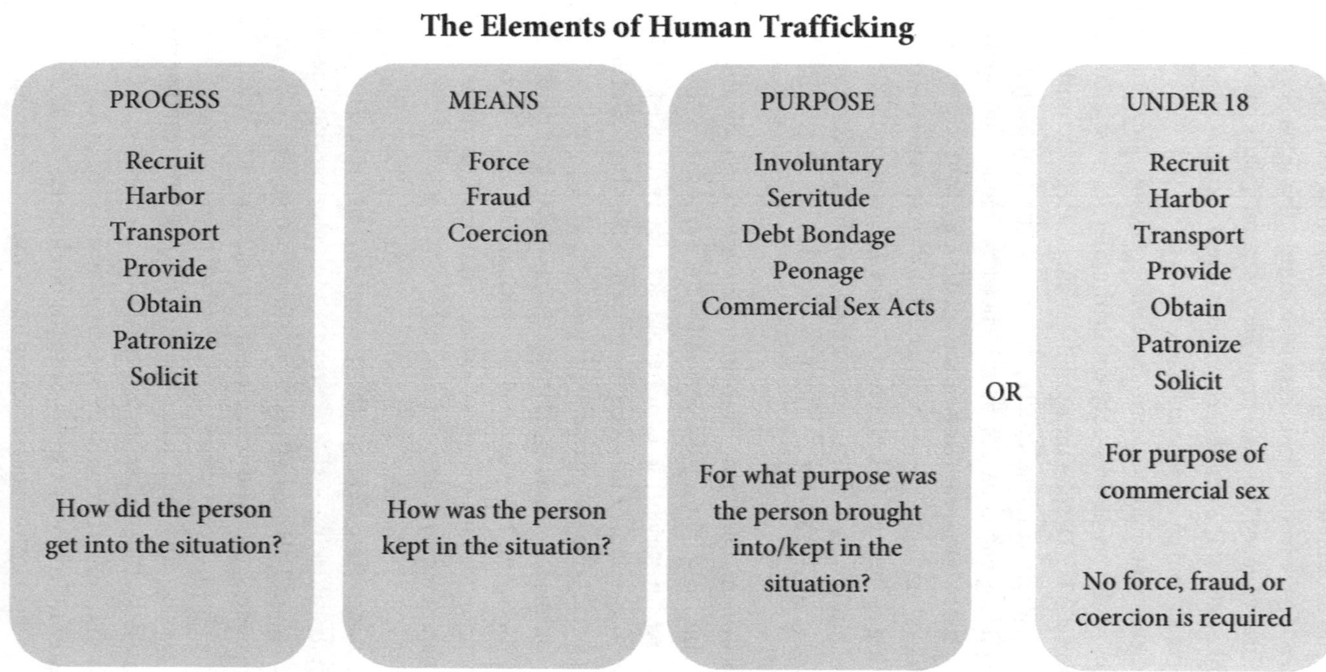

Figure 3. The Legal Elements of Human Trafficking Under the Trafficking Victims Protection Act

all the survivors I interviewed recognized themselves as survivors of trafficking, few used that language themselves, and most referred to their abusers as pimps rather than as traffickers. Many other scholars have documented the feminist debates about the definition of trafficking and the conflation between uncoerced sex work and trafficking and similarly between pimping and trafficking.[139] My own previous research documented the ways in which this conflation was symbolically incorporated into the TVPA.[140] While revisiting these debates is beyond the scope of this book, I observed that, despite the legal delineation between trafficking and non-trafficking related labor, many of the survivors I interviewed for this project moved in and out of situations involving trafficking where they were compelled and those where their choice to engage in sex work was constrained but nonetheless agentive. While survivors were able to articulate the differences between these experiences, they used the same language of being "in the life" or "working for my pimp" whether the circumstances involved trafficking or not. Unless a particular usage potentially contributed to confusion, I have left this language unchanged throughout the book. Many law enforcement investigators also used the term *pimp* interchangeably or in place of *trafficker*. While some law enforcement agents at times conflated trafficking with pimping that did not involve force or coercion, usually due to discrepancies between state and federal definitions, nearly all of the cases I discussed with them involved severe forms of trafficking as defined under the TVPA.[141]

Depending on context, trafficked persons are referred to as either *victims* or *survivors* of trafficking. The former is favored in legal discourse and reflects that someone is the victim of a crime. This was the term used by most of the law enforcement investigators I interviewed. Throughout the book, I primarily use the term *survivor* to reflect the fact that the individuals I interviewed are complex humans who are more than their victim status. However, in instances where there is specific reference to someone as the victim of a crime, I use that terminology.

Organization of the Book

Reflecting the premise that survivor voices must be at the center of the human trafficking response, the following chapters begin with a series of survivor narratives. The book builds on those accounts by integrating their voices with those of frontline workers to highlight specific examples of structural vulnerability and barriers arising within the current U.S. human trafficking response. Ultimately, I offer a series of policy recommendations that stem from survivors' lived experiences.

Survivors embody structural violence throughout their lives, from the compounding vulnerabilities in the years leading up to their trafficking to the conditions that prevent them from leaving trafficking situations to the challenges they face in trying to achieve and maintain stability post-trafficking. Chapter 2 introduces the survivors I interviewed through a series of nine narratives documenting their trafficking trajectories. The narratives reveal multiple missed opportunities for intervention along the way and also demonstrate how vulnerabilities continue to accumulate during and after trafficking.

Chapter 3 examines the concept of vulnerability as it relates to human trafficking and provides evidence of contributing structural factors, including housing insecurity, lack of treatment for substance use disorder and mental health, and generational trauma. Those factors persist making it difficult for survivors to leave, and they pose ongoing challenges post-trafficking. The chapter reviews various frameworks for understanding vulnerability, including structural violence and social determinants of health. It then scrutinizes two main areas of vulnerability among survivors—substance use disorder and housing insecurity—drawing on ethnographic examples to illuminate the role of failed systems as precursors to trafficking and also as factors that continue post-trafficking, creating an ongoing cycle of vulnerability. The chapter also examines the role of structural vulnerability as a precursor to perpetrating trafficking.

Victims are routinely arrested as a protection strategy in the anti-trafficking response, and law enforcement investigators view arrest as a method of saving vulnerable individuals. Chapter 4 problematizes criminal legal intervention as the U.S. government's primary strategy to address human trafficking. Analyzing the effects of these strategies on survivors, the chapter makes clear that the current approach serves as a barrier to recovery and stability.

Focusing on the lived realities of survivors, and those who encounter them through their work to address trafficking, the following pages illustrate that prioritizing an interventionist criminal legal response to trafficking does little to address the issues that make individuals vulnerable to trafficking in the first place and does very little to end trafficking. The empirical data presented throughout the book make the case for an upstream, primary prevention-focused approach to domestic human trafficking. Addressing structural vulnerabilities will be more effective than the current criminal legal response, and prioritizing prevention will result in better outcomes for survivors. Therefore, the concluding chapter advances a series of specific policy recommendations related to housing, support and treatment for those with substance use disorder, health, youth programs, education, and criminal legal reforms. These are the interventions that will reduce trafficking and create better, richer, safer lives for those experiencing vulnerability.

CHAPTER 2

Survivor Trajectories and Experiences of Vulnerability

> He hands me a business card with every state I ever dreamed of going to, and I'm like, "Maine sucks." I wasn't that easy to get to go, though, because I'm like, "Oh, I signed up for school." But he brought me shopping, bought me this, bought me that. And where I was at in life, that was amazing. I wasn't homeless. I was fed well, I got my nails done, went shopping. I thought he was a respectable man. After he finally convinced me—he's like, "Oh you can go to college any time." And I'm like, "Yeah, actually you're right, and I don't really want to stay here and be homeless going to school."—And he comes in the room and tells me I need to make a thousand dollars a night. What? I'm thinking in my head, "This happens to me? To me?" And I was like, "No, I'm not doing that." And he punched me, very hard. And I just remember—in my head, like, "Oh my god, what is happening?"
>
> —Elliott, Survivor

Over more than twenty years of conducting research with trafficking survivors, it has become astoundingly clear that there is no "typical" victim profile.[1] "Ideal" victim narratives have been profoundly counterproductive in terms of identifying the full spectrum of individuals experiencing human trafficking.[2] Indeed, when I asked case managers and law enforcement officers what a trafficking victim looked like, most alluded to the diversity of individuals they had encountered in their work. Leah, a federal agent, shared, "You know you cannot walk . . . in the mall and go, 'Oh, that's a victim.' . . . No, it can be anybody. . . . I've had a fifty-eight-year-old victim who was a grandmother and a thirteen-year-old girl, and from every age group, from every bracket, every color."

Both the investigators and the service providers I interviewed referred to multiple ways in which diverse identities were represented among the clients or victims they worked with, including race and ethnicity, age, gender identity, income level, degree of family stability, and citizenship status, among others. For example, Mariah, a case manager who worked with survivors, mentioned a recent trans client—one among primarily cisgender women. She continued, "We have one male client . . . that we've been working with . . . But other than that, it's been all women . . . mostly U.S. citizens. We have had a couple folks who are foreign nationals." Resoundingly, I heard that it would be incorrect to assume that all victims come from traumatic backgrounds. Frontline workers provided examples of survivors they had encountered who came from stable, middle-class families—however, these were usually invoked as exceptions. Even if no one could agree on a prototypical victim, they all seem to concede that patterns, and variations on those patterns, do exist.

The exceptions frontline workers encountered were likely more numerous than what was being seen, but the investigative and identification strategies used were not especially effective at identifying BIPOC, LGBTQIA+, or male survivors of trafficking, nor those forced into labor sectors outside of commercial sex work. As Ryan, a federal agent, told me, "There's no defined trafficking victim. We haven't run across one." He then went on to elucidate the gender breakdown of victims encountered as part of investigations he had led: "We don't run across many male victims up here. I'm sure part of it is reporting, part of it is shame. Part of it is it's not what we're necessarily looking for." Eliza, a program director, elaborated on this point: "We get what we look for." She was referring to the lack of racial diversity in the area and admitted that "there's a difference between who we're currently serving, and who the trafficking victims are in the state." Women were more likely to be identified than men; middle- and lower middle-class individuals more than those in poverty; and white people more than people of color. Frontline anti-trafficking workers often see and identify the survivors that fulfill their own perceptions of what a survivor should look like. The cisgender female victims of sex trafficking being identified are the most visible, and the most expected. Their stories are the most scintillating for the public, and research shows that the government has directed the majority of its efforts, resources, and time to identifying that population.[3]

Despite the many references to exceptions to the rule, for the most part, I heard that the survivors identified in the region shared certain characteristics. Anthony, a local prosecutor, shared, "Your textbook case would be . . . a vulnerable woman who [is] probably late-teens to early thirties, who may have housing insecurity, economic insecurity, drug addiction . . . I mean [this] is a very white state. I do see a lot of the young white women involved in trafficking—primarily working-class to very modest means, poverty-line stuff." Grant, and nearly every other investigator I interviewed, echoed a version of this description. "They are primarily mid-twenties. Female. White . . . born [in the state]. Went to [the local] high school. Made some bad decisions. Got into heroin and things got out of control for them. That's our prototypical victim." Service providers shared the same kinds of descriptions:

Maia: Mostly white women from Maine in their mid to late twenties. I think about 75 percent have significant substance use disorder . . . maybe 80 percent do not have safe, permanent housing . . . [a] number of cases have federal law enforcement involvement.

Orla: The vast majority are female. The vast majority are being trafficked for sex. The vast majority are Mainers or from the New England region and the vast majority have some substance use disorders . . . mental health issues, homelessness, poverty.

Angelique: My clients are mostly female, mostly U.S. citizens, mostly sex trafficking clients.

Reflecting the demographics of identified survivors, the individuals I interviewed consisted primarily of white, twenty- and thirty-something, New England-born cisgender women with substance use disorder who had been domestically trafficked for commercial sex, sometimes combined with forced drug trafficking or other forms of forced labor. Overall, I interviewed sixteen survivors of trafficking. Ten were part of the main research study—some of whose narratives I include here—and six whose stories inform the research and were collected as part of action research for an agency receiving federal trafficking funds. One additional survivor shared her story through her caseworkers. I also interviewed three individuals who had experienced exploitation in commercial sex work but did not identify as trafficking victims. Of the nineteen total interviewees, eighteen identified as women and one identified as trans. Of the seventeen trafficking survivors, thirteen experienced forced commercial sex trafficking, two experienced trafficking in another labor sector, and three reported histories of both "sex" and "labor" trafficking.[4] Two survivors were foreign-born and the remainder were U.S. citizens, most from the New England area. Of the two survivors who were trafficked for non-sex-related labor, one elected to share her story through her caseworkers and the other was not a member of the primary study, meaning their accounts did not have the same level of richness as those of the other interviewees whose stories are included throughout the book.

Though I did not ask about race and ethnicity, two survivors were Black, one reported Native American heritage, and the remaining survivors presented as white. I attempted to interview both male and additional BIPOC survivors but was ultimately unsuccessful. One male survivor initially agreed to an interview but later opted out. Two BIPOC individuals who originally agreed to an interview were unable to participate due to being in crisis when it came time for the interview. Intersecting oppression is likely a contributing factor to the underrepresentation of BIPOC individuals both being identified as trafficking survivors and achieving the stability to participate in research interviews.

In what follows I highlight survivor experiences of vulnerability through nine narratives. The accounts are not necessarily representative of the range of individuals being trafficked in New England, but they are consistent with the general characteristics of trafficking survivors who are being identified and the primary population consuming trafficking-specific services in the region. From how these survivors experienced structural violence, we can, if anything, infer that the types of marginalization and oppression that are illustrated here are magnified for those who are not identified.

The women who shared their life histories with me had various levels of education. Several had dropped out of middle or high school, though most reported being strong students who left school due to unstable family circumstances, unaddressed trauma, or drug use. Some had returned to complete GEDs, and still others had completed some college. One survivor reported having received a full scholarship to attend university. As Troy, a law enforcement officer, noted, "For the most part, the women that are getting caught up in this . . . they've graduated high school. They have an education. They're articulate."

A few of the women came from stable family backgrounds, while the majority reported histories of family instability, economic insecurity, abuse, and mental health challenges. Substance use disorder featured prominently in all of the narratives, and the majority of research participants had multigenerational histories of addiction. While most of the women were recruited into trafficking situations via their addictions, which were then used against them as a means of control, others did not begin using substances until traffickers provided them.

Some survivors spent weeks in trafficking situations, while others were unable to escape for years, sometimes experiencing multiple episodes of trafficking. While some of the women only ever experienced situations involving force and were never involved in consensual commercial sex work, others moved in and out of situations involving force and choice. A few individuals walked away when circumstances allowed, while others continued to live in fear of retaliation from their traffickers. Survivors shared varied experiences with service providers, shelters, and residential treatment programs. They also described a range of experiences with law enforcement and the criminal legal system. I heard gratefulness for interventions that allowed them to leave trafficking situations, and I heard long histories of negative experiences involving arrests, lack of respect, and little-to-no assistance from law enforcement.

The narratives below illustrate how survivors embody structural violence throughout their lives. The accounts also highlight how vulnerabilities compound in the years leading up to trafficking, the conditions that keep people in the trafficking situations, and the challenges survivors face in trying to achieve and maintain stability post trafficking.[5] I share these stories not to spotlight or reify victimhood but rather as evidence of failed systems. These accounts reveal how real people embody structural violence and how compounding barriers, or chains of risk, ultimately contribute to the experience of trafficking.[6] The narratives can be hard to read. They make raw the everyday violence—perpetrated both by individuals and the state—that these survivors experience. Multiple opportunities for intervention were missed along the way, and vulnerabilities continued to accumulate during and after trafficking. The individual stories are devastating. Yet it is even more unsettling to see the patterns that emerge in terms of failed systems and the lack of support and intervention available to those at risk for trafficking, going through trafficking, and attempting to achieve stability post-trafficking. These failures are especially apparent in the barriers to comprehensive mental health care and drug treatment and in the lack of stable, secure housing.

In what follows I focus almost entirely on the words of trafficking survivors to illuminate the ways in which failed systems affect both the individual and the collective experience of trafficking. While some of the narratives include discussions of the individual and interpersonal coercive conditions of trafficking, my goal here is to reveal more general trajectories from pre- to post-trafficking, and the structural conditions that increased vulnerability at all stages, making individuals vulnerable to trafficking in the first place and making fleeing their captors and achieving stability all the more difficult.

The narratives illustrate the complexity of victim-trafficker relationships. Many survivors moved in and out of trafficking situations, sometimes experiencing force, fraud, or coercion and at other times, not. Elements of structural vulnerability also followed them in and out of trafficking situations. Most study participants were trafficked by somebody who provided whatever substance they were addicted to and they viewed their traffickers as alternately compassionate and supportive or as violent and coercive. Traffickers both supplied drugs and withheld them as means of control. Traffickers provided a place to stay when potential victims had nowhere else to go, and this made leaving all the more difficult. The types of restraint used were not always physical, and traffickers often exploited their victims' addictions and housing insecurity as ways to maintain control.

Survivor Narratives

Sam

When I met Sam, she had recently moved into an inpatient drug treatment facility. Living there, with twenty-four-hour staff, made her feel secure after being trafficked twice by two different groups of traffickers. She had been forced both to sell drugs and to trade sex for money. In her early thirties at the time of our interview, Sam had grown up in an affluent suburban town and lived with various family members throughout her childhood. Her aunt helped her mother raise her; her "biological father wasn't really in the picture." She had experienced multiple traumatic events throughout her life, including between the ages of six and eight, sexual abuse at the hands of a caretaker's relative. Sam dealt with the resulting depression, anxiety, and PTSD throughout her adolescence, complicated by drug and alcohol addiction. Although she was a strong student, family circumstances led her to drop out of high school and to spend some time unhoused during her late teens. After marrying, having kids, and then divorcing, Sam returned to school and worked to support her family. Following an injury that coincided with some other significant medical issues, Sam started taking painkillers and developed an addiction. When her prescriptions stopped, Sam started seeking drugs on the street and her use intensified.

Sam's entry into trafficking began with her large drug debt. Originally under the impression that she would only have to transport drugs to pay off the group of dealers who had been selling to her, Sam said the situation very quickly changed and her traffickers began dispatching her to deliver drugs and provide sex to customers. "Shocked at first," Sam tried to run away multiple times. Each time, her traffickers tracked her down, made her observe violent assaults of others to show her what they were capable of, and forced her to perform sexual acts at gunpoint. She told me, "I got to a point where I realized that there was no getting away from the situation."

Sam's situation was extreme. Her traffickers kept her under lock and key and took all of her earnings. This isolation, along with restrictions on her communication, effectively severed ties to most of her friends and family. "They still allowed me to take the occasional phone call from my mother because they wanted to keep suspicion down on what was going on," but they dictated when she could talk and what she could say. The traffickers used Sam's addiction as a form of leverage, controlling her access to drugs.

I asked Sam whether she ever considered law enforcement as a resource or as a potential way out of the situation. "No. I was terrified," she said. "I didn't think they had the means to protect me in any way, shape, or form. I figured that one way or another that they [the traffickers] would find me and they would kill me, or they would kill my family . . . The two times that I took off, I was beaten upon return, and I knew how bad that was."

When Sam was arrested as part of a larger drug investigation into her traffickers, the officers asked whether she had been forced to perform sexual acts. After being pressed for some time, Sam did admit that she had experienced some force but refused to provide a statement or offer any details out of fear of retribution from her traffickers. Because she was unwilling to cooperate, Sam remained in jail and was not offered any resources. Following her release, she quickly went back to jail on a probation violation. Once again, investigators pressured her to share what she knew; when she failed to cooperate, she was charged as part of the drug case. She was "basically told that if I was willing to talk about what had happened, then they would be willing to drop the charges, but otherwise I could sit in jail."

Law enforcement offered to reduce Sam's jail time and connect her with resources if she would be willing to cooperate in the investigation. Weighing their promises against the potential risk of retaliation by her traffickers was difficult: "What were the chances of them actually getting a prosecution . . . and how much was I willing to risk my own safety, my family's safety?" Eventually, after spending several months in jail and working with a lawyer whom she trusted, Sam opened up about her experiences and began cooperating with officials. After sharing pertinent information with investigators, she grew frustrated when they did not follow through on their promises and rarely updated her on the status of the case.

Following her release from jail, Sam got clean, which led to more mental clarity and also to more time spent reflecting on her trafficking experience. Fear became a prominent feature of Sam's daily experience: "[I was] living in fear every single day of my life . . . just constantly terrified." She was also grieving, struggling to cope with the deaths of people close to her as a result of violence and drug overdoses. Sam said that she was in desperate need of mental health support and medication to deal with the trauma resulting from her experiences. After an unsuccessful suicide attempt, Sam received inpatient mental health treatment and started to move slowly forward. She was discharged from one program due to a positive urine test and later overdosed.

With the help of a caseworker, Sam entered the inpatient drug treatment facility where she was living at the time of our interview, recounting, "I'm grateful . . . to just have a safe environment." Sam noted the incredible support she received from the anti-trafficking services organization that assisted her. "It's just one of the few places that I felt safe for the longest time." The program helped her return to college, helped pay for her phone and gas, and assisted with basic necessities like groceries, clothing, and toiletries. While Sam continued to struggle with the aftermath of her trafficking as well as some of her pre-existing vulnerabilities, she experienced a positive shift in her well-being and perspective. She attributed the improvement to the support she received from her caseworker, as well as having some distance from her traffickers, working with a psychiatrist whom she trusted, and maintaining sobriety: "I'm tired of feeling like a victim and want to . . . switch . . . to more so feeling like a survivor of this finally." Sam hoped to reunite with her children and family from whom she had been separated due to her drug use. She also intended to continue with school, hopefully pursuing a master's degree and doing "whatever I can to try and help other women going through this or that have been through this."

Ashley

When we met, Ashley was making positive strides toward stability post-trafficking yet continued to face challenges involved with moving on from trauma. "It's very hard for me to live a normal life after something like that . . . It's a totally different life how I live things now. I'm a lot more paranoid." She added, "Being around normal people is really hard because you feel like it's freaking written on your forehead what you did and what you've been through and they would just be disgusted if they knew." Ashley was in her late twenties when we met but implied that her trafficking trajectory had roots in a complicated childhood. She had grown up in another part of New England and moved around a lot as a kid. She survived physical and sexual abuse as well as familial drug use and incarceration. During her early years, her father was in prison, and her mother was an addict; her alcoholic stepfather molested and physically abused her. Exposure to drug use created precarious situations: "My mom used to always be like, I'm going out and getting milk, and not come back for three months." As a result of the adults in her life being largely absent, Ashley worked a number of jobs in her teens to support herself and her siblings and ended up dropping out of high school.

After working in various retail and service industries, Ashley started stripping to make ends meet. One day a friend suggested she go with her to visit her "boyfriend" in another state, claiming that Ashley could make a lot more money dancing there. Shortly after they arrived, the friend's supposed boyfriend pursued Ashley romantically, eventually forcing her into his prostitution ring. Mired in manipulation, she felt trapped. Ashley knew she was in trouble right away because she had just lost her housing and had no place to go as an alternative. She explained, "There was a day that I walked around when it finally hit me that I need to get out of here, but I [didn't] know if I could . . . I just walked around like, 'Is this really happening?'" She paused, and added, "it was."

While Ashley's trafficker largely maintained control over her and a number of other women with promises of money and devotion, he also wielded violence and withheld drugs to ensure they acquiesced to his demands. "You were always on edge." Not meeting the nightly quota of dates and associated cash had consequences: "You could be beaten. You could be locked in a room . . . The girls who are doing drugs, they could not get the drugs they were supposed to get that night. Then they're sick as hell." Ashley did not start using drugs until she had been with her trafficker for some time—the trafficking led to her drug use rather than being a point of vulnerability that contributed to her trafficking. But the ramifications of her addiction were severe and lingered long after she escaped her trafficker.

Eventually, Ashley confronted her trafficker and told him she was leaving. He violently assaulted her and made her show the other women her injuries as a warning for what would happen if they tried to leave. After enduring numerous threats and attempts to deter her, Ashley walked away, no longer afraid of the consequences. She described being emotionally incapacitated for days and screaming in her sleep. Some significant injuries led her to seek medical help. She explained that the scarring became "a constant reminder of strength, but it's also a reminder . . . I let someone do this to me. I didn't *let* him, but you know . . ." (her emphasis).

After escaping her trafficker, Ashley's drug use increased and she transitioned from OxyContin to heroin. Unaware of resources for people in her situation and continuing to receive threats from her trafficker, she became suicidal. One day following a drug purchase, she was intercepted by law enforcement investigators. As she described it, "I . . . kind of had a bring-me-to-Jesus moment . . . and I knew that I was going to die and that I needed help." The encounter was her first positive experience with law enforcement. Ashley had previously attempted to report abuse but had left feeling discouraged. "If something happens, I might as well not go to them, because what are they going to do? Nothing."

Ashley shared that the interaction with the local officers on that day "was really the first time I ever brought up the trafficking. I asked them if they knew any resources." They connected Ashley with federal investigators who, in turn, referred her to an organization providing services for survivors of trafficking that got her into a detox program and then a residential treatment program for survivors of trafficking.

In her words, the treatment program "wasn't for me." The environment felt controlling—"It's almost like you're living with a [trafficker] again." Ashley was fortunate in not having the same vulnerabilities as some of the other survivors enrolled in the program: she was engaged and had a place to live with her fiancé after leaving the program. Her biggest need was therapy to deal with the aftermath of trafficking and to address her addiction; she also struggled with sobriety and finding meaningful employment. Additionally, she faced ongoing dental issues resulting from her trafficking and felt judged by medical providers when she sought help for pain.

"It's never going to go away," Ashley said, "but I'm sure there's a better spot than where I am now." She spoke highly of the services she was receiving; when she was in the trafficking situation she didn't know of any resources for getting out. "When you're in the life you don't think that there's any help. Yeah, you think there's rehab for drugs and stuff like that. What else am I going to do? Where do I go from here? Am I going to go to a homeless shelter? Yeah, right. That's not an option when you leave like that."

When asked about her hopes for the future, Ashley responded, "To be a little bit more normal." She looked forward to getting a job and developing a career, making money, and helping people. "Having kids—I definitely want to do that." Her aspirations are modest but achieving and maintaining stability is challenging post-trafficking. "I just want to live a normal life, a square life, I guess. Those things are important. It's very hard. I would like to just be comfortable with it. Not have so much anxiety about it or be like 'Why am I so nervous for no reason?' . . . It's crazy how something like that can ruin your life the way it did. That's the thing that makes me mad."

Leslie

Leslie did not disclose her age to me, but she had adult children and shared a decades-long series of events leading up to her trafficking, suggesting she was likely in her forties or fifties. Following a fairly privileged childhood outside of New England, she married young and had kids. Her move to New England happened after her husband became abusive and her marriage had deteriorated.

Leslie spent much of her adult life in voluntary sex work. After leaving her husband, "There were times when we really didn't have any money for food . . . and I had two children with me at the time." A friend in the escort business explained the work and got Leslie started as an independent sex worker. For many years, Leslie worked on her own under noncoercive conditions, able to work part-time and make her own hours. She appreciated the financial benefits: "I had money in the bank, I had a car. I had two places I stayed." Advantages extended beyond money. She embraced the autonomy and the flexible schedule that allowed her to travel and to work only when her kids were in school.

Leslie eventually began using drugs, which led her to make riskier choices regarding her work. As her addiction intensified, she moved in and out of periods of agentic work and exploitation: "A lot of times it had to do with my drug addiction . . . and being so dependent on the drug, and then at some points not having anywhere to stay." Both male and female traffickers exploited her addiction and would keep the money she made from dates with clients. Her addiction limited Leslie's ability to work independently. "When you do [sex work] out of desperation for shelter, or food, or drugs it's just a whole different world." Further clarifying, she shared that "addiction changes the element of what you're willing to put up with, or risk. Years ago, when I first started, if I got a bad feeling about anything, I didn't do it . . . What you're willing to do, and to the extent [you're willing to do it], changes so much depending on what you're doing it for. You know, drugs, a place to stay."

Leslie's changing levels of choice and control over time caused her to think definitionally. "I believe I was exploited a lot more than I was trafficked. I think they're two different things . . . Exploiting is using somebody else's vulnerability or weakness for your gain, and then trafficking is somebody that . . . will not let you go, and makes you do things, and makes you give them the money. It's similar, but it's not the same."

Over a period of several years, Leslie moved in and out of trafficking situations. At one point, a trafficker barricaded her in a room: "He barred the opening with doors and furniture, like I couldn't get out." She talked about the complicated relationship with her captor, who sometimes was pleasant and at other times demanded she turn over all her earnings in exchange for drugs. "He'd be great in the beginning, and then over the course of the day he could change so quick . . . be so happy with you one minute, and then the next minute, 'Oh well, we have to pay rent' or . . . maybe say he provided a meal . . . and [later] he'd say, 'Well, you didn't think that was free?'"

Leslie ultimately escaped that coercive situation and went back to working independently, but her drug use made it difficult to maintain stable housing. She stayed in hotels off and on, but told me, "When it was really bad with the drug situation . . . I couldn't afford it more than a day or two at a time . . . It was this just crazy cycle."

Eventually she was arrested, and the officer told Leslie's attorney that he had done so in an effort to help her. Leslie, however, did not immediately encounter any assistance, and instead a long entanglement with the criminal legal system ensued. "Maybe the officers are trying to help . . . but it just causes more problems."

Leslie came into contact with law enforcement again as part of a joint federal-local operation to identify trafficking; this time they connected her with a local victim services agency. Even though Leslie was working independently at the time, her prior history qualified her for anti-trafficking services. She quickly moved into a treatment program and told me that it "saved my life . . . It gave me a lot of life skills . . . Before . . . it was just all about survival. They gave me my life back."

Having recently moved into her own place, Leslie told me she was setting goals for herself and moving forward. Despite her success, leaving her former life behind was difficult, partly financially and partly due to familiarity. As she told me, "It's just what I know." She attributed another element to what she called wanderlust: "I wanna just pick up and go." She added, "My hope for moving forward is that I can really learn how to live my life again. A normal life, or somewhat normal life, and not be scared to do things." Reflecting on all she had been through, she told me, "I think about, 'Oh, it's a bad day because I can't find my thing that goes in my purse,' but a year and a half ago it was a bad day because some guy left bruises all over me. It's just totally tilted in another direction, my life has."

Liana

Liana was in her early thirties when we met in the conference room of an otherwise quiet building on a small college campus. She had grown up in a town a couple of hours away and had been in and out of trafficking situations since adolescence. As soon as we sat down to chat, she immediately launched into her story and her long history of drug use. "It started out when I was about sixteen years old. I started using pretty heavily right off. I started with pills. Then I quickly went to IVs." She was soon deceptively recruited into a trafficking situation. The trafficker had lured her and a friend to a party out of state, bought them nice clothes, and then made an about-face, demanding that the young women stay and "work" for him by selling sexual services. Liana refused and her trafficker responded with violence, isolation, and deprivation. She eventually submitted to her captor's demands. After a short time, she was able to escape. Following a meet-up with a client, Liana had made a run for it and sought assistance from a good Samaritan who provided her with the funds for a bus ticket.

Once back home, Liana started selling sex for money on her own terms. She told me, "I've been doing it for about nine years . . . In the beginning it was forced, and then . . . in between I'd be doing it on my own, then I'd be forced again, then doing it on my own. I wasn't on my own very long until I got to the point where I was back in the hole."

Substance use determined Liana's work history. She spent periods of time exotic dancing but repeatedly returned to on-call commercial sex work as a way to afford her drug habit. "I used to get my drugs, give them my money . . . It was kind of like I was working for them [her pimp and drug dealer] but also working to get my drug habit under control." Over time the relationship with her drug dealer—sometimes pimp—evolved into something involving much more force and control. "He stabbed me because I tried to take off . . . I've got some battle wounds from not giving them enough money or not wanting to participate or being too high that I couldn't do it. I got consequences for that."

Throughout the years, Liana was able to extricate herself from situations involving force and coercion either by running away and relocating or through law enforcement involvement. She had a long history with the criminal legal system, usually in the form of prostitution charges. She shared, "A lot of times [the cops] would let the guy go, and they would charge me. I have probably four prostitution charges, but if they would have looked into it more, they would have seen that I was forced to do those things." She continued, "They just thought I was a drug addict, and charged me. If they would have been more responsive to why I was doing it, I think that I [would] have gotten help a long time ago."

Liana never viewed law enforcement as a source of safety or of help if she needed it, instead asserting, "I didn't think they'd help me. I kind of knew they wouldn't. I thought they would charge me instead of helping me." Indeed, the police did charge Liana, repeatedly, and she spent time in jail as a result, which further compromised her safety. Her pimp-turned-trafficker would call the jail to find out when she was being released and "he was waiting right outside every time." She speculated, "If I would have gotten the help that I needed from the law enforcement then . . . I wouldn't have had to go back to that life."

The control Liana's most recent trafficker exerted over her kept her in the situation. She was able to leave for dates with clients, but was expected to come right back to the house where he provided her a place to sleep. Even if she could have walked away, other vulnerabilities prevented her from leaving. She lacked alternative housing, had inadequate clothing, and was food insecure. Those factors, as well as her drug addiction, all served as barriers to escaping the situation. The fact that Liana lacked these vital resources and knew of no sources of help meant that she was trapped, with no viable alternatives.

Again and again, Liana insisted that she didn't view law enforcement as a source of assistance because of her arrest history. Even so, it was an arrest for a parole violation that ultimately helped her leave her trafficker for good. By happenstance she was connected with a knowledgeable lawyer and a law enforcement officer with extensive training on trafficking. This help came quite late in Liana's trafficking trajectory. Though many previous opportunities for intervention were missed, working with the right professionals finally allowed her to access services and to address multiple unmet needs.

Once Liana was connected with federal law enforcement investigating her case, she noted a drastic difference in the way they responded to her situation compared to the earlier local authorities. The federal officers "will do something about it, but as far as the regular cops go . . . they think it's all the female's fault." Her attorney put her in touch with a treatment program for survivors of trafficking. In addition to receiving treatment for her substance use disorder, Liana was able to work with a therapist, address longstanding medical and dental issues, and prepare for her GED exam—"stuff that you can't do when you're in the life because they wouldn't let you." While in the trafficking situation, Liana's most pressing needs were "drugs and making sure that [the trafficker] gets the amount of money that he wants, or you get hit for it." Once out of the situation, she was finally able to prioritize her own needs and desires, including school and medical appointments.

Liana detoxed while in jail the last time and continued her sobriety once she entered a treatment program for survivors of trafficking. At the time of our interview, she was taking Suboxone, a form of medication-assisted treatment. It took getting sober for her to recognize that she had been trafficked. Her trafficker had forced her to do a certain amount of heroin a day as a way to control her and the other women she worked alongside. At times, she took more as a way to get through the work. "I was using to do the job that I had to do. I had to be high doing it, and I've overdosed like three times. I got pretty beat for that too."

When we met, Liana was enrolled in a GED program. She had a job interview scheduled and spoke highly about the staff in the treatment program who had helped her get to that point. "It's just a beginning . . . not being dependent on anybody else for my money, that's a huge step for me. Normally

I had to depend on men for what I needed. Now it's doing it on my own, and it feels good. They've helped me to get to that point, you know?" I asked what was next for her and what felt achievable. Liana told me she soon hoped to be reunited with her child and also planned on "getting housing, getting my own place, getting my schooling, holding a job, holding sobriety . . . Working on me instead of what [the traffickers] want."

Reagan

Reagan was in her late thirties at the time of our meeting. She had grown up in an affluent New England suburb and described her childhood as "pretty normal," yet the details she shared left me with the impression that her upbringing was far more tumultuous than her initial description suggested. Her parents divorced when she was young and, as she told me, "My mom was in and out. I grew up with my grandparents for the most part." Reagan dealt with a significant family loss and subsequently dropped out of high school. She went on to get her GED and enrolled in college briefly but "started hanging out with people who weren't doing great things" and "everything went on a downward spiral from there." She ended up in prison shortly thereafter. After her release, Reagan was doing well until a back injury put her on oxycodone. She quickly developed an addiction. She reconnected with an old friend who introduced Reagan to doing dates on Backpage and quickly reneged on a promise of free rent. Having already taken her up on the housing offer, Reagan felt trapped and acquiesced to a demand to turn over half of what she made.

The friend-turned-trafficker also provided Reagan with drugs and used threats of cutting her off from the supply and taking away her housing to maintain control and Reagan's continued compliance. Reagan had heard the term *trafficking* and associated it with foreign-born women being kidnapped and sold for sex, but she didn't realize it could apply to the form of control she herself was experiencing. When she was arrested on an old warrant, her lawyer explained the connection.

Reagan felt stuck and was not aware of any services that would help her meet her needs. She had thought, "How do I get out of here? Where am I going to go? How am I going to make money? Then I had an addiction too.

How am I going to support that?" The addiction became a major consideration, and she recalled "wanting to leave but you don't want to leave because you're going to get [dope]sick. It's just a really bad cycle." Emphasizing the vulnerabilities she was experiencing, Reagan listed all the unmet needs that she had no way of fulfilling: "Housing would have been big . . . a way to walk away from it and have somewhere else to go. When you walk away from something like that you are walking away from any kind of money you had; [you have] nowhere to go; you have to start your whole life over. There's really not anything put in place, I don't think anyway, to help somebody like that."

Once Reagan was identified as a trafficking survivor, the organizations she worked with helped her meet some of those needs, something which had seemed impossible while she was actively being trafficked. "When you're in fear for your life you can't go down and talk to somebody about it or call somebody when your pimp is sitting right next to you . . . If you're going to get help or need to leave the situation, you need to have somewhere to go where nobody knows where you are. There's no place like that." Reagan's point was one reiterated by multiple survivors—they needed crisis services in the period between leaving the trafficking situation and beginning case management services provided by nonprofits.

Reagan also expounded on the challenges of seeking help with her addiction. "I've tried to do that like a ton of times. When you're out there by yourself it doesn't really work when you're trying to do it on your own. Twenty-eight-day programs don't work because they just kind of throw you right back out there when you're at your most vulnerable." Her experiences left her with a strong sense of the link between housing and sobriety. "There's just not a lot of places to go get help for an addiction where you can stay and get yourself better and stronger before you go back out . . . like longer than thirty days, helping you get a plan in place . . . at least get on your feet and have a job . . . before you're just thrown out there." Being discharged into a world where one doesn't have a job or financial resources essentially undoes the effort put into detox.

Reaching out to the police for help was never an option for Reagan. She described multiple instances of being harassed by police. The disrespect she felt "just walking up the street, going to the store" foreclosed that option in her mind. "If I would have known I could go to law enforcement and not had anything to worry about and felt safe I'm sure a lot more people would do it. It's not like that."

Even though an alternate pathway would have been preferable to her, being arrested for a parole violation was what ultimately connected Reagan with extended wraparound services and the treatment she needed to achieve sobriety. She had only been in the program a short time when we met and was optimistic about her future prospects. "I just started working . . . I start school next month. I'm just pretty excited to get my life back on track . . . Things are happening. It's pretty great."

Sophia

Sophia radiated confidence. When we met, she was in her thirties. She had been free from trafficking for a couple of years and was living independently. She had grown up locally. Like many of the other survivors I interviewed, she had a turbulent childhood and had endured periods of physical and emotional abuse, as well as familial drug use and incarceration. Nonetheless, Sophia had been a good student and a hard worker. She graduated from high school and attended college for a bit.

Sophia first took OxyContin as an adolescent following an injury. In her late teens she rediscovered it, and then heroin, and was hooked. Soon she was "working all the time to basically just pay for drugs." She described her recruitment into trafficking as a gradual, almost casual, process. Her dealer became her pimp and eventually her trafficker. "At first he was giving me my money, or like part of my money for it, but slowly he just ended up keeping all the money himself." She continued, "At first it was great . . . He paid for everything." Noting the complexity of the relationship, she told me, "It seemed like he was this really friendly, compassionate, like, I-care-about-you kind of guy."

Ultimately, Sophia's trafficker became violent and controlling and forced her to engage in sex for money, to sell drugs, and to turn over all her earnings to him. He would retaliate for missed quotas and other presumed indiscretions by withholding drugs: "If [trafficker] would get mad at me, he'd be like, 'Oh, I'm not giving you any dope' and . . . 'You can be fucking sick,' and 'you can do your dates.'" Emphasizing the extreme control her trafficker exerted, Sophia added, "He would like rape you if he was really mad, or he'd like beat the shit out you." Sophia received a minor reprieve when her trafficker ended up in prison for drug-related crimes, leaving her under the control of a less violent co-conspirator.

Eventually Sophia spent time in jail for parole violations related to other crimes and came into contact with an organization providing support for trafficking survivors. She knew what had happened to her was "kind of messed up" but she had never heard the term *human trafficking*. Upon her release, the organization continued to assist Sophia, but structural barriers left her vulnerable. The group offered to help get her into a sober living facility, but there was a waitlist at the time. The alternative was to stay at a shelter, which Sophia declined. She felt she would be more at risk staying at the shelter, not least because her traffickers would easily be able to find her there. Sophia also noted that the organization's case management model and schedule didn't correspond to her needs, which often arose outside of typical working hours.

While Sophia was seeking treatment for substance use disorder, her trafficker found her and punished her violently for leaving. Sophia tried to seek help unsuccessfully several more times, and her trafficker responded by completely isolating her and keeping her under constant watch. During that time, Sophia's drug use intensified and her health declined severely. She shared, "I was using really heavily . . . I was a lot more reckless with my whole life overall . . . I just really didn't have the will to live and keep myself in safer situations anymore."

One day, based on an anonymous tip, law enforcement showed up at the door. One of the officers suspected trafficking. Sophia initially turned down the officer's offers of assistance, and he arrested her for drug possession, supposedly to keep her safe. Sophia ended up in jail as a result. She went from there into a treatment program for survivors of trafficking, which helped her cut ties with her trafficker for good.

Sophia's experiences with law enforcement were very mixed. Correctional officers made derogatory comments based on their assumptions about her work. One probation officer had a victim-blaming mentality and chided her for her drug use, telling her, "You're just gonna get murdered by a John, or you're gonna OD on heroin if you don't stop." Another probation officer initially did not pick up on the signs that Sophia was being trafficked but was sympathetic to her situation after she was arrested for a parole violation.

While Sophia was distrustful of her arresting officer, she viewed her arrest as her way out of the trafficking situation she had been trapped in for so long. She said she told the officer, "I don't even want your help. I would rather just go to prison and get this over with. I'm happy to spend a year in prison peacefully and not deal with any of this shit." Nonetheless, the officer continued to show up throughout her court proceedings and offered ongoing support in the form of phone cards and meals once she moved into a treatment program.

After spending a little under a year in the treatment program, Sophia had a job and a new baby. Enrolled in college, she had hopes to move on to a master's program. She considered herself lucky to be moving forward in this way and noted that several of the other women from the treatment program had not been as successful in leaving their former lives behind. Despite her relief at being safe and moving toward stability, there were still certain aspects of "the life" that were enticing. "There are fun things about being at the huge parties and being all dressed up and being able to do all these drugs and everybody thinks you're so pretty . . . But then you have to stop and weigh it out . . . and . . . it's not really that appealing." Considering the challenges of being out of that life, Sophia admitted, "It actually kind of really sucks to be out of the life sometimes. You're going to be like eating Ramen noodles and riding the bus . . . but you just kind of have to work through those times, and you'll start to succeed more and more."

Insurance had always been a barrier when Sophia was "in the life" and dreaming about rehab as a potential exit. Post-trafficking as well as after completing the treatment program, Sophia still experienced a range of vulnerabilities. "It's hard rebuilding . . . I kind of left the program with nothing." She didn't qualify for subsidized housing, food stamps, or state-funded healthcare, all of which posed major challenges to moving forward. She moved in with her fiancé, which solved her housing issue, but she struggled in other areas. Broadening her commentary to other survivors, she continued, "Housing is a huge issue. Income is a huge issue, then like food and healthcare . . . And especially for people that do relapse . . . because that comes along with addiction."

Emma

Emma was in her mid-twenties and had lived in one of the state's more significant metropolitan areas her entire life. During her childhood all of her adult caregivers struggled with addiction, and drugs and alcohol were ever-present. Her mother and stepfather were both addicts, so she spent little time with them: "When my mom's heroin use really took off, I went to go live with my grandmother, so I was separated from my . . . siblings." Her grandmother was an alcoholic and her grandfather was an addict, so Emma "was around it 24/7." She moved around a lot due to the changing custody circumstances. In her mid-teens, Emma began using with a family member and then dropped out of high school. She entered foster care shortly thereafter, got clean, and then had a child of her own. After moving back in with a family member in her early twenties, Emma started using again. She described her life as "rough, in and out of treatment, in and out of jail, all that sort of stuff." She had been trafficked twice.

Shortly after Emma started using again, she met a drug dealer who became her boyfriend. She did not initially grasp that he was also a pimp. She told me, "I was just so heavily into using and so self-absorbed that I didn't even realize what was going on around me." At one point the police came and Emma reported that they arrested her on a nonsense charge because they believed she was being trafficked and wanted to remove her from the situation. The boyfriend was pimping other women at that point, but it wasn't happening to her, "at least not at that point."

The separation was helpful, for a time, and allowed Emma to get clean. After a few months, she encountered her ex again, and things changed quickly. Emma's former boyfriend responded violently when he saw her. She said the last thing she remembered about that encounter was seeing him, and then she woke up in another state where she was forced to perform sex acts along with multiple other women. Emma remained in the situation for a number of months and told me, "Nobody knew where I was, and I wasn't going to call my family because that would put them at risk." She revealed that her former-boyfriend-turned-trafficker and his associates would inject her with drugs, and she did not remember a lot from that time. She was always being watched and there were constant threats of and actual physical and sexual violence.

What Emma recalled with most detail was her point of exit. While she was with her traffickers during a drug deal, law enforcement had descended on them. "They knew everything, which is why I was so pissed off with law enforcement, because if you knew, why didn't you come get me?"

After being identified by law enforcement, anti-trafficking service providers assisted in Emma's admission to a residential treatment program. She found the program helpful, but it closed before she completed treatment, leaving her vulnerable and without housing. Thus began a whole new phase of instability. She relapsed and moved in and out of various shelters before ending up in another trafficking situation where her addiction was used as the means of control. Emma described how the trafficker would say "I've given you all these drugs. You owe me all this money."

Emma once again was able to leave the trafficking situation when law enforcement got involved. The investigators were familiar with human trafficking and connected her with targeted services. She spoke highly of the assistance she received. When I asked what the organization had helped her with, she told me, "Oh my god, everything . . . I lost all my clothes and everything. They replaced everything. They got things for my kids, case management, counseling, everything. I feel like if I didn't have that I probably would have been dead . . . They really helped me get into a treatment program, and even when I screwed up and had to leave that program, they would help me get into another one."

Coming out of the trafficking situation, Emma's biggest need was dealing with her addiction and trying to access treatment. She continued using and started trading sex on her own terms to make money and meet her basic needs. She found the work dangerous, but the area lacked economic alternatives. "I felt like I couldn't do anything else," she told me. "This is what I know . . . It's just been a struggle to break the cycle."

After a drug overdose, Emma spent time in another substance use program, hoping it would be enough to help her recover, though she asserted, "It wasn't. I needed a long-term thing because I've never dealt with it [the trauma of her past experience]. I just kept pushing it down and down because I [didn't] want to deal with it." When we met, she had just entered a treatment program for trafficking survivors and was looking forward to finally addressing the complexities of her addiction and mental health needs.

"To move on and figure out who I am and get my shit together"—these were her hopes for the program. Emma wanted serious counseling for her post-traumatic stress disorder: "I'm so done with being stuck in that. It's time to do something about it instead of letting it control me and ruin me . . . I want to rise up out of it, and I want to help other girls."

Taryn

Taryn was in her late twenties when we met and had lived in the area all her life. She told me that "school was always really difficult for me" and that she had dropped out before even entering high school and had moved in with her boyfriend.

Her extended drug use included multiple attempts at getting sober followed by relapse. Despite being uneasy about it, a desperation to maintain her addiction was what initially led Taryn into sex work. She told me, "I knew what was happening wasn't right, but I had a drug addiction . . . [and] still did it because of my addiction." Taryn ended up in situations that turned into trafficking twice and chose not to share a lot of details about either instance. She did mention that, after her first trafficker went to prison, she got sober for a period but then got caught up in another trafficking situation. "I got clean one time, but other than that, I honestly didn't think that I could. Because what I was doing, I needed to get high to do it." The futility vexed her. "In my head, from being clean one time for over a year, when I was back in the life I would get so upset about it. I remember what I felt like to be out of the life. I remember what I felt like to be sober, and then to be back to the point that I was, where I couldn't just walk away from it, was a scary feeling."

Taryn, like many of the other survivors I spoke with, had a long history of arrests and incarceration related to drugs and theft. Apart from the cops she had seen as clients, interactions with law enforcement had actually been mostly positive and "They just always tried to help me." It was law enforcement who had connected Taryn with anti-trafficking services, and she spoke with gratitude about the support she received from her caseworker. "When I came out of jail, I had nothing. I had lost everything, and they helped me get clothes, they helped me get back on my feet."

Housing proved to be an enormous hurdle, but Taryn's caseworker eventually helped her get into a residential treatment program for trafficking survivors. Taryn wished she had connected with her caseworker sooner and emphasized how the program had provided unconditional and nonjudgmental support. "No matter what, I always had them. Whether I was still in the life, whether I was out of the life. Just because I was in the life didn't mean they left me." The program "made me feel safe even when I was in the life, when I was really unsafe." Even when she drank to excess to cope, "They would always talk to me and do what they could to help me . . . It's important to feel that no matter what you do, that somebody's gonna have your back."

Taryn had reluctantly agreed to do an interview because she saw it as a way to help others and shared, "I hate to talk about being in the life . . . Sometimes I have to close my eyes and shake my head just so I don't have to see what I'm thinking." When I asked about the positive aspects of the residential program, she responded ardently. "Oh, everything's the best part. Just waking up without being sick. Not always looking over my shoulder. Not being hit." When we spoke, she had been sober for seven months and told me, "I'm pretty happy about where I'm at now."

Mia

Mia was from another New England state. Her parents divorced and she grew up separated from her siblings. She completed high school and attended some college. Tracing her pain-pill addiction back to a teenage injury, she said she didn't realize the "type of issue that that was going to cause because it was doctor prescribed; there wasn't any thought that anything was going to go wrong with that until two years into it when they took me off of them, and I realized that, obviously, there was an issue and I needed to find outside sources [for the drugs]." She had to look elsewhere for her supply.

Mia moved around a lot throughout her twenties and went in and out of treatment for her substance use disorder. Her drug habit led to her first experience with trading sex for money. An acquaintance had introduced her to the idea and told her she would arrange the date and they would split the money. "I didn't quite understand what the deal was until I was in it, and I was like, 'Well, I'm already here and I don't feel good' because I was [dope]sick and there was $100 at the end of it, so I just kind of went with it." Recognizing the profit to be made, Mia continued engaging in sex work as a way to feed her drug habit.

Following a period in rehab for her drug addiction, Mia met someone and, in the beginning, understood their relationship as being romantic. "What I didn't notice until I looked back at it," she said, "is I was pretty much groomed for a solid two months. And the red flags that I see now, I didn't see then." After a short time, "he just pretty much went psychotic, and basically kidnapped me." Mia's friends reported her missing, but her boyfriend-turned-trafficker held her phone and made it impossible for her to contact anyone. He took her up and down the East Coast, selling her for sex and tracking her every move.

Physical and sexual violence were constants. "I would fight back in the beginning, but it just got to the point where I wanted it to just be over. So I would just take the beatings and hope that they would end quicker if I just didn't do anything." Mia's trafficker kept her isolated and forbade any outside contact. "I was never allowed to talk to people about myself. I had asked somebody for a lighter, and I literally got in so much trouble for that, that I never spoke to another soul." Following her escape, people kept asking why she didn't just run away, and Mia would explain, "Because it's not that easy and every time I would attempt to do something, I would just get hurt violently and I just stopped because I was done getting beat up over it."

Mia shared that on account of the trauma she experienced, "There is still a good period of time that I don't remember . . . Some days I wish that I could and then there's other days that I'm glad that I don't. But what I do remember is when I finally was able to escape." After a particularly intense beating, Mia made the decision to leave, despite the risk. She waited until her captor was asleep, retrieved her phone, and made a run for it. She "had reached that point where I was just so hopeless that I would rather have died than to keep doing it." Within a short time, Mia's trafficker awoke and tracked her down, but she used her phone to contact law enforcement and eventually got help and medical attention.

Mia was grateful to one law enforcement official in particular who went out of his way to assist her, but overall, the criminal legal system failed her. In multiple instances, she had reached out to law enforcement to report what was going on, to no avail. She described the excruciating process of trying to get anyone to take her story seriously. Mia was not using during the time of her trafficking but said "Because I was an addict, I was looked at that I just took off with my boyfriend." She participated in extensive interviews recapping her experiences, but her trafficker faced minimal prosecutorial consequences. "I was mortified . . . like I literally went through this for nothing, and nobody cares and nobody believes me. And because I have had drug problems in the past, it's [assumed that it's] my own fault that this happened."

Not only did Mia feel there was little justice served in the case, but law enforcement officials also never referred her to anti-trafficking services, and she was left on her own with no support. Officers asked her to stay in touch so she could support their court case, but they did not offer to support her; they did nothing to connect her to an anti-trafficking organization. As she told me, "There was no services. There was no, 'Here, reach out to this person,' there was nothing." On her own, Mia did not have the tools or skills to resolve the trauma of trafficking. "I tried to go back into normal life and try to deal with it on my own and it just led me to not being able to deal with it. I tried to work full-time again. I tried to do all these things to get back into the regular swing of life, but I just couldn't do it. And I didn't know that there was help . . . I really didn't."

After her experience, Mia lived in terror. "For the first two months I couldn't even leave the house . . . I was literally afraid of my own shadow." She was terrified of her trafficker and the possibility that he might retaliate following her escape. Mia shared, "I started using again because I didn't know what else to do . . . I got to the point where I would go to work and then I would go home and I would hide and I would do drugs trying to forget that any of it was going on."

Finally, Mia couldn't take living in fear anymore. "I was just done running from it," she told me. "I was done using because I didn't even want to, and something needed to happen, so I checked myself into detox." Mia explained everything to her case manager, including her concerns about safety, and he helped her get into a residential treatment program for trafficking survivors. At the time, she "just need[ed] some place to be safe and to try and rebuild my life." The program delivered and provided Mia with "more opportunities than I could have even dreamed of." The staff were incredibly supportive, helping her to get medical care and access other much needed services.

Prior to entering the program, Mia's greatest needs were "housing, safety, and . . . trying to stabilize my mental health on top of my recovery." Life had been pared down way past the bare essentials and Mia "went into detox with $10 to my name and a couple pairs of clothes and that was it. I had nothing and I knew that I needed to start over, and I knew it wasn't going to be easy, but I knew that it needed to happen."

At the time of our conversation, Mia was working full-time and pursuing a degree in criminal justice "because," she told me, "I've seen the absolute disaster on the other end, and something needs to change about it." She went on, "I want to help the next person because I remember what it felt like to be so alone and that nobody understood or nobody believed me, and that's miserable and I don't want anybody to have to go through that."

CHAPTER 3

Structural Vulnerability Before, During, and After Trafficking

There's a lot of barriers. We have a lack of substance abuse services in our state. The cost of housing is skyrocketing. Getting jobs that have livable wages is difficult. I think there's a lot of things that contribute to somebody being vulnerable to trafficking, and not having their basic needs met, or feeling like they can support themselves is one of those. And I think that [our state] is a place where it's really hard to do that . . . There's a significant need for affordable housing. There's a significant need for available and easy-to-access substance abuse services. I mean, we have a frickin' drug problem that's off the charts, and . . . the size of our treatment does not [correspond to] the size of our problem. They don't mirror one another.

—Eliza, Program Director

When risk and blame are individualized, the solutions imagined and interventions planned focus on changing the behavior of the individual. However, attempting to intervene on an individual behavior in such contexts draws attention away from the structural forces producing mortal danger and death in the first place.

—Seth Holmes, *Fresh Fruit, Broken Bodies: Migrant Farmworkers in the United States*

Public health and social medicine accept that a person's health is not determined solely by individual biology. The concept *social determinants of health* encompasses the wide range of social, economic, and demographic conditions that also influence well-being. Social determinants include place of residence, education, work opportunities, healthcare quality and access, housing, transportation, exposure to racism, and access to healthy foods and community resources.[1] Evidence shows that these factors impact health outcomes for conditions such as cancer, heart disease, and diabetes and also affect how people are able to cope with long-term challenges and trauma. Vulnerability to, and ability to recover from, human trafficking is intricately linked with the social determinants of health.

Medical anthropology emphasizes these same principles through the framework of structural violence. This concept is especially useful with regard to human trafficking because it corrects an over attention to the individual proximal risk factors and de-emphasizes interpersonal violence and the narrative of individual traffickers and victims.[2] A structural violence lens reframes the issue: the paradigm is no longer one of bad people doing bad things to innocent victims that necessitates criminal legal solutions. Rather, human trafficking becomes a subject of social injustice, failed systems, inequitable economic arrangements, and poor social policies that require policy interventions and a radical rethinking of the status quo. Structural violence goes a step further than the framework of social determinants in that it explicitly calls out the violence of hierarchical power structures and directs attention to the state as a key force in creating and reproducing inequality.[3] As Shannon and colleagues note, this framing accounts for "the mechanisms by which social forces such as poverty, racism, and gender inequity become embodied as individual experiences and health outcomes."[4] Violence at the structural level works itself out on—and in—the bodies of the vulnerable.

The narratives in the previous chapter reveal the ways that survivors experience structural violence before, during, and after trafficking. It became clear over the course of my research that the structural problems, including insufficient systems and supports, that were present before trafficking persisted during and after the period of trafficking. The survivors I encountered experienced multiple intersecting vulnerabilities, many of which had contributed to their trafficking but which also remained following their exit. Even after escaping, survivors struggled to achieve stability because the same failed systems that factored into their trafficking in the first place remained, even with support from experienced and knowledgeable service providers. To be clear, while each of the survivors experienced vulnerability at the individual level, the barriers they encountered—and that will be discussed here—were structural, and structural interventions are necessary to prevent trafficking moving forward. Throughout their interviews, survivors, service providers, and criminal legal authorities expressed remarkable agreement about the greatest challenges facing trafficking survivors: lack of housing; lack of treatment for substance use disorder; insufficient access to wraparound health care and transportation; and unavailability of economic alternatives. Widespread barriers and the lack of corresponding solutions reflect the inadequate systems in place to address inequality and prevent trafficking (see Figure 4).

Contextualizing Vulnerability

What the survivors in this study have shared is echoed by findings of the National Survivor Survey (2023)—the vast majority of surveyed survivors face trauma, abuse, poverty, mental health challenges, and other struggles in childhood. According to survey findings, 83 percent of survivors experienced poverty, 69 percent ran away from home, 96 percent experienced abuse (physical, sexual, emotional), 93 percent experiences substance abuse and mental health challenges, 93 percent lived with someone who experienced substance abuse and mental health challenges, and 96 percent experienced other family or household instability.[5] These are high numbers and suggest specific areas of vulnerability where intervention is needed. A growing body of research has examined the connection between adverse childhood experiences (ACEs) and human trafficking (particularly for U.S. citizens) and has shown that ACEs have a significant impact on future violence, victimization, and perpetration. Children and youth who experience high levels of traumatic situations have an increased risk of mental health problems, teen pregnancy, violence, and involvement in human trafficking situations.[6]

When asked about their clients' pre-trafficking experiences, caseworkers often cited childhood adversity and trauma as key points of vulnerability. Chloe, one caseworker, described parental neglect and abuse as predominant: "I can't think of really any of my clients who have talked about having good

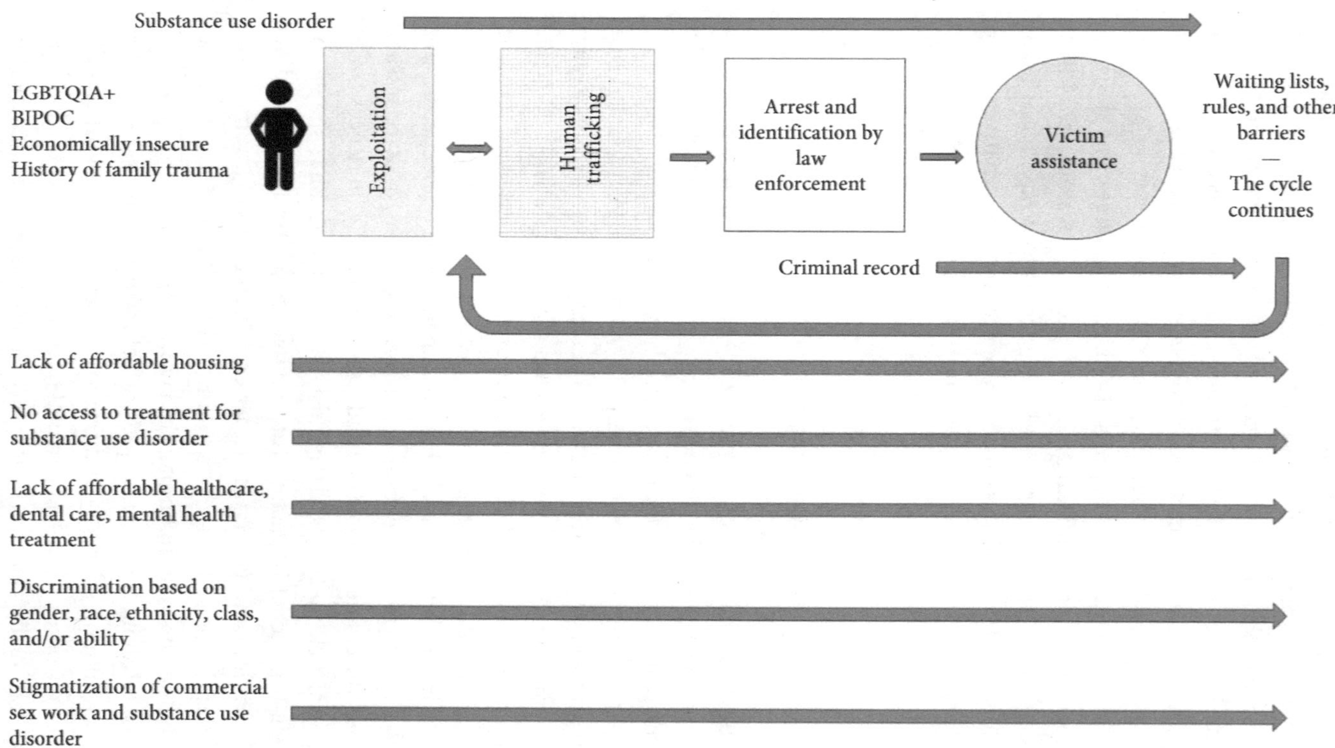

Figure 4. Trafficking Trajectories: Structural Violence Before, During, and After Trafficking

parenting experiences." Involvement in the foster care system is another common complication. For example, many of the cases Mariah oversaw involved foster youth "who then are themselves mothers who are involved in DHHS," describing the vicious cycle many of her clients experienced.[7] "That is a very, very traumatic thing that people a lot of times will talk about that experience of themselves being taken away from their family's custody, being in foster care, potentially having not good providers or caretakers, potential abuse there, and then themselves going through the process of losing their children." On top of the trauma of losing custody of their children (usually due to substance use disorder), Mariah's clients often subsequently lost their health insurance that was tied to their children. The parents were thus unable to access treatment for substance use disorder, and the cycle continued.

As their own words illustrate, many of the survivors I interviewed had lived through multiple, and often exceedingly traumatic, adverse childhood experiences. While not predictive of trafficking, research suggests that the risk of trafficking increases as adverse life events accumulate over time—what Schwarz and coauthors refer to as chains-of-risk. Proactively identifying these accreting risks and offering services and resources may disrupt and break patterns of vulnerability and exploitation, yet far too few resources are available to meet these needs.[8]

Of course, individual experiences do not occur in a vacuum but rather within the context of unequal structures and social conditions, and it is important to consider the complex roles that race, social conditions, and generational trauma play in relation to adverse childhood experiences (see Figure 5).[9] Broadening the concept of vulnerability and risk-taking beyond individual behavior and choice, and placing it within the context of inequity creates space to acknowledge that "risky" behaviors, including substance use, may be ways for coping with previous and ongoing trauma.

Examining the role of social conditions and inequality through a public health lens, Elaine Alpert and Sharon Chin draw on the social-ecological model as a framework to understand the factors that "push" individuals into at-risk situations or that "pull" them into coercive ones.[10] As was evident for several of the survivors I interviewed, many of these factors are experienced at the individual level, including the need for basic necessities; a history of child abuse, neglect, or maltreatment; a history of being involved in the juvenile justice, criminal justice, or foster care system; poor education or

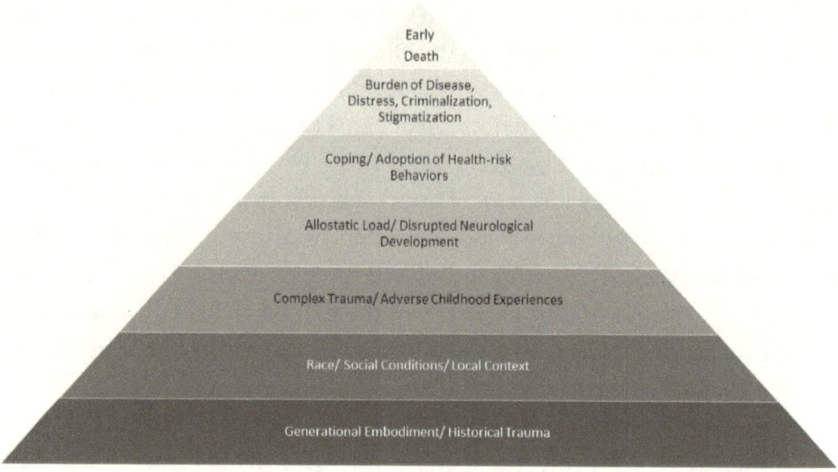

Figure 5. The ACE Pyramid as adapted by RYSE to account for social conditions, historical trauma, and embodiment, https://static1.squarespace.com/static/58ece61644024383be911a95/t/593e579b37c58172ed51340c/1497257886219/ACEs_social-location_2015.pdf.

illiteracy; minority gender, ethnicity, and/or race; stigma and discrimination; and extreme familial poverty. These are compounded by social factors at the relationship level (familial conflict, disruption, or dysfunction; lack of supportive adults; social isolation; and familial poverty), the community level (under-resourced schools, neighborhoods, and communities; bias against marginalized or vulnerable individuals), and the societal level (inequitable distribution of opportunities and resources; health and economic disparities). Compounding vulnerabilities also become key to understanding potential responses to trafficking. Indeed, it is the societal, structural, and systemic barriers that are the root causes, and that are the primary contributors to individual vulnerability to trafficking.

Substance Use Disorder and Intersections with Trafficking

Maine and New Hampshire have witnessed some of the highest overdose death rates in the country, as was certainly the case during the ethnographic study period. Both states ranked between third and twelfth highest nationwide each year between 2016 and 2018. Overdose deaths continued to climb in the two states through 2022, a sign of the inadequate resources and insufficient systems in place to address substance use disorder, though both states followed the nationwide decline in overdose deaths in 2023, likely because of the increased availability of Naloxone.[11]

The survivors I interviewed reported using a number of prescription and illicit drugs. Heroin was the most commonly used substance, and survivors also reported using fentanyl, OxyContin, cocaine, crack, methamphetamine, Klonopin, marijuana, and alcohol. Untreated substance use disorder was one of the biggest vulnerabilities among the clients Mariah served, and it played a key role in their trafficking trajectories. She noted, "For many of the people their use was one of the vulnerabilities that led to their traffickers or to their trafficking . . . For some people they might have had a more casual, occasional use, and then [during] the trafficking, part of the means of the control was just tons of access to opiates specifically [and] also cocaine and crack." In the absence of connecting to mental health services, Mariah's clients also reported increased drug use as a way of coping, not just with the trafficking situation itself, but also with previous trauma.

In numerous cases, survivors were recruited into trafficking through somebody who had been supplying them with drugs. In most cases, the relationship started with the individual meeting a dealer who initially provided them with free product and later made clear that the person owed money for the drugs they consumed. When the person had no money to pay for the drugs, the supplier then told them the type of work they needed to do to pay off the debt and used that debt and the threat of cutting them off from drugs (and the accompanying withdrawal symptoms) as means of control.[12] "For someone with an opiate addiction," Mariah explained to me, "those withdrawals are very intense. And for someone without any access to get treatment, that's a huge terrifying thing." Grant, a federal law enforcement investigator, called sex trafficking "one of the products of the opioid epidemic," adding that, with Maine and New Hampshire having some of the highest rates of opioid addiction in the nation, "folks are desperate and they are vulnerable to exploitation," leading to trafficking. Grant also shared that they were seeing cases that they classified as labor trafficking in which traffickers forced individuals to transport drugs on their behalf to minimize their own risk of being arrested. "They will enroll couriers that are drug addicts, and they'll use much the same tactics that a sex trafficker uses to force or coerce a mule to drive down to [a nearby city] and back with a bag of dope."

Drug Use, Trading Sex, and Choice

Of the survivors I encountered, some had been involved in sex work consensually and others had only participated within the context of trafficking. A few individuals were introduced to drugs during their trafficking experience, but most were trafficked as a result of their preexisting substance use disorder which had made them vulnerable to exploitation and abuse. In interviews, survivors raised complicated issues around the intersections of drug use and choices surrounding their entry into sex work.

Among frontline workers, there was some sense that drugs were indeed *the* primary impetus for women entering sex work. Absent their addiction, Hannah, a law enforcement investigator, told me that "these women" would "go out and get regular jobs and live regular lives." Some survivors echoed this sentiment but conveyed varied experiences with and nuanced attitudes toward sex work. Reagan, who had battled addiction her whole life, viewed it as a constrained choice: "You're out there for a reason. Either you have a really terrible situation at home, money issues, but most of the time you have a drug problem." While she had participated in commercial sex work as a way to support her drug habit for a long time, Reagan (and other women she had encountered prior to her own trafficking experience) had largely done so of her own free will. "Yeah. In my experiences, the people that I was around mostly . . . did it because they had a drug addiction. That's how they fed it; that's how they supported it. That's what I saw. I never knew anybody that had a pimp, that went out and did that, and was in fear for their life. Until now."

Conditions leading to sex work also include a lack of alternatives and economic precarity. Harsh economic and labor conditions factor into individuals' vulnerability. Emma told me, "There's really nothing in [the state], nothing. It's hard." A state politician, Rita, reinforced the point, stressing the economic drivers of trafficking: "There's a lot to be said for the idea that prosperity really helps, but to have prosperity, you have to have jobs. To have jobs, you have to have skills. And you also have to have an environment where businesses are able to thrive so they can offer jobs to those people with skills . . . There's [*sic*] too many places in [the state] where that's just such a challenge." Focusing overly on individual drug use and risk-taking ignores these larger structural factors. The lack of economic opportunity, of safe affordable housing, and of jobs constrained survivors' opportunities and made them susceptible to both drug use and trafficking.

A few of the survivors communicated that sex work had preceded their addiction. Others entered sex work as a way to pay for a drug habit they could not sustain through other forms of employment. Some individuals had found ways to engage in commercial sex work safely and appreciated the flexibility it provided, for example allowing them to work during school hours while raising kids as a single parent. It was when addiction led to desperation that sex work became less safe. Leslie, for example, started selling sex by choice and spoke about the level of control she had over her work that she could not find in other sectors. But as her drug use intensified and she struggled to meet her basic needs, her sense of control diminished. "It was a cycle of events, like the drug use," Leslie said. "And then with drug use, you know, unstable circumstances or situations would lead to me having to go back where I knew it wasn't going to be pleasant and have this person try and take advantage of me or take over." I talked to many survivors whose substance use led them to make increasingly unsafe choices. In multiple instances they first encountered their traffickers as drug dealers who provided drugs in exchange for sex or on credit, resulting in the accrual of large debts that were not easily repaid.

Sophia reported being less attuned to safety as a result of her drug use, both leading up to and while she was being trafficked. "I was using really heavily . . . between five to ten grams of heroin a day," she told me. "I was just like a lot more reckless with the dates that I did. Before I was kind of more like . . . 'Oh no, I'm only gonna do dates that like wear condoms,' and I just had all these different standards and stuff." In this progressive way, human trafficking became an additional form of structural violence experienced by the women I interviewed whose drug use, high rates of STIs and other health issues, and lack of safe and secure housing had preceded their trafficking. "What you're willing to do, and the extent, changes so much depending on what you're doing it for," Leslie explained. "You know, drugs, a place to stay. I mean, there's twenty-some-year-old girls, young girls, eighteen-to-nineteen-year-old girls staying out and having sex with people so they can use their shower." One of the survivors I interviewed, Andy, told me her first experience of being trafficked was the result of housing insecurity: "I was sixteen years old. I was by myself. My mom was in prison. I remember I just met this girl and I needed a place to go. She's like, 'Well, I need you to have sex with this guy for our rent' . . . I remember walking down the street with her. I remember her showing me what I should do, how I should walk, what I was supposed to do in order to get this money."

Andy's need for shelter serving as an entry point into the sex trade illustrates a common trajectory. A study of 641 homeless youth ages seventeen-to-twenty-five found that "sixty-eight percent (68 percent) of the youth who had either been trafficked or engaged in survival sex or commercial sex had done so while homeless. Nineteen percent (19 percent) of all youth interviewed had engaged in survival sex solely so that they could access housing or food."[13] Respondents reported challenges finding paid work, affordable housing, and support systems to assist with meeting their basic needs, all of which made them vulnerable to trafficking. The study also reported that nineteen percent of youth had experienced sex trafficking, labor trafficking, or a combination of the two. Force and coercion were used in many of these situations, where a person's addiction would be exploited or they would be threatened with homelessness for noncompliance.[14]

Exploiting Substance Use Disorder as a Method of Coercion and Control

No matter how the survivors I met had been introduced to sex work, weaponizing their addiction was a near-universal tactic of their traffickers. Ryan, a federal investigator, called it an "extreme method of control," adding that survivors are "so afraid of getting dope sick that they will do anything." He explained that traffickers will withhold drugs until a certain number of transactions have been completed, at which point they provide substances in an amount that will stave off the sickness, but only temporarily. Then things get even more complicated, even more compounded. "We see [victims] that come in with an opiate addiction and come out with both addiction to heroin and addiction to crack because they're being fed this cocktail to keep them moving throughout the day," he said. Traffickers isolate their victims and control every aspect of the victim's life, including access to the addictive substance. Grant, another investigator, said, "It is just an endless cycle at that point. It can take years. It is so easy to get sucked into the life, but it is harder than hell to get out." He provided a recent example: "We had a case where two trafficking victims who were being controlled by the trafficker were getting dope sick into a garbage can. The trafficker held a bag of dope over the garbage can while these girls were getting dope sick and he said 'if you get back to work, you can have this,' right? That's the type of control . . . They allow their victims to get to the edge of dope sickness and then they feed them a little bit of dope, a little bit of heroin or fentanyl to keep them going, to keep them from becoming dope sick. That's how they control the addiction."

Traffickers also used debt and threats of violence and arrest to ensure victims complied with their demands. Mariah had been working with a client whose trafficker manipulated her even as she was managing her own sex work independently. "She disclosed that she had been consensually engaging in sex work for many years on her own, with no one controlling her. And then parallel to that, she had this very controlling relationship with her drug dealer who is holding over her a debt in the five figures and is using that as a way to control her to traffic drugs across state lines." If she did not comply with his orders, the trafficker threatened to violently harm the victim's family members and to report her to law enforcement when she was transporting drugs for him. Mariah's client "did not see a way out at all. She was like, 'He has so much control. If I stop doing this, if I get any help or resources he's going to my mother's house and [will] hurt her.'" Mariah was limited in what she could offer the client. "There wasn't a lot we could do for her in that moment because she just completely felt like there was no safe thing that she could do." In this case, the client was so terrified of retribution from her trafficker that she did not believe law enforcement—or anyone else—had the means to protect her or her family if she left.

Criminalized Survival

Already vulnerable from substance use disorder and the control exerted by their traffickers, survivors face additional barriers in the criminal legal system. A 2016 National Survivor Network survey found that over 90 percent of

130 respondents had been arrested at least once in the course of being trafficked. Respondents reported being arrested for prostitution, solicitation, intention to solicit, drug possession, drug sales, and other crimes. Over half of all respondents believed that all their arrests, charges, and convictions were directly related to their trafficking.[15]

These findings align with what I heard from survivors about their experiences. The majority of them could be categorized as what legal scholar Leigh Goodmark terms *criminalized survivors*—"women, trans people, and gender-nonconforming people whose punitive encounters with the criminal legal system are directly linked to their own gender-based victimization (rape/sexual assault, intimate partner violence, or trafficking—or some combination thereof, given the co-occurrence of these forms of violence)."[16] The survivors I interviewed were engaged in criminalized behavior in at least two sectors—drugs and commercial sex work—and often under duress by their traffickers. They had encountered the criminal legal system in a variety of ways. A small number had sought help from law enforcement officials, which did not always turn out well. When Mia, for example, reached out to police, they did not believe her story and viewed her as an addict who had run off with her boyfriend rather than as a victim under the control of an abusive trafficker.

Other survivors initially came into contact with the criminal legal system because they were arrested for selling drugs, sex trading, as part of sex trafficking investigations or stings, or as a result of probation violations for other crimes such as theft. Some individuals were grateful for those interventions and viewed their arrest as the only way out of the trafficking situation. One survivor, Andy, shared, "I just remember I just was so grateful when I was all done. I remember feeling that relief . . . When they took me in that police car, I'm like, 'Thank you.'" Others only experienced negative consequences as a result of arrest and viewed the police as putting them in more danger. Despite the violence and control they endured as part of their trafficking, these survivors' fear of law enforcement officials—often based on previous interactions—also meant that they did not feel safe seeking help from the police. They might be arrested for crimes related to their trafficking, but survivors were also arrested for criminalized activity that they had engaged in as a way to cope or survive, including uncoerced commercial sex work, drug use and selling, theft, and assault in self-defense.[17]

Sex workers often avoid reporting abuse to police out of deep-rooted mistrust and fear of criminal charges, stigma, or further abuse.[18] Some survivors that I spoke with recounted having cops as clients while they were trafficked. Others feared arrest. Many endured continued abuse from their traffickers because their lived experience had led them to see the police as a source of harm rather than help. The criminalization of sex work and drugs posed barriers to seeking assistance, sometimes because police harassed survivors on account of their presumed status as sex workers or drug users. "There's only a few [cops] that really know what's going on. Some, they're just so judgmental, they just look at you like you're just a prostitute . . . A lot of them shame you for it." In Emma's experience, law enforcement did not consider trafficking a potential reason for her participation in commercial sex work; they viewed her as a criminal breaking local prostitution laws. When individuals are not identified as victims of trafficking at the time of arrest, they often end up with a criminal record that can create barriers to achieving long-term stability, including finding stable employment and safe housing once they leave the trafficking situation.[19] Rather than addressing the underlying cause of sex trading and trafficking, criminalization increases the likelihood of individuals remaining in coercive situations.[20] Ostensibly intended to prevent sex trafficking, local law enforcement policies often focus on arresting trafficking victims and others engaged in commercial sex trading. These strategies, temporary relief on the individual level notwithstanding, are not only ineffective in combating trafficking, but they can also be extremely harmful to survivors and sex workers both in terms of the short-term disruption of arrest and detention and the long-term implications such arrests have on victims' abilities to secure work and housing; they also make survivors more vulnerable to re-trafficking.

Unmet Need: Accessing Treatment for Substance Use Disorder

A number of challenges confronted survivors attempting to escape trafficking situations, particularly when survivors remained addicted to drugs. Survivors need help accessing appropriate treatment and connecting with services to stabilize other aspects of their lives. Inpatient drug treatment was an urgent matter for many survivors in my study, but there were not enough spots available to meet the need.[21] The lack of open beds—regionwide, not just in any one state—limits what can be done because part-time support doesn't cut it when survivors aren't able to live day to day without drugs. "There aren't a lot of safe places for people in the midst of addiction to be while they wait for help," Audrey, a program director, shared with me. Clients sometimes enrolled in outpatient programs while they waited for inpatient beds to open up, but those programs were generally insufficient for the clients her program served. "We're talking about people who have significant long-term addictions, so showing up every day to a program, that's . . . not a realistic plan for them."[22] Addicted sex workers also encounter a blame-the-victim mentality that frames addiction as an individual problem rather than as a structural one. Angelique, a caseworker, put it this way: "Different services that you might apply to all are treating you as not really human, not like somebody who needs help, but like somebody who is responsible for what's happened to them." Preconceptions and lack of empathy provide additional barriers to addressing the needs of survivors living with substance use disorder.[23]

When spots were unavailable in long-term residential treatment programs, survivors were referred to detox programs as a stopgap measure. The limitations of this approach and the need for long-term treatment were not lost on Tony, a government official who supported survivors. "The biggest challenges are [that] the detox programs don't do anything for them. They're three or four days long, and you're talking about someone who might have been on drugs for three or four years. So what is three to four days going to do? Nothing. You put them in a detox center, you'll be lucky sometimes if they last through the four days [before returning to drug use]," he said. Barriers to round-the-clock treatment frustrated him too. "They [residential treatment programs] won't take anybody until they get through detox or until they have a length of time of sobriety." Survivors had to jump through hoops to be accepted into human-trafficking-specific treatment programs, he said. "You have to fill out a referral form, and you have to set up an interview, and then you have to set up a second interview. And in the meanwhile, this girl could be either in a detox program or in a substance abuse program, they're wanting to move her out. Her wanting a place. The possibility of her going back on the street, and you still don't have an answer about the safe house, you know?" The system was not set up for smooth transitions, meaning many survivors faced additional vulnerabilities as they attempted to recover from substance use disorder.[24]

Even if treatment spots were open, finding specialized residential treatment programs that fit the needs of human trafficking survivors is its own challenge. The entry requirements can create a catch-22. Maia, a program director, voiced a common frustration, explaining, "Most sober houses in [the state], you have to be completely sober and substance free." Despite evidence of the effectiveness of medication-assisted treatment (MAT) programs, many residential treatment programs will not admit individuals taking methadone, suboxone, or other such forms of treatment, arguing that complete abstinence is the only acceptable treatment goal.[25] Ultimately, many drug treatment programs that have sobriety requirements and kick out participants for relapse pose additional barriers for trafficking survivors.[26] Most survivors with opioid dependence who are unhoused require more flexibility and the option of medication-assisted treatment.

An evidence-based, integrative treatment approach is what Grant, a federal agent, viewed as the greatest need in the anti-trafficking response: "The answer is always going to be safe housing, and that includes counseling for substance abuse and suboxone treatment, drug recovery. . . . The biggest thing is safe housing with some kind of recovery component, both for trauma and for drug abuse." Echoing the need for programs that address the complex needs of trafficking survivors, Emma told me that the drug treatment she had entered "was good for the drug piece, but it wasn't good for the mental health piece because that's really what I need to focus on." In her estimation, she "needed a dual diagnosis program."

Treatment access aside, frontline workers recognized the up-and-down aspect of recovery and the challenges it posed for survivors. Tony, a government official who supported survivors, noted, "Working with them is sometimes one step forward and four or five steps backwards. It's the drugs you have to get through." Survivors were not always ready to commit to treatment, which could make accessing other services difficult, Maeve said.

> The clients that are ready to let go of their past . . . they totally have more stability . . . and then there's other clients that are still in those stages of change, of like, contemplation . . . going back and forth, relapsing . . . So, it makes it harder to have hope . . . in their future

> stability, because . . . you're not seeing that client really utilize the services that are in place. Our role as case managers is to be that constant support system and cheerleader for them and hopefully give them some of that hope. It's just a matter of, do they continue to connect with us or not?

Systemic barriers sometimes made moving forward even more challenging for Maeve's clients. "When housing really can't be established, and their mental health trauma or substance abuse can't be treated, then there's a lot less stability for them." Similarly, Orla, a program director, reflected, "If the goal of our service provision is stability and security, then one of the biggest barriers to achieving that with a client is . . . if they're using opioids, because it puts them in such precarious situations and compromises their ability to think rationally and make empowered and centered choices." She continued, "This program is a way to help them get the services . . . as well as the case manager who will not abandon them if they fall off or they go back to the trafficking situation again . . . or they can't maintain housing. We're not going to just leave them in the lurch."

This nonjudgmental approach was so important to supporting survivors whose paths to stability were often arduous, turbulent, and unpredictable. One client in the program Eliza directed was not ready to leave her trafficking situation and stop using drugs due to all the barriers she knew stood in the way of moving forward:

> We have a young person who we know is being trafficked. She openly admits that she's being trafficked. But she's not ready for help. She's not ready to change it right now. And when you talk to her about other options, she has been in and out of substance use for a long time, and her teeth are in a really, really bad condition. And she will say to you, "Look at me. How am I gonna get a job? Nobody's gonna hire me. I dropped out of high school. This is my option." So, for her, it's just about reinforcement. "Nope. I believe there's something different for you. I believe that you have the ability to do any of the things that you want to do. Here's my thoughts about what we can do about your teeth. Here are my

> thoughts about what we can do about school." And she continues to say, every time she comes in to take a shower, or do laundry, or get food, "When I'm ready, you guys will be the place that I come to." So sometimes it just means that we're trying to keep them safe until they're ready to say, "I want to do something different."

One of the women I interviewed, Tanya, who did not identify as a trafficking survivor but who had substance use disorder and had been exploited in commercial sex work and had accessed anti-trafficking services, told me that her interactions with supportive service providers helped her to leave sex work when she decided she was ready to do so:

> They were my first interaction with the public that cared about my safety and my wellbeing. I was just dealing with other girls in the business, with other drug dealers and people that used, and my parents that were so ashamed of me. There was nobody that had a solution . . . or had a hand that I could reach for that provided me with the solution. They [the anti-trafficking program staff] didn't expect me to do anything to get clean, to stop using. They didn't push me. They treated me like a human being . . . It was a perspective change. I can't say it was one incident or one specific conversation that stands out in my mind, but it was just the act of them being present to me and showing love and concern for me that I didn't have for myself . . . There was [*sic*] no ultimatums. It was, "Here's a way out. Even if you're not on your way out, these are people that can help you. Here's some counselors. Here's some food. Here's some supplies. Here's some stuff for you."

Caseworkers worked tirelessly to support their clients' needs but were often constrained by a lack of available resources designed to address the messiness of addiction. Few systems are built to support the complicated needs of clients with substance use disorder. Angelique, a caseworker, told me:

> They struggle with homelessness. It's so hard to get housing, to access resources because at the same time they are struggling with

> substance use and it blocks everything for them . . . I have many clients who got stable housing and stable work for a while, but then lapsed. Lost the housing and lost the job and they're homeless right now . . . They got kicked off from work because they were using. Then they got kicked off where they were living because they were using. Then, since they got kicked off from that housing, which was a residential service, they couldn't access treatment anymore.

Throwing up her arms in frustration with the lack of flexibility built into the systems her clients depended on for moving forward with their lives, Angelique added, "So [I'm left] telling them, 'You're just on your own now. Nobody can help you anymore.'"

Serving clients with co-occurring disorders is a complex undertaking. Maia, a program director described it succinctly: "It's like people that are existing in crisis all the time and it's all about survival." She told me about one of her clients who was:

> involved in the criminal justice system, struggling with significant trauma, and there's more mental health, and substance use. [Her case manager breathes] a sigh of relief when she gets a text from her and she knows she's alive. It's like working with her to try to help her get into a shelter somewhere away from here because she feels so unsafe. Then it's hearing from probation officers, and law enforcement [that] she overdosed in this car and was found. It's just crisis all the time. It's homelessness, it's substance use, it's mental health, it's having this involvement in the criminal justice system generally as a victim and then also as a criminal, which also complicates things. I think that's like the majority of what we're seeing and not a lot of systems and services that they'd fit into.

Caseworkers and program directors alike highlighted the complexity of survivor trajectories and how survivors' nuanced needs and the limitations on services and resources don't always make exit an easy or attractive option when housing, drug treatment, and other systems are insufficient.

Housing Insecurity

One of the biggest unmet needs precipitating trafficking and preventing exit cited by survivors, caseworkers, and criminal justice officials was lack of safe, affordable housing. For many survivors, unstable housing was what made them vulnerable to trafficking in the first place, and it was one of the biggest barriers to leaving once they were in the situation.[27] Similarly, once survivors did escape trafficking, lack of safe short-term shelter, transitional options, and affordable long-term housing all posed challenges to achieving stability. Nearly every person I interviewed—survivors, service providers, and law enforcement officials—referenced housing as one of the biggest challenges for survivors post-trafficking, especially when they were still struggling with substance use disorder or had felony records. Ava, a prosecutor, acknowledged how limited the resources were and what an obstacle housing was to survivor stability:

> The thing that keeps getting repeated at every group I've ever been to is, "Where are they going to go?" Suppose you do everything right. You have a caring law enforcement team and the court is on board. We get them a lawyer and everybody says, "This person has had a horrible thing happen to them. They want to change their life. How do we help change their life?" Everybody's on board and we all care and we're all doing the best we can. We say, "Okay, she can't go back to living in the house that brought her to this place. She has no insurance. She only knows people who are involved in the criminal world, so she's probably not going to be productive if she goes to live at their house. Where can she go? Where can she lay her head at night? Where can she be around other people who are going to support her efforts to deal with the trauma that's happened to her and move on?"

The northern New England area had only one safe house for trafficking survivors, with a very limited number of beds. This meant there was usually a weeks- to months-long waiting list, necessitating survivors seek other options. Domestic violence shelters were sometimes considered, but they are not designed to deal with the specific needs of trafficking survivors and often have requirements that are inappropriate for this population, such as mandatory group counseling or disqualifying survivors with histories of substance use. Other survivors sought admittance to residential drug treatment programs or sober houses, though there too waitlists were often a problem. Survivors who were more stable could seek out housing vouchers and try to identify their own accommodations, but criminal records made many of them undesirable tenants in the eyes of landlords. The shelter options that did exist were also subject to funding restraints and closures. One survivor whom I interviewed reported being referred to a local homeless shelter when the safe house she was staying at closed its doors on short notice. The shelter was ill-equipped to address her complex needs. Orla, a program director, noted another barrier, telling me, "I wish there was a house that offered temporary housing for men and women and families of all different forms of trafficking because right now the only housing that's offered is for women who've experienced sex trafficking." Housing did not accommodate a diverse enough range of survivors.

The unavailability of resources meant survivors sometimes stayed in dangerous situations with safety planning as the only option. Eliza, a program director, for example, had a client who was a victim of labor trafficking in the form of forced drug selling for whom the program could not secure housing. "Obviously, you want to remove them out of the situation, try to get them housing. But . . . sometimes there's no housing . . . It could be months where you're on a list." The client had to continue living under coercive conditions, prompting Eliza to take creative measures. "When we can't find her, it's tough. What do you do? So you just keep reaching out. I'll tell the local PD, 'Hey, can you just do a couple of drive-bys every once in a while to the house? Make sure there's no weird cars in the driveway trying to threaten her?' So I just keep doing the little bit I can to make sure . . . because I can't be there every day, sitting outside their house to make sure that they're safe." From a survivor perspective, the same challenges exist. While caseworkers waited for a spot in a sober house, they suggested Sophia stay at a domestic violence shelter, a prospect that she said made her feel like she "would be even more at risk." Sophia's concerns were not just about finding a place to stay where she could receive treatment; she also wanted to feel safe from her traffickers, whose retaliation she feared. She felt like she had no viable options for safe and secure housing.

When I asked Audrey, a program director, what the biggest challenge was for clients in her program, she responded, "Not having anywhere to go. They don't have any safe people. They don't have any backup, or they don't have their own place to be. When we're looking at where can you go right now, or if they get kicked out of somewhere, cause trauma's messy, then they have nowhere else, so that's it." Many of the domestic violence shelters were full. Another option was temporarily housing clients in hotel rooms, but many survivors felt unsafe living independently or had been trafficked in hotel rooms and were triggered by those spaces.

Chloe, a caseworker, also named homelessness as one of her clients' biggest challenges and described the barriers to addressing it. Recounting the hazards of the screening process—like criminal records and biased landlords—Chloe explained: "If they're trying to figure out where they're going to sleep every night, and how they're going to shower and feel clean and fed, then they can't really focus on other things. The shelter is a big piece. From a caseworker's perspective, trying to advocate for clients over and over and over again . . . Landlords don't really want to hear it, and don't trust that the clients will be good tenants and stuff . . . Then you're hitting a roadblock a lot as a caseworker, especially around housing."

Caseworkers worked hard to support survivors. They were often able to cover basic necessities to help survivors get back on their feet, but larger systemic issues like housing were beyond their control. Taryn, a survivor, spoke glowingly of the support she received from the anti-trafficking program she worked with: "When I first came out of jail, I had nothing. I had lost everything, and they helped me get clothes, they helped me get back on my feet." Asked whether she needed anything that the program was not able to provide, she responded, "Housing. Housing's the biggest thing." Unique circumstances allowed her to secure housing when most of her peers could not. "I'm a felon, and being a felon, I'm lucky because my family owns a business that I can always fall back on if I'm doing the right thing . . . but some people have nobody, and how can they ever get out of the life when they have to go back to a homeless shelter?" A felony history was a huge impediment to securing employment and housing for many survivors if they had no other support.

Indeed, intersecting barriers could complicate housing exponentially. In one very thorny situation, Angelique was working with a client whose trafficker ran up a credit card in the survivor's name—charging hotel rooms, for example. It negatively impacted this survivor's credit which, along with their criminal record, repeatedly foiled their chances of securing housing. Many survivors had criminal histories that posed barriers to housing, but even without a criminal history, survivors faced obstacles. One of Mariah's clients, whom she described as a "textbook 'perfect victim,'" was on a solid path until racial bias hindered her progress.

> She got a job; she got a housing voucher faster than anyone I had ever seen. And she had such a hard time finding an apartment and getting things moving that she ended up getting really frustrated. She identified racism on the part of the landlords as part of it . . . And she just was like, "You know what? Thank you for all your help, I've given a good three months, I'm going back to him [the trafficker]." And that was really hard, because it was hard seeing someone use the resources so well, work really hard on their own, and then just see that community not be there for her in the way that she needed it.

Ironically, the survivor viewed her former trafficker as a more reliable source of support than the housing system that failed her.

"Traffickers Are People Who Are Always There When You Need Them"

Survivor narratives made clear that addiction—frequently combined with a lack of stable and safe housing—often precipitated trafficking, and lack of housing was one of the biggest barriers to leaving trafficking situations. Even though most traffickers wielded physical violence against their victims, actual physical restraint was not necessary in most cases. When I asked Reagan, a survivor, whether her trafficker ever threatened to hurt her, she told me, "Nope. I mean, other than, 'You're not going to have a place to stay.' [I was] going to be pretty much screwed as far as my addiction at that point . . . Physically, I wasn't threatened." Several survivors talked about how traffickers offered a safe place to stay as a coercive recruitment strategy and maintained control by using homelessness as a threat. The reality was that even when survivors' movements were not restricted, safe housing alternatives were rarely available. Sophia described how she had come in contact with an anti-trafficking organization while still under the control of her trafficker, but the group was unable to meet her biggest need: safe housing. The organization had offered to put her up at a shelter, but she did not believe she would be safe from her trafficker there. "That's not really a safe place for somebody. You know what I mean? That kind of just doesn't really make you feel very good about yourself either . . . Like why am I staying in the shelter, when I could just live with my [trafficker] in a house and have everything. You know? It's like you kind of have to almost make leaving the life seem a little bit better than being in it." In this case, Sophia believed she was safer staying with her violent and controlling trafficker than if she left and he later found her at an unsecure location.

Traffickers not only take away control from their victims, but also fulfill needs left by inadequate systems. One of Chloe's clients described the relationship succinctly: "Traffickers are people who are always there when you need them." Traffickers provided a way for survivors to meet their most pressing and basic needs—housing, drugs, food, and other essentials—when no one else could. Unfortunately, traffickers were often able to meet those needs in a timelier way than those trying to assist survivors programmatically and altruistically.

An issue that came up again and again in discussions with frontline workers was how to handle the immediate crisis that occurs when a survivor is trying to exit the trafficking situation and is suffering from opioid withdrawal symptoms. Inpatient beds were extremely limited, and it was difficult to find an available treatment slot for survivors who wanted it after identification. Law enforcement investigators talked about trying to find resources for victims they had identified. Grant, a federal agent, would reach out to the sexual-assault nurse examiner at a local hospital in hopes that the patient might meet the criteria for admission following a psychological and medical assessment. "If they don't . . . now what do we do? We call a crisis center, domestic violence crisis center type of places, which isn't ideal. This girl is going to be dope sick pretty soon. How is she going to be cared for?" Ted, a local officer, was emphatic: "The immediacy of the problem when it's identified is astronomical, and there is limited, basically no resources other than an emergency room somewhere . . . These girls are sick . . . when they're trying to get off [heroin] cold turkey, they are sick, sick, sick." Immediate twenty-four-hour assistance is crucial, Ashley, a survivor, said. "We need to know that there's a place out there that we can at least go for that night . . . It's safe to sleep here. It's safe to eat here, go to the bathroom, do whatever . . . and then they can tell you what the next steps are from there . . . People have to be able to know that there's a place they can go and get help and receive help immediately."

Law enforcement officers often viewed crisis intervention as a service that federally funded anti-trafficking programs should take on, but the reality is that the federal government does not fund crisis intervention for human trafficking. Highlighting this disconnect, one caseworker, Mariah, noted, "One of the things people want, law enforcement and the potential clients themselves, is immediate response to an immediate, like crisis vulnerability situation. And that is not what we have set up. We're set up to do case management, to help people access services, to help people potentially find legal remedies, and or access benefits, and or work on goals of their choosing that will help them sort of stabilize after this crime." Caseworkers provided a vital service to assist survivors with moving forward and achieving stability, but a gap remains for assisting survivors when they are arguably at their most vulnerable and trying to transition between trafficking and what comes next. Chloe explained, "One of the big major points of the program is to make sure that clients have their basic needs met, but if you can't do something immediately, they know who to go to, who will meet their needs even if they have to do certain things to get that need met, but they can get that need met." Structural barriers to receiving services can make the trafficking situation seem more appealing than the alternatives available when the person can't meet their needs any other way. The lack of viable options for survivors meant that some remained acutely vulnerable to re-trafficking.[28]

In addition to fulfilling financial needs, and providing drugs and a place to stay, traffickers also sometimes provided a sense of stability that their victims could not find elsewhere, particularly for those with rocky family ties. Several survivors described their relationships with their traffickers starting out as romantic. When I asked Ashley whether she thought she loved her trafficker, she responded, "At first, yeah. Of course, I did at first." She spoke of the guilt she felt when she finally left her trafficker because of the other women who remained in the situation. She told me, "Some of them are in love with him. Some of them are in love with the drugs. Some of them just need a place to stay or need food or whatever the case. If there were more resources out there for people to get help, this kind of shit wouldn't even be happening. I mean they [traffickers] prey on people that are vulnerable." It was very clear to Ashley that a lack of services and inability to meet basic needs, rather than any real love, was what was preventing the other women from leaving.

The complexity of victim-trafficker relationships came up often during my discussions with frontline workers. Ross, a local cop, spoke of one particularly memorable case: "It's extreme psychological stuff going on . . . This is a person who showed compassion and caring to them at one time and choked them [nearly] to death on several other occasions. It's a really dynamic relationship." The deep emotional processes at work also struck local officer Lauren, who shared, "I feel like . . . that feeling of loyalty and love, whether it's real love or not, that weird sense of family bond because that's their family, because a lot of them come from broken homes, that's the common denominator I see." Sometimes the relationship with the trafficker preceded the actual trafficking. For example, one of Naomi's clients had been trafficked by her parents and yet wanted to go visit her mother in prison. When Naomi asked about her motivations, the client responded simply, "I miss her." Despite enduring years of abuse at the hands of her parents, the client still felt a strong bond with her mother. In many cases, traffickers used their relationships with victims as a way to maintain control, providing the illusion of love and demanding, "If you love me, then you will do x, y, z."

The Ongoing Cycle of Vulnerability

Post-trafficking survivors expressed a mix of relief at being out of the situation and concern about returning to their pre-trafficking challenges. The survivors who had engaged in anti-trafficking case management or who were enrolled in a trafficking-specific recovery program received additional support with finding housing and accessing drug treatment and medical and mental health care, but these programs were limited by many of the same structural constraints that created vulnerabilities for survivors in the first place. Survivors who came from marginalized communities remained marginalized, and the options for safe housing, substance use treatment, and affordable health care continued to be limited. As May, an advocate, emphasized, "You have someone who's been the victim of human trafficking . . . That person is still in poverty, still lacks the skills to engage in formal employment, might still be undocumented, might still have an open warrant, is definitely still a trans person, a person of color, a person from a background of poverty who still has to support an entire family. You haven't dealt with any of those things." No matter how good interventions focused on victim protection are, the response will always be inadequate without addressing root causes.

Survivors had a wide range of needs when exiting a trafficking situation. In her casework, Maeve was "dealing with people who have experienced severe trauma, and a good handful of clients struggle with substance abuse, and [lack of] transportation is a huge barrier, as well as a lot of them struggling with mental health issues." The intensity of needs Maeve's clients faced often made it difficult to get them in for services. They were so consumed with daily survival that things like goal setting and working toward future stability took a back seat. Repeating a similar refrain, Celeste, a program director, rattled off a list of challenges: "They [survivors] need insurance. They need to be able to see the doctor . . . To be able to have a safe place to be where they're able to eat, where they're able to . . . get healthcare. Those would be the immediate [needs]." Insurance, Mariah told me, was key to several paths out of trafficking: "We want people to be able to feel like they can survive and thrive on their own and build up their natural supports . . . But people have so many basic health care needs as well as mental health care needs, substance use issues, and when they're not able to access [healthcare and treatment] it's really, really hard to get them to be able to move forward."

The service providers I spoke with were clear that trafficking was often only one among many devastating experiences in their clients' lives. In addition to dealing with the trauma of trafficking, as one program director, Maia, noted, many survivors also were struggling to overcome other longstanding traumas and vulnerabilities:

> A lot of what we're seeing with the clients that we work on behalf of . . . is that the issues that have made them vulnerable to trafficking, like poverty, like intergenerational violence, mental health, substance use, all those things, there is very little infrastructure or

> resources to help them resolve those issues. It's not a matter of just being able to find housing and a job and things get better. It's recovery from their trafficking experience, but it's really all the other stuff that has led them to this place to be as vulnerable as they are to be trafficked that there's little ways to address, without addressing these major, major issues . . . We have clients that we've been working with and could probably continue working with because they're still struggling with housing, all of those things where they started, which is what made them vulnerable to begin with and they're still struggling with it.

Maia continued, explaining that for many clients losing their state-funded health insurance had a domino effect. Losing funding for drug treatment led to increased drug use and increased criminal activity to pay for drugs, which meant survivors acquired felony records, which in turn inhibited their ability to secure housing and employment—the exact things that need to be in place to support recovery. Maia spoke not just of drug recovery and recovery from trafficking but also of recovering from the experiences of vulnerability and structural violence. "It's a really long process to recovery from all of that. Then just the recovery from the trauma of poverty. That in itself is a trauma and getting out of that may take someone forever." Maia's comments gestured toward the chains-of-risk that survivors continue to accumulate post trafficking, and the inadequacy of systems to address survivor needs and to help them move beyond trafficking.[29]

Human trafficking services in the U.S. are delivered through an intensive case management model. According to the Justice Department's Office for Victims of Crime, "The case manager performs multiple roles as point person, victim advocate, and facilitator of communication in order to help the victim navigate complex criminal justice and social service systems."[30] Under this model, federally funded anti-trafficking organizations help connect survivors to existing services but do not generally provide the services directly.[31] This means that anti-trafficking services are only as strong as the underlying systems—housing, substance use treatment, mental health care, and so forth—and depend on those systems being not only available but also adequately funded. For many survivors, federally funded, human-trafficking-intensive case management became a way to finally begin to access resources and to address some of their preexisting vulnerabilities. There were simply no other programs designed to help with the co-occurring histories of trauma, economic insecurity, and mental health issues that survivors were struggling to overcome prior even to the start of their trafficking trajectories. "Sometimes the trafficking experience," Angelique, a caseworker, said, "is not the worst thing they have experienced in their lives."

When I asked Orla, a program director, how much the complexity of victim needs could be attributed to trafficking versus preexisting factors, she responded, "The vast majority [of needs] are not due to the trafficking [but rather] are due to the other vulnerabilities." Referring to some of her clients' complex past experiences, Naomi, another caseworker, concurred: "A lot of them [survivors] have very significant histories outside of the trafficking itself. And a lot of them have mental health issues." Sometimes those early experiences are more salient than the immediate exploitation. "Working with clients," Maeve said, "I hear more often about their childhood traumas than I do [about] their traumas from their trafficking experience . . . Because a lot of those childhood traumas never were addressed, and now they're thirty- or forty-year-old adults, and they're still struggling with that pain."

Indeed, many survivors had complex mental health needs that required responses beyond what an anti-trafficking program could offer. It was always hard to make decisions about limited resources when it meant deciding between taking on a client with needs related to their trafficking or taking on a client with a history of trafficking but whose needs were related to other pre-existing vulnerabilities, Maia, a program director, said. "Times when we've got a ton of capacity we can take that on. Then at times when our capacity is so limited we have to say how much of this is related to trafficking and how much of this is about trafficking versus all this other stuff, but they don't have access to other services." In a recent referral, a twenty-three-year-old had "one of the most horrific trafficking stories I've heard as a child. She's a young adult with acute mental health issues and a history of suicide attempts, history of multiple psychiatric hospitalizations. Her mental health needs are so acute and so big and we're a program that provides intensive case management to survivors of trafficking, but we're not a mental health program." The referring agency made the referral as a last-ditch effort. Because there were no other services available to the survivor whose trafficking had occurred many years ago, the anti-trafficking program appeared to be her only option. Victim assistance programs provided critical case management services for survivors exiting trafficking and worked tirelessly to connect them with resources but also were constrained by inadequate systems that limited how much support they could offer their clients.

Traffickers and Structural Vulnerability

While I did not interview traffickers as part of the research for this project, I take seriously that the perpetrators of trafficking are often subject to the same structural constraints and social determinants as those they exploit. Criminal legal authorities described traffickers as coming from diverse backgrounds, just as survivors do. As Ryan, a federal investigator, told me "We've come across both male and female traffickers. They've been of any race or ethnicity." Several law enforcement officials that I spoke with referenced a female trafficker whom they described as vicious in her tactics, but for the most part the traffickers they investigated and prosecuted fit a profile of being poor men of color. When asked to describe the typical trafficker, Grant, a federal investigator, responded, "Black, male, gang member. Often up from Boston, sometimes local. Yeah. I mean we prosecuted female traffickers as well." While recognizing the disproportionate number of Black male traffickers, Leah, another investigator, was seemingly aware that this imbalance reinforces the human trafficking narrative and the role of the Black or brown villain. "Oftentimes we do find that they're men of color targeting white women . . . [but] there are white pimps out there too. Oftentimes I think the majority are Black males. I hate saying it." The fact that most trafficking arrests and prosecutions involve Black males is especially notable in the context of Maine and New Hampshire—two of the whitest states in the country—and is a striking vestige of the nineteenth-century "white slavery" narrative in which white women were believed to be the victims of foreign and Black men.[32]

Communities of color in general, and Black men especially, are disproportionately subjected to police surveillance and incarceration. Many of the cases under investigation during my fieldwork involved drugs as well as human trafficking. Criminal legal authorities' responses to trafficking mirror the racial disparities in drug arrests more broadly. According to a Bureau of Justice Statistics (BJS) report, of the 201 defendants charged with peonage, slavery, forced labor, and sex trafficking in fiscal year 2021, 77 percent were male, 58 percent were Black, 18 percent were Hispanic, and a mere 21 percent were White, reflecting a massively disproportionate representation of racial minorities among those federally charged with trafficking crimes.[33]

In her best-selling study *The New Jim Crow*, Michelle Alexander argues that discrimination against Blacks and other minorities did not end with legal segregation but rather shifted to other legally sanctioned forms of racial control, including the American criminal legal system that targets Black men through the so called "War on Drugs" (and now the "War on Trafficking") and perpetuates a racial class system via mass incarceration.[34] Characterizing people of color as criminals justifies discrimination, exclusion, and other forms of oppression in the name of fighting crime. These new forms of discrimination also inflict structural violence in employment and housing discrimination, loss of voting rights, denial of educational opportunities, and denial of myriad other public benefits.[35]

Criminal legal authorities also often referenced family dysfunction as a common precipitating factor among traffickers. Nico, a local investigator, noted that many of the traffickers he had encountered "come from broken childhoods. They are doing things that are immoral and clearly against the law but have had hard lives." The description evokes the role of adverse childhood experiences, often referenced by caseworkers. Ryan, a federal investigator, recalled often hearing traffickers recount their backgrounds during the sentencing process—for example, saying, "I know I did this bad thing, but this is how my childhood looked. I was abused at this age. I moved around at this age. I was a ward of the state." Ryan noted, "That's a running theme that's not someone just decides one day to become a pimp after a completely normal life . . . There's been a lot of people that we've sentenced that even the judge will say 'you've done horrific things, but I can see that you've had a horrific childhood, too. You failed to rise above it, and you'll be sentenced accordingly.'" Indeed, I sat in on a sentencing where this very scenario occurred.

Lauren, a local cop, expressed empathy for the traffickers she encountered. "These offenders are the worst people in the world, but they probably came from a really shitty environment too, and so what happened along the way that they decided to start doing this, and getting girls, or drugs, and selling them?" Social and family background, combined with race and economic position—the same social determinants that put trafficking survivors on a trajectory of vulnerability—also influenced the trajectories of their traffickers.[36] For example, a local investigator, Ross, shared with me, "One of our most prolific violent sex traffickers to date is a female who . . . was raped from a young age, who was exploited herself, who has just done horrendous things." One survivor talked about her trafficker who had come from a history of familial drug use and sex work: "He had all these plans about how he was going to be this new pimp that would have this whole new way of doing things . . . he kind of worked his way up . . . he says that he . . . 'rose from the crack smoke.' His mom was [a sex worker with substance use disorder], and he had just kind of rose up from that and made this big empire for himself." Much like Philippe Bourgeois' research on Hispanic men turning down office jobs to sell crack in the context of a white supremacist system that offered them no respect, trafficking can be understood as a harmful but logical alternative to the suspicion and lack of alternatives that young Black men face as part of their lived experience.[37] Research also shows that many individuals start out selling sex, sometimes being exploited or trafficked, before transitioning to facilitating or victimizing others.[38]

Multiple people whom I interviewed considered social and family background as "push factors" to becoming a trafficker, but few went so far as to suggest that prevention efforts to address gaps in the system could be implemented to support potential perpetrators in addition to potential victims. One investigator, Troy, expressed empathy for perpetrators, to a point: "I get why people sell drugs. I get what it's like to grow up in an inner city, have nothing, turn to a gang because you don't have a family. Selling drugs, yes, all of that is wrong. It is all socially bad. There's violence involved in it, but I understand the concept behind how the person gets there, because I've worked in the environment and I've seen it . . . people growing up in that environment." While Troy appreciated the role of social context in a person's life, he saw human trafficking differently. "I look at human traffickers and I personally think that they are the closest thing to a sociopathic, psychopathic, just bad people. Taking another human being and treating them as if they're an animal, is right up there with murdering somebody." For most individuals engaged in the criminal legal system, the goal was to protect victims from traffickers—essentially, following the narrative of innocent victims and evil perpetrators. As the director of an anti-trafficking program, Maia noted that her take was different in that her organization's mission was human-rights based and focused on ensuring access to food, shelter, and safety for all. As she told me, "We serve everyone." Her agency's clients were just as likely to be traffickers as they were trafficking survivors, which could create uncomfortable dynamics. Nonetheless, Maia recognized the vulnerabilities and structural barriers shared by survivors and traffickers—they were both often victims of the same failed systems.

Acknowledging how social vulnerability impacts traffickers is in no way meant to condone the violence or abuse inflicted by these individuals upon others. Abusing and removing autonomy from another human being is inexcusable. At the same time, it is critical to consider not only the structural factors that make people vulnerable to trafficking but also the factors that lead individuals to see trafficking as a reasonable way of responding to oppression or of moving out of poverty. Both trafficking survivors and their perpetrators often experienced the same types of traumatic childhood incidents and structural vulnerabilities, perhaps one of the reasons why they sometimes shared such strong bonds. As perpetrators, traffickers channeled their trauma and need in deeply harmful ways. As will be seen in the next chapter, both victims and perpetrators also suffer as a result of the carceral approach to trafficking. Recognizing the role of structural vulnerability for both victims and perpetrators means that prevention can be doubly effective in reducing trafficking.

CHAPTER 4

"You Can't Arrest Your Way out of Trafficking"

Intervention Versus Prevention

There's all these resources and things for survivors, so you have all these programs that are there to pick up the pieces, but you don't have any programs to get it before it breaks. And that's like a huge issue. I mean it's great that we have all of these resources, but wouldn't it be even better if we could stop it before it gets to that level?

—Mia, Survivor

The problem that we're facing right now is that everything is still . . . victim-service led . . . That means that people have to be victimized before we care about them . . . It's so disconnected from root causes. It's so disconnected from anti-poverty work. We're told that this is happening, and we have to identify it. It's "see something, say something." It's those stupid posters in the fucking airport that have people just profiling Asian women on airplanes. It is so predicated on that moment of intervention as the only important moment. We also don't actually care about the services that we give to

> people afterwards, and we definitely couldn't give a fuck about them when they were just poor.
>
> —May, Advocate

> When the focus is on "rescuing" a person, we fail to confront the drivers of exploitation and a lot of potential change is thereby never even acknowledged.
>
> —Aubrey Lloyd, "What Does Real Healing Look Like for Trafficking Survivors?"

On the surface, the federal government's 3P's paradigm presents as a balanced and holistic approach, presumably utilizing prosecution, protection, and prevention in equal parts to combat trafficking.[1] In reality, the government's strategy is overwhelmingly interventionist—with a disproportionate focus on the criminal legal goal of prosecution and moderate attention paid to the goal of protecting victims. Prevention has proven a mere afterthought, a catchphrase in the government's attempt at alliteration but lacking many observable efforts to meet the objective.

The U.S. government's 2021 fiscal budget lays out this lopsided focus in monetary terms.[2] Given the criminal legal focus of the response, the government allocated a whopping $160 million to human trafficking investigations and prosecution efforts through the Department of Homeland Security and the Federal Bureau of Investigation. An additional $40 million was designated to fund the Enhanced Collaborative Model Task Force to Combat Human Trafficking program, the model in place in the state of New Hampshire, which brings together state and local law enforcement and victim service partners and combines the goals of the first two P's, prosecution and protection.[3] The budget also included $77 million solely for victim protection via victim services funded through the Department of Justice. Another $28 million was directed toward the Department of Health and Human Services primarily to provide case management services and benefits for victims of trafficking, along with support for the Human Trafficking Data Collection Project, and a small amount—in the single-digit millions—earmarked for prevention.[4] It is difficult to decipher the exact ways in which all these allocations are divided between agencies, but some basic calculations suggest that nearly 60 percent of spending on the domestic human trafficking response is directed to criminal legal initiatives, with less than 10 percent going toward prevention.

Most prevention funding in the U.S. has been funneled toward public outreach and awareness campaigns despite little evidence of their success.[5] Outreach is of course vital for connecting potential survivors with resources, especially for those who may not recognize that they have been trafficked, but it is a reactive approach that depends on reaching individuals *after* they have been harmed. Primary prevention is proactive and seeks to decrease vulnerability *before* trafficking occurs, but to date almost no U.S. government funds have gone toward addressing the root causes of trafficking.

Policing Sex Work to Address Trafficking

The carceral approach to trafficking is intricately tied to the legal response to commercial sex work. Countries around the world have taken a variety of legal approaches to the issue, ranging from criminalization to partial decriminalization of sex sellers (but not sex buyers) to legalization with government regulation to full decriminalization (see Figure 6). The model used overwhelmingly across the U.S., and in both Maine and New Hampshire at the time of my fieldwork, was that of criminalization.[6] Since the passage of the Trafficking Victims Protection Act (TVPA) in 2000, the U.S. response to trafficking has emphasized sex trafficking over all other forms of trafficking and has focused its approach around policing prostitution.

Leading up to and since the passage of the TVPA, a group of self-proclaimed human trafficking abolitionists—comprised of anti-prostitution feminists and conservative and evangelical Christians—has conflated human trafficking with sex trafficking, and all sex work with sex trafficking. Anti-prostitution feminists object to both sex work and sex trafficking as affronts to women's equality while the conservative and evangelical Christians hold moral objections to any and all sex work and seek to protect the sanctity of heteronormative marriage. With a shared goal of the complete elimination of all forms of sex work, this strange-bedfellows coalition has promoted a gendered law and order response focused on protecting innocent female

The Four Legal Approaches to Sex Work

CRIMINALIZATION—Criminalization is the current model in most of the U.S. and was the model in place in Maine and New Hampshire at the time of this study. It prohibits prostitution and places criminal penalties on individuals who buy or sell sexual services.

- → Can result in fines, arrest, incarceration, criminal records, and deportation.
- → Leads to greater isolation, less ability to negotiate with clients, and increased violence and exploitation by law enforcement, managers, and clients.[a]
- → Contributes to stigma and discrimination that pose challenges to seeking healthcare and other services as well as accessing housing and employment.[b]

PARTIAL DECRIMINALIZATION (also known as the "Nordic model" or end demand)—This approach criminalizes the buying of but not the selling of sexual services such that those buying sex are subject to criminal penalties.

- → Advocates of this model seek to eradicate sex work by ending the demand for sexual services and believe that criminalizing clients will end men's demand for sexual services from women. Sex workers' rights advocates do not support this approach.
- → Evidence indicates that sex workers continue to be arrested under this model, though under different charges.[c]
- → In order to arrest buyers, the model focuses law enforcement attention on the areas where sex workers conduct business. This exposes sex workers to many of the same risks of violence, exploitation, and arrest as criminalization.[d]
- → Results in increased isolation as buyers seek to avoid law enforcement attention.

[a] Michele R. Decker et al., "Human Rights Violations Against Sex Workers: Burden and Effect on HIV," *Lancet* 385, no. 9963 (January 10, 2015), 186199. doi:10.1016/S0140-6736(14)60800-X.

[b] Erin Albright and Kate D'Adamo, "Decreasing Human Trafficking through Sex Work Decriminalization," *AMA Journal of Ethics* 19, no. 1 (January 1, 2017), 122126. doi:10.1001/journalofethics.2017.19.1.sect2-1701.

[c] Nina Luo, *Decriminalizing Survival: Policy Platform and Polling on the Decriminalization of Sex Work.*

[d] Kate D'Adamo, *Attacking Demand, Escalating Violence: The Impact of Twenty Years of End Demand Implementation on People Who Trade Sex, (Reframe Health and Justice [2021]).*

→ Evidence suggests this model does not reduce violence against sex workers and can lead to less choice surrounding who they accept as clients and less power to negotiate over condom use and location.[e]

LEGALIZATION OR REGULATION—Under this model city or state government regulates the sex trade by setting specific conditions, such as licensing or registration requirements, under which the exchange of sexual services is permitted. Sex work outside of these conditions remains criminalized.

→ Many sex worker advocates and allies oppose this model.

→ Grants excessive power to managers, brothel owners, and third parties and limits sex workers' autonomy and control over strategies to stay safe.

→ Those who fall outside the legal designations remain subjected to policing and criminalization. Immigrants, refugees, LGBTQIA+ people, and individuals engaged in survival sex remain at risk for criminal penalties.[f]

FULL DECRIMINALIZATION—This approach involves the complete removal of criminal penalties related to selling sexual services for both sex workers and sex buyers.

→ Trafficking and other forms of violence and abuse as well as sex acts involving minors all remain illegal under this model.

→ Sex workers are less subject to violence from law enforcement and clients under this approach.[g]

---

[e] Albright, "Decreasing Human Trafficking through Sex Work Decriminalization," 122–126; Graham Ellison, Caoimhe Ní Dhónaill and Erin Early, *A Review of the Criminalisation of the Payment for Sexual Services in Northern Ireland* (Belfast, Ireland: Queen's University Belfast [2019]); Hélène Le Bail and Calogero Giametta, *What do Sex Workers Think about the French Prostitution Act? A Study on the Impact of the Law from 13 April 2016 Against the 'Prostitution System' in France*, (Saint Denis, France: Médecins du Monde [2018]).

[f] Mariëlle Kloek and Minke Dijkstra, *Sex Work, Stigma and Violence in the Netherlands*, (Edinburgh, Scotland: Global Network of Sex Work Projects [2018]); Joyce Outshoorn, "Policy Change in Prostitution in the Netherlands: From Legalization to Strict Control," *Sexuality Research & Social Policy* 9 (2012), 233–243. https://www.nswp.org/sites/nswp.org/files/fulltext1%20%282%29.pdf.

[g] Lynzi Armstrong, "From Law Enforcement to Protection? Interactions between Sex Workers and Police in a Decriminalized Street-Based Sex Industry," *British Journal of Criminology* 57, no. 3 (2017), 570588. https://academic.oup.com/bjc/article/57/3/570/2623927.; Gillian M. Abel, "A Decade of Decriminalization: Sex Work 'Bown Under' but Not Underground: Criminology and Criminal Justice," 14, no. 5 (2014), 580–592. https://journals.sagepub.com/doi/pdf/10.1177/1748895814523024.

→ Lifting the threat of arrest results in both sex workers and buyers being more willing to report suspected trafficking to law enforcement.[h]

→ Research from New Zealand suggests that decriminalization improved health outcomes for sex workers and did not result in an increase in sex trafficking or in an increase in the number of minors involved in the sex trade.[i]

[h] Dean Peters and Giles Griffin, *Sex Work, Human Trafficking & the Harm of Conflating the Two* (Asijiki, 2015).

[i] *Prostitution Law Review Committee, Report of the Prostitution Law Review Committee on the Operation of the Prostitution Reform Act 2003* (Wellington: New Zealand Ministry of Justice [2008]).

Figure 6. The Four Legal Approaches to Sex Work
Adapted from Sex Workers & Allies Network and Yale Global Health Justice Partnership, "The Law and Sex Work: Four Legal Approaches to the Sex Sector" (2020).

victims from male aggressors. Coined the "antiprostitution sphere" by political scientist Barbara Stolz, the group draws on old narratives of sexually pure and innocent victims first circulated during the white slavery panic of the late nineteenth and early twentieth centuries and also on ideas introduced by anti-prostitution feminists, including sociologist Kathleen Barry.[7] In her book *Female Sexual Slavery*, Barry argued that all prostitution is sexual slavery and called for the use of state power to criminalize the purchasing of sex as a means of abolishing "slavery in all its forms."[8] During the drafting of the TVPA, another group of human rights, public health, and migration advocates pushed for a rights-based approach that addressed trafficking in all labor sectors.[9] That approach prevailed in the way trafficking was broadly defined in the law, though the views of the anti-prostitution sphere have strongly influenced the ways the law has been implemented in practice. One of the primary forms government response has taken has been the enforcement of state-level prostitution statutes against both buyers and sellers of sex.

Sex work is criminalized, or partially criminalized, based on the belief that the consequences will deter people from engaging in it. Laws punishing sex work are often justified with moral or religious beliefs that condemn the work as inherently immoral or consider it so exploitative that no one would freely choose to engage in it. Relying on the policing of sex work to control trafficking depends on the mistaken belief that sex work and trafficking are one and the same, but not all people who work in the commercial sex trade are trafficked. Involvement in commercial sex work occurs across a spectrum of choice, circumstance, and coercion with some choosing to do sex work, others finding it to be their only option on account of poverty or lack of economically viable job opportunities, and still others at the far other end of the continuum involved due to some form of force or control.[10] In addition to conflating sex work with trafficking, anti-trafficking strategies that depend on policing sex workers overlook the fact that trafficking occurs much more frequently in sectors outside of commercial sex work. While law enforcement authorities identify more cases involving sex trafficking than those involving other forms of labor trafficking, significantly more victims of labor trafficking are ultimately identified (usually through channels outside of law enforcement) than those being trafficked for both commercial sex alone or in combination with labor trafficking.[11]

The criminalization and associated stigmatization of sex work results in violence and violations of the rights of sex workers, both trafficked and not. Far from reducing instances of exploitation, as outlined in the survivor narratives, criminalization creates an environment conducive to trafficking when sex workers are afraid to report experienced or observed abuse to law enforcement.[12] This is especially true for foreign nationals who do not have a path to status and who are afraid to report abuse out of fear of deportation.[13] Due to the harms associated with criminalization, a number of organizations, including Amnesty International, the World Health Organization, the American Civil Liberties Union, the Human Rights Campaign, Human Rights Watch, the Global Alliance Against Traffic in Women, Freedom United, and Freedom Network USA, along with hundreds of academic researchers, have advocated for and supported full decriminalization to improve safety, decrease stigma, abuse, and exploitation, and protect the health of sex workers.[14]

Arrest as Protection

Of the investigators I spoke to, many were invested in arresting and supporting the prosecution of traffickers but admitted that such investigations were challenging and time consuming. As a result, they often would turn their attention to those being trafficked or potentially trafficked. Over and over throughout my research I heard the same kinds of statements from law enforcement officers—that they were encountering women with addiction issues engaged in commercial sex work and who were deeply vulnerable and in danger of overdosing. They seemed to think the only way to ensure the safety of these women was through intervention by the criminal legal system, usually involving arrest and detention. In some cases, the women were trafficked, and in other instances, they were trading sex consensually for some combination of money, drugs, and a place to stay.[15]

This way of speaking about vulnerability on the part of law enforcement officers marked a shift from my research a decade prior. Those in the criminal legal system this time around had more complicated observations that reflected at least a partial recognition of systematic vulnerability and the likewise systematic failure to address it. Ross, a local police officer, contemplated the shift in his own mentality from viewing sex workers as criminals when he was working vice to seeing them as victims after being introduced to the concept of trafficking:

> It was a lot easier back then because . . . you would essentially in your mind solve a crime. Somebody would be out there under their own free will . . . engaging in sex for money. It was criminal behavior so they were arrested and adjudicated through the system. There was no personal story behind it when we were doing that. Once you slow down and start talking to people that are involved in it, it becomes personalized so it becomes very different. Then you start to see the human side of it, like well this girl is somebody's sister—you know, daughter, mother, cousin, what have you. It becomes a lot more difficult to separate yourself from it.

In how they approached potential victims, other members of law enforcement joined Ross in conveying a combination of compassion and paternalism. Their conceptualizations of potential victims frequently revealed this paternalism; law enforcement lauded arrest as one of the most useful tools—sometimes the only tool—at their disposal.[16] Many also staunchly defended the criminalization of prostitution and believed it was necessary, despite the collateral harm that sex workers and trafficking victims experienced as a result of arrest, detention, and prosecution. As outlined in the preceding chapter, significant barriers to securing housing and employment on account of a criminal record are inflicted as a result of this "help."[17]

The presumption was that law enforcement had an absolute duty to intervene by arresting those they assumed to be victims due to the severity of their substance use disorder. Investigators seemed concerned for potential victims' safety on account of their engagement in commercial sex work and the potential for overdose—and not because of their trafficking per se. "I'm not against prostitution being illegal, being used on a situational basis," Troy, a local investigator, shared. "If the person can't identify themselves as a victim, or they're just a complete train wreck spiraling out of control . . . the safest thing for them is to charge them with prostitution, try to get them [in] jail, a safe place for the night, and then trying to put services in place for their rehabilitation. I think [that] is the best that you can do." For Troy, arrest was a means of keeping potential victims alive, and saving them not only from potential traffickers but also from themselves. Ted, another local investigator, said he and his colleagues would "use whatever we can. I have locked girls up multiple times, the victims, to keep them straight . . . I'll lock anybody up to keep them alive. Sometimes you have to."

Ted's use of "girls" to refer to potential victims was standard parlance among the law enforcement officials I interviewed and reflected the belief that all women involved in commercial sex, and especially those being trafficked, lacked the autonomy to decide for themselves when to get sober and when to disengage from commercial sex work. Much has been written about the conflation of women and girls in regard to trafficking and the ways in which adult women are conceptualized as childlike victims who are passive, fragile, and in need of intervention and support.[18] Most of the women whom law enforcement investigators encountered did not fit the ideal victim profile in that they were adult drug users, many of whom had, initially at least, entered commercial sex work of their own accord. Referring to them as "girls" instilled a sense of innocence and vulnerability that was incongruous with their recognition as fully agentic adults.

On arresting sex workers and trafficking victims for their own protection, one officer, Ross, shared that he relied on the tactic

> sometimes because you're afraid that if you let this person go they'll be dead within twenty-four hours, which is a tough call . . . It's like, all right, do I want to help this person? Absolutely. But if we let this person go right now, they're going to be dead, probably from a drug overdose or through self-harm or what have you . . . Sometimes keeping them alive means they're sitting in a safe place somewhere where they don't want to be . . . i.e., jail. If it gets them to a place where they can make a rational decision, I don't necessarily think that's a bad thing. That is my opinion and it is not shared by most advocates.

Law enforcement officials repeatedly acknowledged that their use of arrest as a protection strategy conflicted with the beliefs of most advocates and victim service providers, who viewed arresting victims as a human rights violation. Doug, a local officer, asserted, "These liberal social workers, their belief is none of these women should ever go to jail. They're victims. I disagree. I think there are times when they have to go to jail, because that is the only thing that is going to keep them alive. That is the only way that they're going to get some services. That is the only way they're going to get off the drugs, even if it is to go to jail." The idea was that stopping trafficking required intervention, and it had to happen immediately, as soon as law enforcement encountered a woman involved in commercial sex work whom they believed was in danger of overdose. In this way, law enforcement officials who were "tuned in" to trafficking based on experience and training at once both acknowledged and overlooked the importance of social determinants by conflating the identification and "rescue" of victims with the prevention of trafficking. As Doug told me, "There are several women that I daresay are alive today because of our intervention and the fact that we didn't give up on them."

While several officers spoke about how relieved they were to have social service providers available to assist with survivors in meeting their needs, many others, like Doug, inserted themselves into the lives of the women they arrested and identified far beyond what their roles as investigators would require. They usually justified their actions by citing the vulnerabilities the victims faced. Sometimes officers would drive them to appointments, offer monetary assistance, or provide emotional support. During one local network meeting that brought investigators and service providers together, Paul, one of the officers present, talked about inequality and the vulnerabilities it created for the victims he encountered, asserting, "I am a social worker; I just wear a different uniform." At the time, I was sitting next to Maia, a program director, who muttered under her breath, not loud enough for Paul to hear, "In that case I should be pretty good at police work." Maia was frustrated at the continued claim on the part of investigators that they were meeting survivor needs when in actuality they were creating additional vulnerabilities through the ways that they encouraged dependency, sometimes in very similar ways to how traffickers did.

Certainly, there were survivors who appreciated law enforcement intervention and believed it was their only way out of trafficking. "I've never been so relieved to be in jail," Elliot told me. "I felt so protected. Nobody could touch me. I didn't have to wake up. I didn't have to do dates. It was . . . a relief to be in jail. Officer [last name] probably saved my life." Others, like Liana, however, expressed their distrust of the police because of their use of arrest as an identification strategy: "I was afraid to even say anything because I'd get arrested for it, so I can't talk to the cops. If they were more there to help you get out of the situation or I would feel that they would help, then I would have talked to them about it, but I just didn't feel like I could." Even though Liana knew she needed help, her earlier interactions with police led her to doubt their commitment to her safety.

Through the stories I heard, I came to realize that police officers and investigators used what Jennifer Musto terms an "arrest to assist" model to keep potential victims safe. In her book *Control and Protect: Collaboration, Carceral Protection, and Domestic Sex Trafficking in the United States*, Musto observes that nonstate actors support the carceral framework in the name of protecting youth.[19] What I found, however, is that victim service providers resisted "managing" their primarily adult clients in support of law enforcement goals. Rather, providers supported these efforts when aligned with what their clients wanted but in general focused on protecting clients' rights, sometimes much to the dismay of law enforcement investigators.

Indeed, nearly all of the advocates and service providers that I interviewed decried arrest as a form of so-called assistance, citing the unnecessary entanglement in the criminal legal system and the barriers it poses to recovery and future stability. Advocates like Cat understood the ways that fear of arrest eroded trust in the criminal legal system, noting, "If people don't feel safe to report, they won't. If people don't feel that they'll be served by the criminal justice system, they won't report. If they don't feel that accountability and justice can be accessed in that way, they won't report. If they aren't stable enough to be able to go through that process, they won't. There are lots and lots of reasons people don't access criminal justice, and until we tend to those reasons that will continue to be the truth." The law enforcement officials she interacted with cared about the victims they worked with, to be sure, and Cat emphasized that advocates and social workers were coming from a similar place of care but that they viewed survivors through a human rights lens that centered their decision-making power. "Grownups can make all the bad decisions they want, even when we know it's going to result in dreadful outcomes," she said. "It's not an endgame solution but it's a solution in the moment to offer someone a caring ear and a cup of coffee and to say we're going to be waiting for you when you want to talk and not throw them into jail to save them." As a caseworker, Mariah came to a similar assessment: "There is great need in our community for a number of reasons. And there is an inadequate systems response for that . . . and it's understandable [that] people are seeing somebody really struggling and . . . they want to immediately fix it right there, [but] that individual might not be ready to be working on solutions at all."

Cat and Mariah, like many advocates and service providers, believed that survivors—especially those in need of treatment for substance use disorder—needed to make empowered decisions for themselves in order to leave the trafficking situation and seek assistance. While some survivors were held by their traffickers truly under lock and key, most had freedom of movement. Survivors' physiological need for opioids, combined with their traffickers' exploitation of their addictions, is what kept them in human trafficking situations. Providers encountered some of these individuals while still in the throes of trafficking and worked to ensure they knew that other options were available, granting survivors more autonomy and decision-making power around how and when to leave.

Some investigators acknowledged that arresting victims was not an ideal solution but justified it as an intervention strategy in a variety of ways. Lauren tried to avoid arresting potential victims when possible but explained,

"We also have to produce some results. When we're taking a week or three days to investigate something, there's an expectation from somewhere, supervisors or something, that something's going to come out of it. And we have had, I think, great success when we do charge some of these girls." She continued justifying the carceral approach very paternalistically, asserting that victims benefited from the structure of incarceration:

> These girls are used to having someone control them all the time, and so then if we do separate them from their pimp . . . it's just like when people get out of prison and they've had their whole days constructed for them, and then they commit suicide when they get out because they're having a hard time. It's easier for them to function in jail. It's kind of that same principle. So, if we charge a girl and she has bail conditions, and someone is keeping tabs on her who wants what's best for her, who's getting her counseling, who's finding her a place to live; and sometimes the only way to do that is with a charge being over their heads, unfortunately. Ideally, we would be able to come in and say, "Hey, we have a healthy lifestyle for you, come to this side." And they would say, "Absolutely," but that's not the reality.

In their view, investigators' arrest strategies were meant to keep potential victims safe and came from a place of care as Lauren, the investigator quoted above, went on to describe:

> When we do charge or arrest, the intention is wholesome and it's not to get a charge on them. It's to make sure that we're doing everything we can, which includes that tool sometimes of a charge to keep them as safe as we can . . . I think it gives them some space and time to heal, from their pimp. Even if it's just a weekend, if it's one night that they're not working and they're not going to have to worry about where their food is coming from, or that their phone's ringing . . . We're not busting them and saying, "Oh good, screw you." It's more of an intention of our compassionate response, even if from the outside it doesn't seem empathetic or compassionate at all.

Lauren was emphatic that her approach was driven by concern for victims, yet she and other investigators were quick to dismiss the harms of arrest that often persisted throughout a survivor's lifetime. The cost of having a lengthening criminal record was seemingly insignificant compared to Lauren's sense that arrest got victims "out of the life."

"We're treating them with respect, and hopefully they understand it," Terry, another local investigator, said. "When we've had to take them and bring them to jail and book them, we drop their child off at daycare. We're trying to help out; we're not trying to be really mean." While Terry viewed his actions as helpful and compassionate, he failed to recognize the long-term effects of arresting a mother of young children who was herself the victim of a crime, including the resulting trauma and future obstacles to securing housing and employment. Others, like Matt, a prosecutor, extended empathy to potential victims only when they were cooperative about agreeing to drug treatment or assisting with the prosecution of their traffickers: "We can charge them, get them an attorney who is sort of understanding of the situation, and we can get them services . . . [but] if somebody tells us to, 'Go pound sand. We don't want your help. I'm just going to go back to doing it,' I can say, 'Okay, my only recommendation on this is that you get found guilty [of drug or prostitution offenses].'"

The focus on arresting victims rather than traffickers was intentional and practical. As Lauren noted, "It's not as easy to get the pimp as it is to get the girl." This strategy not only means that victims are being punished as a way to keep them "safe," but also that their traffickers often continue to abuse others. Gavin, a local investigator, asserted, "Ninety-nine percent of the time I'll charge the female . . . I will take them to jail if I think it's a safety issue. And if they're transient, they got nothing and I can't find the trafficker, I know he's around here somewhere but I can't find him . . . I'll take them to jail." From Gavin's perspective, removing the potential victim was a way to keep her safe and to ensure she received the services he believed she needed, whether she requested them or not. Seeming not to understand that trafficking victims were being scapegoated for their exploiters, he added, "I always charge them with whatever I can . . . So, I charge them with engaging in prostitution. I charge them with a drug possession if they have it. I charge them with violation of bail if they have bail . . . Give her the resources, get her that help she needs. I don't care at all if she's found guilty, I don't." Gavin's concern was that the potential victims may fall out of the system's view entirely, and he wanted to "keep a hook on them." His approach was an attempt to keep victims under the supervision of the carceral state, even when they did not want that form of protection.

In talking to members of law enforcement about their reliance on arrest as a mechanism to "rescue" victims—albeit with the hope of getting them access to resources, especially drug treatment—it became clear that this was an imperfect response to a series of broken systems. Lauren, a local investigator, stated that "now they're being held accountable to somebody else that's not their pimp, which necessarily isn't the most healthy thing either, but it's a segue into trying to build a life without them . . . It might seem short-sighted to people on the outside, but it's a long-term goal of trying to get someone healthy." Drug treatment while in jail offered criminal legal authorities a preferred, if convenient, justification. Ava, a prosecutor, shared, "It's tragic to say, but being swept up in the criminal justice system sometimes is the only way a . . . person gets access to services." She called arrest a way to "pause" their lives long enough for intervention to occur—it was "an extraction method."

The assumption that victims need to be subjected to the violence and trauma of arrest and incarceration in order to access resources throws into stark relief just how broken the system is. U.S. and state anti-trafficking responses are set up to intervene after the trafficking occurs rather than creating supports and preventing it before it reaches that level of exploitation. There are certainly cases where this approach helps individual victims and proves life-changing by providing a way to separate some survivors from their traffickers and help them access services. However, the impact of these strategies can be devastating for survivors as well. There is no evidence to support the effectiveness of arresting survivors as an identification strategy or as a way to access services. The TVPA itself provides that "victims of severe forms of trafficking should not be inappropriately incarcerated, fined, or otherwise penalized solely for unlawful acts committed as a direct result of being trafficked."[20] Even so, victims are sometimes charged with crimes they were forced to perform as a result of their trafficking based on the belief that it is the only way to identify and help them. As May, an advocate, told me, "The idea that you can only find people in the sex industry if you arrest them . . . It's not true. You just have to go to where people are in a way that people feel comfortable with you and develop those relationships to identify people."

Criminal legal anti-trafficking strategies often result in high rates of low-level prostitution arrests and few prosecutions of traffickers, negatively impacting both consenting sex workers and trafficking survivors.[21] Additionally, reliance on arrest as a victim identification strategy fails to recognize the need for non-carceral prevention strategies that avoid traumatizing survivors and address vulnerability long before trafficking occurs. As Poppy, a survivor advocate, noted, "For me, the problem is that if everybody agrees that [the potential victim] is in high danger, whether it's because of drugs or because . . . people are looking for her and would love to get rid of her because she's a big witness . . . where's the recognizing that and saying, 'we need a safe place, not jail, to help her and resources to help her detox, and resources to help her long term'?"

Service providers also questioned the benefit of these strategies. To Orla, a program director, the approach her law enforcement colleagues lauded was far too imperfect to be worth the harm it caused survivors:

> I say bullshit. One, I don't see excellent services being provided in jails or prisons. So I'd really like to know when they're saying "access to services," what they are talking about. Are they talking about AA [Alcoholics Anonymous] and NA [Narcotics Anonymous] coming in, or are they talking about being able to have three meals a day? Are they talking about supposedly not having access to drugs? Not having to pay for housing? Because having any kind of arrest record, certainly even being charged with anything, is going to cause so much more damage than someone continuing to not be arrested. As far as finding housing, it's a huge, huge hurdle. Just that one little thing. You could have a voucher; you could be on all of the welfare systems that the state offers and people would still not rent to you. If you have a criminal charge, no.

For Orla, the fallout from a criminal record was monumental and created lifelong barriers for her program's clients. She continued, "To me, it's just completely irrational. It just makes everything worse. And clearly shows to me the lack of understanding around trauma and around what it even feels like to be arrested, or to be processed." With its intent to neutralize dangerous people, the criminal legal approach is, in Orla's words, "a very narrow view." She said, "It's brutal on our clients. It's really, really brutal."

A small minority of law enforcement officials whom I interviewed also pushed back against arresting victims as an anti-trafficking strategy. "The focus should be on trying to end trafficking," Paul told me. "We're not gonna put trafficking out of business by focusing on pimps or prostitutes." He was concerned about failing victims and questioned, "If you truly believe that every day they wake up is survival, why are we arresting them? Why would we do that? The criminal justice system, it's based on fines and jail and none of those help . . . It doesn't help them get out." He described how his thinking had evolved based on interactions with sex workers and survivors, telling me about, "A woman who[m] I had arrested over and over again for engaging in prostitution . . . I guess I realized that I had done nothing to help her, as a police officer . . . Arresting her didn't help her at all. Kept her in . . . She was trying to survive and I was arresting her for trying to survive . . . If you're trying to survive, every day is survival. Who am I to try and use the law and try and stop that cycle? Time and time again it's proven not to work." The approach of arresting victims runs counter to how investigators approach other crimes, he said. "We don't go out seeking . . . sexual assault cases but the doors are always open to come in. That's the way it works. When you're ready to tell your story, we're here to listen, but for some reason law enforcement goes out for these specific people and targets them for enforcement in a hope to elicit information about drug dealers and pimps. Depending on who you get, you might get arrested. If you don't admit to being a victim of trafficking, you might go to jail. My goal now is to try and convince law enforcement that targeting women is the wrong way to go." Adding that officers employed varied strategies, he said, "You just don't know what you're gonna get, so why trust anyone? Why trust law enforcement anyway?"

In some instances, officers believed that arresting someone would help them but later realized they had no control over how the case moved forward. Once when Leslie, a survivor, was arrested, the officer communicated to her lawyer that he had done so in hopes of helping her and had assumed the charges would be dropped. When Leslie's attorney conveyed that the district attorney was moving forward with prosecuting her, the officer was flabbergasted and told her, "I didn't know all that was gonna happen. I just thought maybe she'd get offered some help." Leslie recognized the officer's good intentions but faced serious repercussions as a result of the charges and being prosecuted.

As detailed in their narratives, many survivors distrusted law enforcement because of these strategies, often suffering additional trauma and harm as a result. By perfunctorily jailing trafficked people, cops can exacerbate the situation at several levels, Liana shared. "They're actually traumatizing you even more, and they're making it worse because when you get out of jail the pimp will say, 'You didn't do this right, and you got . . . caught' and you'll get hit for it." Once an arrest has happened, the wheels of the system take hold in ways that some law enforcement investigators clearly don't consider. "When a girl gets arrested," Taryn told me, "she gets put in the paper, and when she gets out, she gets beat for that." In addition to the immediate consequences survivors faced if and when they returned to their traffickers, they also faced long-term repercussions once they exited trafficking and attempted to rebuild their lives. As discussed previously, having a criminal record complicates efforts to secure an apartment and meaningful work, in turn constraining a survivor's attempts to achieve stability.[22]

Still, most of the law enforcement officials I spoke with were in favor of keeping prostitution a crime. Ross shared that although he rarely arrested women—only if he thought it was absolutely necessary—he did not support decriminalization. "Until we can figure out an alternative that will keep them alive in the meantime, I would be against decriminalization. If you decriminalize it, you lose complete control over it." Acknowledging that control is already tenuous, Ava, a prosecutor, said, "When we have so few other tools and options, I just don't want to surrender that tool right now." Ava recognized that she spoke from a place of privilege, not having the lived experience of arrest and detention, but from her perspective criminalization helped get individuals off the streets, at least temporarily, and theoretically connected them with the services she believed they needed.

Support for criminalization was certainly not universal, and advocates, and even some officers, decried the criminalization of sex work and the effects of the carceral approach to trafficking on sex workers more broadly. "The way that it has increased stigmatization of the sex trade and the incredible amount of violence and discrimination and abuse that result from that stigma has absolutely been huge," May, a policy advocate, told me, pointing to the "unintended consequences." Even Hannah, a local officer, noted some of the repercussions of her unit's anti-trafficking work. "When we do our John stings, inevitably, women that are walking the street end up getting locked up too, 'cause you have to clear them all out so we can put our cops out to pretend. You know what I mean? If the real prostitutes are out there and all the sudden these three girls show up that they don't know, that's a giveaway." From Hannah's perspective, these arrests were worth it as part of efforts to "reduce demand"; however, sex-worker rights activists have called these tactics ineffective and research shows that they put sex workers and trafficking victims alike at increased risk for abuse because they push their work to increasingly less public spaces.[23]

While the criminalization of sex work does create opportunities for "extracting" suspected trafficking survivors from conditions of harm, at the same time the approach violates the rights of those who law enforcement officials are seeking to protect and exposes all sex workers (forced or not) to increased abuse and exploitation. At stake is the health and safety of trafficking survivors and sex workers more broadly, as criminalization contributes to the ongoing cycle of vulnerability. Alternatively, by removing punitive laws that prevent sex workers from reporting abuse and exploitation and treating sex work as any other form of work, decriminalization enables safer working conditions for sex workers and reduces their vulnerability, marginalization, and stigmatization. Full decriminalization would create an environment of safety and increased acceptance that would allow those being victimized to come forward without fear of repercussions from police or of a future criminal record. Furthermore, it would create conditions where sex workers feel safe reporting the abuse of others, and themselves. Protecting the rights of all sex workers, including their health and safety, and teaching them about human trafficking helps prevent trafficking rather than creating additional vulnerabilities.

Coerced Cooperation

When trafficking victims are identified, whether as a result of arrest or through other investigative methods, federal and state anti-trafficking initiatives often prioritize the prosecution of perpetrators over the rights of victims. Viewed as "instruments of criminal investigation," victim-survivors are frequently expected to cooperate in the prosecution of their traffickers if requested.[24] The TVPA conditions eligibility for certain benefits for trafficking survivors, including immigration status and access to other services, upon cooperation with law enforcement.[25] Sometimes prosecutors also pursue criminal charges against victims if they feel they were not offering sufficient cooperation in the prosecution of their traffickers. Anthony, a local prosecutor, talked about a case involving a "young girl who had a drug addiction, who very much fit the mold of a victim, but her level of cooperation was wavering from day to day." He ended up prosecuting her on a drug charge. "I think some of the officers were a little upset with that because they said she was obviously the victim in this, so why would you . . . incarcerate her?" Anthony felt the need to maintain credibility as a prosecutor with individuals who straddled the line between criminal and survivor. Nico, a local officer, questioned this strategy. Sharing his logic, he told me, "You have somebody who's already vulnerable. You have someone who's been trafficked and then you're charging them saying . . . do what I say and you won't have this charge. You're pretty much utilizing the same control wheel that their trafficker did." Indeed, many investigators and prosecutors expected these "girls," as they called them, to be compliant in return for their arrest and rescue.

Prosecutors using the threat of criminal charges in order to get victims to assist in an investigation made survivors and caseworkers hesitant to cooperate with police. Sometimes, investigators could be sensitive to the safety issues that survivors faced when assisting in an investigation but at other times, Chloe, a caseworker, found that "law enforcement has been really pushy with clients, and maybe asking them to do unsafe things so that they can get a case." She said, "it can seem pretty transactional, and in a way that feels a little unsafe for clients." Law enforcement did not follow through on their promises of assisting Sam, a survivor, for her cooperation. She shared, "I was told actually when I was arrested that if I gave them the information . . . that they would make sure that I, one, didn't stay in jail, two, possibly didn't even get arrested and, three, that if I was in jail that I would be given medications while detoxing, none of which occurred." Sam's case was just one example of how U.S. anti-trafficking policies prioritize prosecution of traffickers over preserving victim rights and preventing trafficking.

The Need for Prevention

The rescue mentality around both forced and noncoercive commercial sex embedded within the criminal legal approach to trafficking has a way of masking the structural roots of the problem. As I interviewed investigator after investigator who endorsed arresting survivors as a way to address their vulnerabilities without acknowledging the possibility of an alternative, I kept wondering why no one was advocating for other solutions. One day, during a conversation with Cat, an advocate, I brought up the question.

AWP: There seems to be this piece missing of providing alternatives to commercial sex work before it reaches the level of trafficking. How do you intervene? Where does that prevention occur? How do you provide alternative pathways? It seems like people skip over that step and are like okay, we have to just arrest and prosecute.

Cat: We skip over it because if we ask that question, we then have to unmask everything that is really problematic about the way we've structured our society, right?

This hit me hard and made me start thinking about all of the conversations I had had with investigators. Almost without exception, they focused on trafficking for forced commercial sex and the exploitation that occurs in that sector. My previous research showed how this centering of so-called sex trafficking makes other forms of trafficking, and the people forced into them, invisible.[26] Out of all the survivors I interviewed this time around, only two had not been trafficked for commercial sex, and they had been identified through channels outside of law enforcement. Some investigators believed the focus on sex trafficking was warranted and saw all sex workers as victims, regardless of the presence of force or coercion. For Doug, a local investigator, trafficking was less about whether an individual met the legal definition of a victim and more about the type of work in which they were engaged. When I pushed him to explain, he asked me, "Have you ever met a woman that says, I love selling my ass?" Like many of the other local investigators I interviewed who were not limited by the federal definition of trafficking that requires force, fraud, or coercion, Doug viewed the women he encountered working in commercial sex as possessing a special type of vulnerability.[27]

As I continued my conversation with Cat, she addressed this line of thinking:

> I guess the problem I see with the approach of "But you shouldn't have to make these choices; but this choice is the result of no choice. What are the alternatives?" . . . I totally agree with that and also, lots of people are making dreadful choices every day that are terrible for their mental health and their family's well-being. I guess I'm not sure why we've decided that having to make the choice to engage in commercial sex is so much more degrading and terrible than having to be a fucking coal miner, because that's awful . . .
>
> Let's just talk about what it means in today's world to have experienced trauma and instability and violence as a routine, to have no education, no prospects, no mentoring, no stability. Literally, what are your options for any human of any kind to say nothing about adding on other layers of marginalization? Why don't we get to have a conversation about why all these folks in our community are turning to dealing drugs small time or panhandling or engaging in commercial sex or whatever else? Just killing themselves with drugs because it beats the alternative of having to stick around. Anyway, I guess to me the high energy around "how do we fix the commercial sex problem" is ignoring all the other things that it's connected to.

In intersectional ways, structural vulnerability affects families and communities, and solely addressing one result of that vulnerability—commercial sex, with or without force, primarily through one line of attack, the criminal legal system—without addressing all of the other associated issues results in an incomplete response.

A carceral approach not only fails to prevent human trafficking; it also perpetuates the system of mass incarceration for, predominantly, Black and brown men as well as adding to the growing number of incarcerated sex workers and trafficking survivors. Resources directed at arrest and detention continue the cycle of trauma, when what is needed are accessible community resources that lift people up and help them overcome adversity. A response rooted in primary prevention would invest in systems that build healthy families and communities and that ensure all members have equitable access to adequate food, stable housing, gainful employment, and quality education regardless of race, income level, or immigration status.[28] Investing upfront in stronger systems would require fewer criminal legal and victim services interventions and those resources could be directed elsewhere.

A prevention-oriented approach would also eliminate the tensions around the definitional line between exploitation and trafficking, and address questions about helping those who are in need of services but who do not meet the statutory criteria as victims of severe forms of trafficking. While the federally defined criteria serve an important purpose—to ensure that those experiencing the worst forms of abuse have access to services—they also frustrate investigators who are encountering vulnerable individuals and have few resource options to suggest. As Doug told me, "Women have to fit into a category and if they don't fit into that category, they get no services."

Multiple providers shared that they often received improper referrals from law enforcement that did not involve trafficking but in which the person being referred was vulnerable, engaged in commercial sex work, living with substance use disorder, and had unmet needs. Mariah, a caseworker, told me, "If we're getting a referral for someone and the most acute thing is that they're continuing to overdose on heroin in the community, and they're really vulnerable, and then they're doing sex work. That's not a referral for us." For Mariah, it was difficult to turn away people who were not being trafficked, given how many were in need of support. "We just have to be really clear on the folks that we serve because when we do have somebody who does meet that federal definition, the needs that they have are huge and take a lot of time." Providers recognized the immense needs in their communities, but they were constrained by grant funding requirements. Shifting from a primarily interventionist approach to a response that starts with prevention and strategically incorporates intervention as needed would address these constraints and benefit both those who are trafficked and those who are vulnerable to trafficking. To decrease vulnerability across the board and significantly inhibit trafficking into all sectors in addition to other forms of exploitation, a structural approach should focus on ensuring worker rights, strengthening access to safe and affordable housing, and making physical and mental health care, including evidence-based treatment for substance use disorder, accessible to everyone.

CHAPTER 5

Making the Case for Primary Prevention

If our national and state policies were more strongly focused on meeting young people's self-identified needs instead of on trying to catch the "bad guys" and prosecute them, we likely would have a better chance of being of service to these youth. None of the federal or local responses adequately attend to the root factors that are associated with young people trading sex.

—Alexandra Lutnick, *Domestic Minor Sex Trafficking: Beyond Victims and Villains*

The safest communities are not the ones with the most police, prisons, or electronic monitors, but the ones with quality schools, health care, housing, plentiful jobs, and strong social networks that allow families not merely to survive but to thrive.

—Michelle Alexander, *The New Jim Crow*

Over the course of nearly two years of fieldwork, I asked almost everyone I interviewed some form of the question: What does prevention look like to you? One response from Eliza, a program director who worked with youth, encapsulated the ideas expressed by many others:

> Prevention is so many things. The trajectory of somebody being a seventeen-year-old or an eighteen-year-old who's trafficked, that trajectory started when they were like two. So, I think when we prevent poverty, and we prevent child abuse, and we provide services that stabilize families, and we provide affordable housing options, and we teach people how to have careers instead of trying to make it on low wage jobs in a way that does not have a million barriers to it . . . When we can decrease somebody's vulnerability and we can increase their protective factors then we're preventing trafficking . . . They're not going to be vulnerable to trafficking if they have all of those protective factors in place. When people grow up feeling like there's adults who care about them, who are safe, and responsible, whether that's their family by blood or not, where they feel like they're connected to their communities, and they have places where they belong, and they're safe, and they're provided for . . . I think prevention takes a lot of work. It's like a restructuring of . . . how we understand family and community.

The protective factors that Eliza described as effective prevention were some of the same that other frontline workers lauded as the keys to survivor recovery. For example, when I asked Celeste, another program director, about some of the most positive survivor outcomes she had observed, she shared, "People being able to get housing has been incredible. Having babies. Having babies sober. Having babies who are healthy. That's been really cool . . . Getting jobs . . . and being successful in their jobs and being able to have a paycheck . . . Seeing women reach sobriety mile markers . . . Literally like get up and go through the day and have the day be okay." All these milestones were major achievements that required hard work and intense navigation of systems, but they also involved resources that most survivors lacked for the majority of their lives and only had access to as a result of an interventionist response to trafficking. Celeste shared that, even with the resources earmarked for trafficking survivors, moving forward was often laborious. "Sometimes, each day, the women have to climb a mountain just for that day . . . We see that . . . either they make progress climbing their mountain or sometimes the mountains that were once mountains for them are no longer mountains. It's just getting up and climbing a hill for that day."

Restructuring the human trafficking response to focus on prevention would eliminate many of the vulnerabilities that the survivors in this study faced before, during, and after trafficking. It would also replace the many mountains these survivors encountered with occasional hills and flat terrain. Shoring up systems—for example, making safe, affordable housing a given and ensuring families have equitable access to healthcare and financial stability—would stop trafficking trajectories before they commence and would decrease the need for programs like those run by Eliza and Celeste that struggled to meet the needs of those exiting trafficking. A prevention-oriented approach would also ensure that criminal legal investigators are not put in a position where arresting potential victims appears to be the most effective way to ensure their safety. Primary prevention that addresses structural vulnerabilities requires upfront investment and reframing of the U.S. human trafficking response but will be more effective than the current criminal legal approach and result in better outcomes for survivors and for the communities they come from more generally.

As illustrated in the preceding pages, survivors faced a number of vulnerabilities and associated unmet needs over the course of their trafficking trajectories, many of which hindered their ability to achieve stability. When asked about her clients' most pressing needs, Maeve, a caseworker, recited what sounded like a monumental list: "Housing, substance abuse treatment, access to mental and dental and physical health, transportation," each one connected to the others. The vulnerabilities of trafficking survivors are just that—intertwined. While addressing these vulnerabilities is by no means easy, the consistent reference by survivors and frontline workers alike to the same issues, again and again, as precursors to trafficking, and as ongoing challenges post-trafficking, suggests that successfully preventing trafficking is not all that mysterious. The reality runs counter to what most people assume will end the exploitation, and where most resources have been directed to date—arresting pimps and traffickers, rescuing sex workers and victims, and attempting to "end demand" by arresting sex buyers. Indeed, the path to ending trafficking lies in addressing root causes and in the banality of building stronger systems.

A number of critical feminist scholars have made the case for a shift from the carceral state to the welfare state in addressing trafficking.[1] Under Elizabeth Bernstein's careful analysis, carceral feminism and the carceral response to human trafficking that it spawned stand in opposition to the types of economic, gender, and racial justice that necessitate an overhaul of the punitive neoliberal state.[2] We might also look to anthropologist Carole Vance, who, in her article "States of Contradiction: Twelve Ways to Do Nothing about Trafficking While Pretending To," exposes the key elements of the current antitrafficking response as primarily distractions that do little to actually stop trafficking.[3] Survivors who meet the federal definition of victims of a "severe form of trafficking" have received services, which have been meaningful, but prioritizing the carceral approach above a human-rights-based public health approach has resulted in few convictions of traffickers and most certainly has not ended trafficking.[4] What's more, the current carceral approach completely overlooks trafficking into labor sectors beyond commercial sex that are not criminalized and does almost nothing to identify those cases.[5] The one survivor of nonsexual labor trafficking whom I interviewed through her caseworkers was identified not via law enforcement investigators, but rather through a general assistance office where she had gone to try to meet her basic needs. That survivor's experience is illustrative of the importance of identifying people's vulnerabilities and addressing them to prevent trafficking.

During my previous fieldwork on the implementation of the TVPA, one prosecutor contended that, "things that involve sex are just different." While this is certainly true in the way that sexual victimization resonates with the American public, as evidenced by the staying power of the human trafficking narrative, what survivors in all labor sectors have in common are the precarity and intersecting vulnerabilities that contribute to their trafficking. In either case, responding to the structural conditions that create vulnerability and result in structural violence—rather than trying to arrest or deport our way out of it—is what will end trafficking.

After more than two decades of attempting to address trafficking, the U.S. government is at last taking baby steps to incorporate prevention into its response. The Biden administration's National Action Plan to Combat Human Trafficking, released in 2021, has placed a greater emphasis on prevention.[6] The plan is novel in its comprehensive governmental approach that includes specific priority action steps for each of the 3P's. Notably, the plan indicates that advancing gender and racial equity, focusing on prevention of labor trafficking in global supply chains, and promoting safe, orderly, and humane migration are essential to the effort to combat trafficking. Yet wording within the plan is vague, emphasizing "reviewing" and "monitoring" already well-documented deficiencies.[7] Acknowledging these issues is an important first step, but funding ambitious initiatives that prioritize preventions must be included in future budget cycles.

In the genre of programs like the American Rescue Plan, which was implemented during the global COVID-19 pandemic, a holistic response to trafficking would tackle the issue from multiple angles and, perhaps most importantly, it would address root causes.[8] Such an approach would not only help remove the vulnerabilities faced by survivors like those included in this book, but it would also do much more. By creating programs that address inequality and are accessible to all, a strategy that addresses root causes has the potential to reach individuals in sectors outside of commercial sex work who are not currently being identified due to institutional barriers, and also to eliminate the existing schism between those who are trafficked and those who are exploited but fall just short of the definition of trafficking. The goal is to prevent violence and abuse before it occurs and to decrease reliance on the criminal legal system. Within the domestic sex-trafficking context, a structural response addresses issues to help keep those out of sex work who don't want to be there and creates opportunities that provide alternatives ways to earn respect and income for would-be traffickers. Beyond sex trafficking, a structural approach should focus on shoring up worker rights and providing pathways for safe migration. In either context, preventing trafficking also looks like reducing exploitation more broadly.

Prioritizing Primary Prevention

The interventionist anti-trafficking model depends on the narrative of innocent victim and evil trafficker in which the victim must meet certain conditions in order to be worthy of assistance. As a society we have decided that exploitation in many sectors is acceptable, though not ideal. We accept abuse among farm workers, domestic workers, sex workers, and many other low-wage workers.[9] Policies could decrease abuse and protect worker health, but there is no impetus to intervene until the harm has already occurred and those abuses cross the line and become trafficking. Preventing trafficking means rooting out exploitation before it reaches the level of force, fraud, or coercion. It means addressing the intersecting raced, classed, and gendered inequities that result in marginalization. It means putting antipoverty work at the center of anti-trafficking campaigns, supporting worker rights—even for those in informal and criminalized labor—and ensuring supports for LGBTQIA+ individuals. It means investing in strategies outside of the criminal legal system and relying less on policing and mass incarceration as antipoverty strategies and investing more in expanding the safety net and creating healthy, flourishing communities. Intervention is essential to interrupting human trafficking when it occurs, but it should be the last line of defense, and prevention the first, in the U.S. response to trafficking.

Primary prevention is not exciting. In fact, it is the opposite of the thrilling and sensational types of rescue that are central to the dominant trafficking narrative. Rather, primary prevention recognizes and addresses as rights the mundane everyday needs that all humans should be entitled to, regardless of their level of power or privilege. The strategies I outline below emerged from the many conversations I had with survivors and frontline workers and reflect the needs articulated in those discussions. The following proposals would help in ways that are not immediately visible and would result in fewer flashy investigations and prosecutions. But they have the potential to help more people, many more, than the current carceral approach. The goal is to strengthen systems and put policies in place to stop trafficking so that criminal legal interventions that merely pause trafficking are needed much less frequently. An expanded approach to prevention should incorporate initiatives to disrupt patterns of exploitation before trafficking occurs and address factors that make survivors vulnerable to re-trafficking after they exit.[10]

An Upstream, Primary Prevention-Focused Approach to Domestic Human Trafficking

Housing

- Increase funding for housing services, including emergency, transitional, and long-term housing.
- Expand affordable housing. Research has demonstrated a strong link between housing instability and trafficking.[11]

- Increase safe housing options for survivors and those in crisis situations.[12] A housing-first model allows survivors the chance to obtain stable housing without preconditions such as sobriety or employment.[13]

Support and Treatment for Those with Substance Use Disorder

- Expand access to comprehensive, evidence-based treatment for substance use disorder, including medication-assisted treatment (MAT).[14] Such an approach would provide a full continuum of treatment and recovery services, integrate care for co-occurring physical and mental health conditions, and connect people with other social services.
- Prioritize harm-reduction programs that reduce the negative consequences associated with drug use, including overdose, and improve safety for drug users.[15]
- Decriminalize drug use and possession. Research shows that criminalization has little or no effect on rates of use and results in mass incarceration, racial disparities, and social exclusion.[16]

Health

- Ensure access to high-quality, comprehensive medical, dental, and mental health care for all who need it. Research suggests that over 90 percent of Americans face at least one major barrier to healthcare access.[17]
- Increase capacity to provide mental health care and sufficient support to make it affordable. More than one-fifth of American adults have a mental illness.[18]

Youth Programs

- Provide expanded support services for at-risk, homeless, and LGBTQIA+ youth.[19] Research shows that youth report practical needs like housing and job preparation and specialized needs like trauma-informed counseling and harm-reduction programs.[20]

- Address inequities and vulnerability in child protective services.[21] Raising the age that youth "age out" of the foster care system and combatting neglect and violence within the system could decrease the risk of trafficking.[22]
- Expand family support services to provide parents with skills and the ability to build stronger foundations during childhood. The two-generation approach offers a holistic strategy to support youth and families, increase economic security, and reduce adverse childhood experiences.[23]
- Fund community organizations that understand community barriers, needs, and potential pitfalls.

Education

- Ensure equitable access to high-quality education for all students.[24]

Criminal Legal Reforms

- Prohibit the arrest of suspected victims as an anti-trafficking strategy. Ample evidence suggests that arrest causes more harm than benefit to survivors.[25]
- Implement consistent and comprehensive state and federal criminal record relief to vacate all trafficking-related convictions for survivors, whether related to prostitution, drug offenses, theft, or other crimes, so that survivors are not doubly burdened by their trafficking and crimes they were forced to commit while trafficked. Current relief varies from state to state and depends on the crime committed.[26]
- Fully decriminalize consensual adult sex work. Criminalization makes sex workers vulnerable to violence and abuse, including human trafficking. Partial decriminalization (often referred to as the "Nordic model" or the "equality model") that punishes the buyer but

not the seller of sex is insufficient in that this model often pushes sex workers into unsafe locations to avoid law enforcement.[27] Decriminalization will make it easier to assist those who want to leave abusive situations and will remove barriers that keep sex workers from seeking help and reporting abuse.[28]
- Establish policies and practices to address police violence and discrimination against sex workers to ensure that they have equal access to protections.
- Provide alternatives to incarceration, especially for youth offenders.[29]

This list is certainly not comprehensive, and the suggestions I make here are specific to domestic sex trafficking. While my research primarily focused on women trafficked for forced commercial sex, it also has implications for those vulnerable to trafficking in other labor sectors. Primary prevention is needed to address trafficking in all labor sectors and of foreign-born and U.S. citizen survivors alike. In addition to building stronger and more effective housing, healthcare, and criminal legal systems, primary prevention must address the racist capitalist labor system that depends on cheap, unregulated immigrant labor to meet the needs of American consumers but that fails to protect, or even recognize, the workers who produce our food and goods, clean our homes, and care for our families. The U.S. must implement immigration reform to address the demand for migrant labor. Reforms must include making temporary guestworker programs safer, shoring up worker rights, and eliminating abuses within the global supply chain.[30] Additionally, survivors and impacted communities must be included in designing and determining the details of any major policy response, including ensuring it is implemented as intended.[31]

The strategies I suggest are not groundbreaking—and many others outside of the human trafficking field have advocated for similar policies in each of the named areas—but it would be truly transformative to prioritize prevention in such tangible ways in the U.S. human trafficking response. These proposals have added urgency when viewed through the lenses of those who have been trafficked and those who endeavor to help them; the lived experience of survivors and the very real patterns of need documented in the preceding pages must inform the path forward. A structural approach to human trafficking prevention does, however, require a significant financial commitment. The investment need not be entirely new; much could be accomplished through redistributing funds—for example, reallocating the massive budgets dedicated to arrest and detention to housing and healthcare, a move that would be more in line with the perspective of survivors. In an Urban Institute study of survivor perceptions of justice—including 80 survivors of trafficking from eight metropolitan areas in the United States—less than a quarter defined justice as incarceration of their traffickers. On the contrary, most survivors viewed prevention and victim healing as more important than incarceration of the perpetrators.[32] Such a shift in focus requires reframing the human trafficking narrative so that solving trafficking looks less like arresting bad guys and rescuing victims and more like decreasing precarity and strengthening housing, substance use treatment, and health care systems. While the criminal legal approach makes for good crime drama, it fails to adequately address the needs of those who are trafficked.

Investing in strong, thriving communities will be more cost effective and will have a much more far-reaching impact than continuing to pour funds into the criminal legal system. According to one study, the annual economic burden of incarceration in the United States is $1 trillion, when the costs to incarcerated persons, families, children, and communities are factored into the equation.[33] I encourage my colleagues in economics to carefully study the potential implications and benefits of reallocating resources to address the social determinants of trafficking and of exploitation more broadly. The stories of the survivors I met powerfully convey the need for such a restructuring and the potential impact that rethinking and reallocating resources could have. Additionally, more conversations that engage survivors and affected communities are needed at the local, state, and federal levels to move forward initiatives that create structural change.

Given the strong interconnections between domestic sex trafficking and substance use disorder, another potential source of funding for primary prevention lies in opioid settlement money. Like many other states, Maine and New Hampshire will receive hundreds of millions of dollars over the next eighteen years to allocate toward prevention, harm reduction, treatment, and recovery.[34] Much like trafficking, the best path forward in lessening suffering from opioids lies in addressing root causes, and directing funds to primary prevention has the potential to address both trafficking and opioid addiction at once.

It is important to acknowledge that addressing structural vulnerability via primary prevention threatens to put the very individuals who have committed themselves to assisting trafficking survivors out of a job, or at the very least requires that they shift their approaches. Besides the frontline workers and direct service providers, many of the charitable organizations whose claimed mission is to end trafficking rely on the dominant narrative of evil trafficker and innocent victim that obscures the structural factors at the root of trafficking. If the goal truly is to end trafficking, then those workers and organizations will need to reframe their objectives to align with effective prevention strategies and the needs of survivors.

In my previous work I was skeptical about the possibility of trafficking-related policy recommendations moving forward due to a lack of political will, and indeed many initiatives have not found traction. However, there has been a slow and steady recognition of (if not a response to) the root causes of trafficking. I remain hopeful about the path forward because preventing trafficking is about building a stronger, more just, and equitable society. It may sound utopian, but lifting the floor for everyone benefits everyone. There is momentum among youth, and more are questioning neoliberal capitalist values and the status quo. My hope is that the electorate will push for these changes and that our elected officials will acknowledge the complexity of trafficking and move forward with the multidimensional solutions needed to address it at the root. I am optimistic that the Biden administration's National Action Plan to Combat Human Trafficking truly is the first step in a more nuanced and effective response to the issue that moves beyond tired constructions of victims and villains. Primary prevention will never eliminate all trafficking, but it will create detours from and alternatives to the trafficking trajectories documented in these pages and will lessen significantly the need for criminal legal intervention and the associated harms to survivors caused by the current framework.

NOTES

Preface

1. Alicia W. Peters, *Responding to Human Trafficking: Sex, Gender, and Culture in the Law* (Philadelphia: University of Pennsylvania Press, 2015).

2. Peter Billie Larsen et al., "Repositioning Engaged Anthropology: Critical Reflexivity and Overcoming Dichotomies," *Tsantsa* 27 (2022), 4–15. https://www.redalyc.org/journal/6647/664772596002/html/.

3. Peters, *Responding to Human Trafficking*; Elena Shih, "Not in My 'Backyard Abolitionism': Vigilante Rescue Against American Sex Trafficking," *Sociological Perspectives* 59, no. 1 (2016), 66–90. http://dx.doi.org/10.1177/0731121416628551. Carrie N. Baker, "Racialized Rescue Narratives in Public Discourses on Youth Prostitution and Sex Trafficking in the United States," *Politics & Gender* (November 28, 2018), 1–33, https://scholarworks.smith.edu/swg_facpubs/14.

4. *Victims of Trafficking and Violence Protection Act of 2000, Public Law 106–386, 22 U.S.C. 7101 Et Seq*, 2000.

5. Peters, *Responding to Human Trafficking.*

6. As quoted in Tracy Kidder, *Mountains Beyond Mountains: The Quest of Dr. Paul Farmer, a Man Who Would Cure the World* (New York: Random House, 2003).

7. For a discussion of the way the Trafficking Victims Protection Act symbolically directs attention toward victims of forced commercial sex and away from victims of other forms of forced labor, see Peters, *Responding to Human Trafficking.*

Chapter 1

1. U.S. Department of Justice, *Federal Prosecution of Human Trafficking Cases, 2015.*

2. See the Raymond Jeffreys case for an example involving Maine. U.S. Attorney's Office, District of Massachusetts, "Dorchester Man Sentenced to 30 Years in Prison for Sex Trafficking of Minors," press release, May 19, 2016, https://www.justice.gov/usao-ma/pr/dorchester-man-sentenced-30-years-prison-sex-trafficking-minors#:~:text=Raymond%20Jeffreys%2C%20a%2Fk%2F,five%20years%20of%20supervised%20release.

3. Throughout the text I refer to the "criminal legal system" as opposed to the more commonly used "criminal justice system." The American criminal legal system encompasses policing, prosecution, courts, and corrections, and the processes involved often do little to provide justice. The outcomes are in fact unjust in many instances. Erica Bryant, "Why We Say 'Criminal Legal System,' Not 'Criminal Justice System,'" *Vera*, December 1, 2021, accessed May 29, 2024, https://www.vera.org/news/why-we-say-criminal-legal-system-not-criminal-justice-system.

4. Office of Public Affairs, U.S. Department of Justice, "Defendant Who Exploited Opioid Addictions of Young Women Convicted of Crimes Related to Drug Trafficking and Prostitution | United States Department of Justice," last modified March 25, 2019, accessed July 19, 2023,

https://www.justice.gov/opa/pr/defendant-who-exploited-opioid-addictions-young-women-convicted-crimes-related-drug.

5. Erin O'Brien, *Challenging the Human Trafficking Narrative: Victims, Villains, and Heroes* (London: Routledge, 2019), 6.

6. Criminologist Nils Christie defines the ideal victims as "a person or category of individual who[m]—when hit by crime—most readily [is] given the complete and legitimate status of being a victim." Nils Christie, "The Ideal Victim," in *From Crime Policy to Victim Policy: Reorienting the Justice System*, ed. Ezzat A. Fattah (London: Macmillan, 1986), 17–30.

7. Charges in federal human trafficking cases do not necessarily reflect the crimes the prosecutors believe the defendant committed and often hinge on the willingness of victims to testify.

8. Office of Public Affairs, U.S. Department of Justice, "New Hampshire Man Sentenced to 21 Years in Prison for Sex Trafficking of a Minor and Other Crimes," June 25, 2021, accessed July 31, 2023, https://www.justice.gov/opa/pr/new-hampshire-man-sentenced-21-years-prison-sex-trafficking-minor-and-other-crimes.

9. Jeanette Hussemann, et al., *Bending Towards Justice: Perceptions of Justice among Human Trafficking Survivors* (Washington D.C.: [2018]).

10. *3Ps: Prosecution, Protection, and Prevention*, U.S. Department of State, Office to Monitor and Combat Trafficking in Persons, https://www.state.gov/3ps-prosecution-protection-and-prevention/.

11. *Victims of Trafficking and Violence Protection Act of 2000, Public Law 106–386, 22 U.S.C. 7101 Et Seq*, 2000.

12. Alicia Peters, *Preventing Human Trafficking*, Gender Policy Report, University of Minnesota, January 25, 2023, https://genderpolicyreport.umn.edu/preventing-human-trafficking/.

13. Alicia Peters, *Responding to Human Trafficking: Sex, Gender, and Culture in the Law* (Philadelphia: University of Pennsylvania Press, 2015). Alice M. Miller, "Sexuality, Violence Against Women, and Human Rights: Women Make Demands and Ladies Get Protection," *Health and Human Rights* 7, no. 2 (2004), 16–47.

14. While it is common to describe problematic substance use as "substance abuse," the Diagnostic and Statistical Manual of Mental Disorders (DSM-5-TR) considers the term stigmatizing—"substance use disorder" or "substance use" is now the preferred language. *Diagnostic and Statistical Manual of Mental Disorders*, 5th ed., Text Revision (2022), "Substance-Related and Addictive Disorders." According to the Substance Abuse and Mental Health Services Administration (SAMHSA), substance use disorders "occur when the recurrent use of alcohol and/or drugs causes clinically significant impairment, including health problems, disability, and failure to meet major responsibilities at work, school, or home." "Mental Health and Substance Use Disorders," Substance Abuse and Mental Health Services Administration, last modified June 29, 2023.

15. I use the term "frontline workers" to encompass the caseworkers, law enforcement investigators, attorneys, and others who are working directly with survivors at all stages of their trafficking and witnessing the everyday violence they encounter and the role of failed systems in their lives.

16. For a discussion of fundamental causes see, Bruce Link and Jo Phelan, "Social Conditions as Fundamental Causes of Disease," *Journal of Health and Social Behavior* (1995), 80–94.

17. Corinne Schwarz, Emily J. Kennedy, and Hannah Britton, "Aligned Across Difference: Structural Injustice, Sex Work, and Human Trafficking," *Feminist Formations* 29, no. 2 (2017), 1–25. https://muse.jhu.edu/article/671715.

18. *Human Trafficking Is a Public Health Issue: A Paradigm Expansion in the United States*, ed. Makini Chisolm-Straker and Hanni Stoklosa (Cham, Switzerland: Springer International, 2017). Jonathan Todres, "Moving Upstream: The Merits of a Public Health Law Approach to Human Trafficking," *North Carolina Law Review* 89, no. 2 (January 2011), 447–506. https://

papers.ssrn.com/sol3/papers.cfm?abstract_id=1742953. Jonathan Todres and Angela Diaz, *Preventing Child Trafficking: A Public Health Approach* (Baltimore: Johns Hopkins University Press, 2019).

19. "Welcome to RightsWork—Empowering Communities, Advancing Rights," Rightswork, Last updated January 8, 2024, http://rightswork.org/.

20. See Peters, *Responding to Human Trafficking*, for a discussion of how conceptions of trafficking influence the types of survivors who are identified by law enforcement investigators.

21. Jacqueline Berman, "The Left, the Right, and the Prostitute: The Making of U.S. Anti-trafficking in Persons Policy," *Tulane Journal of International and Comparative Law* 14 (2006), 269–293.; Elizabeth Bernstein, "The Sexual Politics of the 'New Abolitionism'," *Differences* 18, no. 3 (2007), 128–151; Wendy Chapkis, "Soft Glove, Punishing Fist: The Trafficking Victims Protection Act of 2000," in *Regulating Sex: The Politics of Intimacy and Identity*, ed. Elizabeth Bernstein and L. Schaffner (New York: Routledge, 2005).

22. Wendy Chapkis, "Trafficking, Migration, and the Law: Protecting Innocents, Punishing Immigrants," *Gender & Society* 17, no. 6 (December 2003), 923–937. Ann D. Jordan, "Human Rights or Wrongs? The Struggle for a Rights-Based Approach to Trafficking in Human Beings," *Gender and Development* 10, no. 1 (2002), 28–37. Julie Kaye et al., "Beyond Criminal Justice: A Case Study of Responding to Human Trafficking in Canada," *Canadian Journal of Criminology and Criminal Justice* 56, no. 1 (2014), 23–48. Miller, "Sexuality, Violence Against Women, and Human Rights," 16–47.

23. Dina Francesca Haynes, "Good Intentions Are Not Enough: Four Recommendations for Implementing the Trafficking Victims Protection Act," *University of St. Thomas Law Journal* 6, no. 1 (2009), 77–95. Susan Mapp, et al., "Local Law Enforcement Officers' Knowledge of Human Trafficking: Ability to Define, Identify, and Assist," *Journal of Human Trafficking* 2, no. 4 (2016), 392–342. Amy Farrell and Rebecca Pfeffer, "Policing Human Trafficking: Cultural Blinders and Organizational Barriers," *Annals of the American Academy of Political and Social Sciences* 653 (2014), 46–64. Amy Farrell, Vanessa Bouché, and Dana Wolfe, "Assessing the Impact of State Human Trafficking Legislation on Criminal Justice System Outcomes," *Law and Policy* 41, no. 2 (2019), 174–197, https://doi.org/10.1111/lapo.12124.

24. Amber Horning and Anthony Marcus, "Introduction: In Search of Pimps and Other Varieties," in *Third Party Sex Work and Pimps in the Age of Anti-Trafficking*, ed. Amber Horning and Anthony Marcus (Cham, Switzerland: Springer International, 2017), 1–13. Gregory Mitchell, *Panics Without Borders: How Global Sporting Events Drive Myths About Sex Trafficking* (Oakland: University of California Press, 2022). Edward Snajdr, "Beneath the Master Narrative: Human Trafficking, Myths of Sexual Slavery, and Ethnographic Realities," *Dialectical Anthropology* 37, no. 2 (2013), 229–256. Ronald Weitzer, "The Social Construction of Sex Trafficking: Ideology and Institutionalization of a Moral Crusade," *Politics and Society* 35 (2007), 447–475. Gretchen Soderlund, "Running from the Rescuers: New U.S. Crusades Against Sex Trafficking and the Rhetoric of Abolition," *NWSA Journal* 17, no. 3 (2005), 64–87. D. Hamilton, K. Hodgson and J. Quirk, *Slavery, Memory, and Identity: National Representations and Global Legacies* (New York: Routledge, 2015), 1–219.

25. Jo Doezema, "Loose Women or Lost Women? The Re-Emergence of the Myth of 'White Slavery' in Contemporary Discourses on 'Trafficking in Women'," *Gender Issues* 18, no. 1 (1999), 23–50; Kamala Kempadoo and Elena Shih, *White Supremacy, Racism and the Coloniality of Anti-Trafficking* (New York: Routledge, 2022). Jessica Pliley, "From White Slavery to Anti-Prostitution, the Long View: Law, Policy and Sex Trafficking," in *Human Bondage and Abolition: New Histories of Past and Present Slaveries*, ed. Elizabeth Swanson and James Brewer Stuart (Cambridge: Cambridge University Press, 2018).

26. Janie A. Chuang, "Rescuing Trafficking from Ideological Capture: Prostitution Reform and Anti-Trafficking Law and Policy," *University of Pennsylvania Law Review* 158 (2010),

1655–1728. Laura Maria Agustin, *Sex at the Margins: Migration, Labour Markets and the Rescue Industry* (New York: Zed Books, 2007). Julia O'Connell Davidson, *Modern Slavery: The Margins of Freedom* (New York: Palgrave Macmillan, 2015).

27. Carole S. Vance, "Thinking Trafficking, Thinking Sex," *GLQ: A Journal of Lesbian and Gay Studies* 17, no. 1 (2010), 135–143. Jane Huckerby, "United States of America (USA)," in *Collateral Damage: The Impact of Anti-Trafficking Measures on Human Rights Around the World*, ed. Bandana Pattanaik (Bangkok: Global Alliance Against Traffic in Women, 2007), 230–256.

28. Diya Bose, "'There are no Victims Here': Ethnography of a Reintegration Shelter for Survivors of Trafficking in Bangladesh," *Anti-Trafficking Review* 10 (2018), https://doi.org/10.14197/atr.201218109, http://www.antitraffickingreview.org/index.php/atrjournal/article/view/326. Sealing Cheng, *On the Move for Love: Migrant Entertainers and the U.S. Military in South Korea* (Philadelphia: University of Pennsylvania Press, 2010). Susan Dewey, *Hollow Bodies: Institutional Responses to Sex Trafficking in Armenia, Bosnia, and India* (Sterling, VA: Kumarian Press, 2008). Elżbieta Goździak, *Trafficked Children and Youth in the United States: Reimagining Survivors* (New Brunswick: Rutgers University Press, 2016), 1–183. Alexandra Lutnick, *Domestic Minor Sex Trafficking: Beyond Victims and Villains* (New York: Columbia University Press, 2016). Jennifer Musto, *Control and Protect: Collaboration, Carceral Protection, and Domestic Sex Trafficking in the United States* (Berkeley: University of California Press, 2016). Pardis Mahdavi, *Gridlock: Labor, Migration, and Human Trafficking in Dubai* (Palo Alto: Stanford University Press, 2011). Rhacel Salazar Parrenas, *Servants of Globalization: Women, Migration and Domestic Work* (Stanford: Stanford University Press, 2001).

29. Elizabeth Bernstein, *Brokered Subjects: Sex, Trafficking, and the Politics of Freedom* (Chicago: University of Chicago Press, 2019). Denise Brennan, *What's Love Got to Do with It? Transnational Desires and Sex Tourism in the Dominican Republic* (Durham: Duke University Press, 2004). Susan Dewey and Tonia St. Germain, *Women of the Street: How the Criminal Justice-Social Services Alliance Fails Women* (New York: New York University Press, 2017). Kimberly Kay Hoang, *Dealing in Desire: Asian Ascendancy, Western Decline, and the Hidden Currencies of Global Sex Work* (Oakland: University of California Press, 2015). Sharon S. Oselin, *Leaving Prostitution: Getting Out and Staying Out of Sex Work* (New York: New York University Press, 2014).

30. Philippe Bourgois and Jeff Schonberg, *Righteous Dopefiend* (Berkeley: University of California Press, 2009). Kelly Ray Knight, *Addicted. Pregnant. Poor* (Durham: Duke University Press, 2015).

31. Leigh Goodmark, *Imperfect Victims: Criminalized Survivors and the Promise of Abolition Feminism* (Oakland: University of California Press, 2023). Kimberly Sue, *Getting Wrecked: Women, Incarceration, and the American Opioid Crisis* (Oakland: University of California Press, 2019).

32. Denise Brennan, *Life Interrupted: Trafficking into Forced Labor in the United States* (Durham: Duke University Press, 2014).

33. Jyoti Sanghera, "Unpacking the Trafficking Discourse," in *Trafficking and Prostitution Reconsidered*, ed. Kamala Kempadoo, Jyoti Sanghera, and Bandana Pattanaik (Boulder: Paradigm, 2005), 3–24.

34. Elżbieta Goździak and Micah N. Bump, *Data and Research on Human Trafficking: Bibliography of Research-Based Literature* (Washington, D.C.: Institute for the Study of International Migration, 2008), 9.

35. Janie A. Chuang, "Exploitation Creep and the Unmaking of Human Trafficking Law," *American Journal of International Law* 108, no. 4 (2014), 609–649.

36. J. Gulati, "News Frames and Story Triggers in the Media's Coverage of Human Trafficking," *Human Rights Review* 12 (2011), 363–379. A. Johnston, B. Friedman, and M. Sobel, "Framing an Emerging Issue: How U.S. Print and Broadcast News Media Covered Sex Trafficking,

2008–2012," *Journal of Human Trafficking* 1, no. 3 (2015), 235–254. Jayashri Srikantiah, "Perfect Victims and Real Survivors: The Iconic Victim in Domestic Human Trafficking Law," *Boston University Law Review* 87, no. 157 (2007), 157–186. Carisa Renae Showden and Samantha Majic, *Youth Who Trade Sex in the U.S.: Intersectionality, Agency, and Vulnerability* (Philadelphia: Temple University Press, 2018). For a discussion of core cultural images of victimization, see also Arthur Kleinman and Joan Kleinman, "The Appeal of Experience; the Dismay of Images: Cultural Appropriations of Suffering in our Times," in *Social Suffering*, ed. Arthur Kleinman, Veena Das, and Margaret Lock (Berkeley: University of California Press, 1997), 1–24.

37. See the film *Taken*, for example.

38. Doezema, "Loose Women or Lost Women?" 23–50.

39. O'Brien, *Challenging the Human Trafficking Narrative.*

40. Kerwin Kaye, "The Gender of Trafficking, or Why Can't Men be Sex Slaves?" in *Understanding Sex for Sale: Meanings and Moralities of Sexual Commerce*, ed. May-Len Skilbrei and Marlene Spanger (New York: Routledge, 2018), 180–198.

41. Doezema, "Loose Women or Lost Women?" 23–50; Pliley, "From White Slavery to Anti-Prostitution, the Long View," 190–218.

42. O'Brien, *Challenging the Human Trafficking Narrative*, 4.

43. Carole Vance, "Innocence and Experience: Melodramatic Narratives of Sex Trafficking and their Consequences for Law and Policy," *History of the Present* 2, no. 2 (2012), 200–218.

44. Erin Albright and Kate D'Adamo, "The Media and Human Trafficking: A Discussion and Critique of the Dominant Narrative," in *Human Trafficking is a Public Health Issue*, ed. Makini Chisolm-Straker and Hanni Stoklosa (Cham, Switzerland: Springer International, 2017).

45. The acronym BIPOC stands for Black, Indigenous, and people of color. Marinella Marmo and Nerida Chazal, "The Trafficked Woman: Ideal or Blameworthy Victim?," in *Advances in Sociology Research, Volume 7*, ed. Jared A. Jaworski (Hauppauge: Nova Science Publishers, 2010), 125–140. Srikantiah, "Perfect Victims and Real Survivors," 157–186.

46. See, for example, Jenn Selva Lemos Gregory, "Mom Says Southwest Airlines Thought She Was Trafficking Her Biracial Daughter," *CNN*, November 7, 2021. https://www.cnn.com/2021/11/07/us/southwest-airlines-human-trafficking-accusation/index.html. Scott Budman, "Hayward Woman Suspected of Human Trafficking Accuses American Airlines of Racial Profiling," *NBC Bay Area*, March 28, 2019. https://www.nbcbayarea.com/news/local/hayward-woman-accuses-american-airlines-of-racial-profiling/159441/. Gary Leff, "American Airlines Flight Attendants Calls Cops on Dad, Falsely Report Him as a Sex Trafficker," *View from the Wing*, May 13, 2023.

47. Lutnick, *Domestic Minor Sex Trafficking.*

48. Showden, *Youth Who Trade Sex in the U.S.*

49. Lutnick, *Domestic Minor Sex Trafficking*; R. Andrijasevic, *Migration, Agency and Citizenship in Sex Trafficking* (London: Palgrave Macmillan, 2010). Sheldon Zhang, "Beyond the 'Natasha' Story—A Review and Critique of Current Research on Sex Trafficking," *Global Crime* 10, no. 3 (2009), 178–195.

50. See also Bernstein, *Brokered Subjects*. Lutnick, *Domestic Minor Sex Trafficking.*

51. Judith R. Walkowitz, "The Maiden Tribute of Modern Babylon," in *City of Dreadful Delight: A Narrative of Sexual Danger in Late Victorian London* (Chicago: University of Chicago Press, 1992), 82.

52. Walkowitz, "The Maiden Tribute of Modern Babylon," 83.

53. Greta Wendelin, "A Rhetoric of Pornography: Private Style and Public Policy in the Maiden Tribute of Modern Babylon," *Rhetoric Society Quarterly* 42, no. 4 (2012): 375–396.

54. Doezema, "Loose Women or Lost Women?" 23–50; Peters, *Responding to Human Trafficking.*

55. Pliley, "From White Slavery to Anti-Prostitution, the Long View," 190–218.

56. Vance, "Thinking Trafficking, Thinking Sex," 139.

57. Kaye, "The Gender of Trafficking, Or Why Can't Men be Sex Slaves?" 180–198.

58. Juan F. Perea, "The Echoes of Slavery: Recognizing the Racist Origins of the Agricultural and Domestic Worker Exclusion from the National Labor Relations Act," *Ohio State Law Journal* 72, no. 1 (2011), 95–138; Jennifer Suchland, *What's Wrong with the US Federal Response to "Sex Trafficking"?* Gender Policy Report, University of Minnesota, January 11, 2023, https://genderpolicyreport.umn.edu/whats-wrong-with-the-us-federal-response-to-sex-trafficking/.

59. Sarah Hamilton-Jiang, *Racially Marginalized Migrant Women: Human Rights Abuses at the Intersection of Race, Gender, and Migration* (New York: UN Women, n.d.).

60. Kimberle Crenshaw, "Mapping the Margins: Intersectionality, Identity Politics, and Violence Against Women of Color," *Stanford Law Review* 43, no. 6 (1991), 1241–1299. doi:10.2307/1229039, http://www.jstor.org/stable/1229039.

61. Cassandra Mary Frances Gonzalez, "'I Went from Being Held Captive to Captivity again': How the Criminal Legal System Fails Black Women and Girl Survivors of Sex Trafficking," *Qualitative Criminology* 11, no. 3 (2022), 300.

62. Shamere McKenzie, "Listen to Black Survivors," *Polaris* (blog), February 1, 2023, https://polarisproject.org/blog/2023/02/listen-to-black-survivors/#:~:text=Victims%3A%20The%20fact%20is%2C%20Black,most%20vulnerable%20in%20our%20communities.

63. Cheryl Nelson Butler, "The Racial Roots of Human Trafficking," *UCLA Law Review* 62 (September 1, 2015), 1464–1514. https://www.uclalawreview.org/racial-roots-human-trafficking/.

64. Duren Banks and Tracey Kyckelhahn, *Characteristics of Suspected Human Trafficking Incidents, 2008–2010,* Washington, D.C., Bureau of Justice Statistics, Department of Justice, 2011.

65. Criminal Justice Information Services Division, Federal Bureau of Investigation, U.S. Department of Justice, "2019 Crime in the United States Tables 43," (dataset), accessed June 7, 2024, https://ucr.fbi.gov/crime-in-the-u.s/2019/crime-in-the-u.s.-2019/tables/table-43; United States Census Bureau, "Race and Ethnicity in the United States: 2010 Census and 2020 Census," Census Database, last modified August 18, 2022. https://www.census.gov/library/visualizations/interactive/race-and-ethnicity-in-the-united-state-2010-and-2020-census.html.

66. Fair Girls, *Amplified Risk Factors to Human Trafficking Experienced by the LGBTQIA+ Community* Washington, D.C.: FAIR Girls, December 11, 2020, https://fairgirls.org/amplified-risk-factors-to-human-trafficking-experienced-by-the-lgbtqia-community/.

67. Lara Gerassi and Andrea Nichols, "Social Work Education that Addresses Trafficking for Sexual Exploitation: An Intersectional, Anti-Oppressive Practice Framework," *Anti-Trafficking Review*, no. 17 (2021), 20–37.

68. *Victims of Trafficking and Violence Protection Act of 2000, Public Law 106–386, 22 U.S.C. 7101 Et Seq.*

69. Bernstein, "The Sexual Politics of the 'New Abolitionism'" 128–151. Elizabeth Bernstein, "Carceral Politics as Gender Justice? The 'Traffic in Women' and Neoliberal Circuits of Crime, Sex, and Rights," *Theory and Society* 41, no. 3 (2012), 233–259.

70. Bernstein, "The Sexual Politics of the 'New Abolitionism,'" 143.

71. For a discussion of interest groups active in the TVPA drafting process, see Barbara Stolz, "Educating Policymakers and Setting the Criminal Justice Policymaking Agenda: Interest Groups and the 'Victims of Trafficking and Violence Act of 2000'," *Criminal Justice* 5, no. 4 (2005), 407–430.

72. Musto, *Control and Protect*, 4.

73. Miller, "Sexuality, Violence Against Women, and Human Rights," 16–47.

74. *Ripe for Reform: Abuses of Agricultural Workers in the H-2A Visa Program*, Centro de los Derechos del Migrante, 2020.

75. Elizabeth Bernstein, "Militarized Humanitarianism Meets Carceral Feminism: The Politics of Sex, Rights, and Freedom in Contemporary Anti-Trafficking Campaigns," *Signs* 35, no. 1 (2010), 57.

76. Niki Monazzam and Kristen M. Budd, *Incarcerated Women and Girls* (Washington, D.C.: Sentencing Project, 2023).

77. Justice Rivera, ed., *Towards Bodily Autonomy Anthology: A Healing Justice Anthology Decolonizing Sex Work and Drug Use* (2022).

78. For example, see Angela Y. Davis, *Are Prisons Obsolete?* (New York: Seven Stories Press, 2003). Julia Sudbury, *Global Lockdown: Race, Gender, and the Prison-Industrial Complex* (New York: Routledge, 2005).

79. Marlihan Lopez, "Opinion: Prison Abolition Is a Feminist Struggle," *CBC News*, November 23, 2020, https://www.cbc.ca/news/canada/montreal/prison-abolition-defund-the-police-violence-against-women-feminism-1.5809912.

80. Peters, *Responding to Human Trafficking*.

81. Vance, "Thinking Trafficking, Thinking Sex," 135–143; Vance, "Innocence and Experience: Melodramatic Narratives of Sex Trafficking and their Consequences for Law and Policy," 200–218.

82. Amy D. Lauger and Matthew R. Durose, *Human Trafficking Data Collection Activities, 2021*, Bureau of Justice Statistics, Department of Justice, published October 2021, accessed August 9, 2023, https://bjs.ojp.gov/library/publications/human-trafficking-data-collection-activities-2021.

83. Amy Farrell et al., "Failing Victims? Challenges of the Police Response to Human Trafficking," *Criminology & Public Policy* 18, no. 3 (2019), 649–673, doi:10.1111/1745-9133.12456.

84. Omar Martinez and Guadalupe Kelle, "Sex Trafficking of LGBT Individuals," *The International Law News* 42, no. 4 (2013), 1–6, https://www.ncbi.nlm.nih.gov/pmc/articles/PMC4204396/. Peters, *Responding to Human Trafficking*; Annie Gilbertson, Aaron Mendelson, and Angela Caputo, "How LA's Fight Against Sex Trafficking is Actually Hurting the Women It's Supposed to Help," *Collateral Damage* (blog), LAist.Com, last modified August 7, 2019, accessed August 7, 2023, https://projects.laist.com/2019/collateral-damage/index.html.

85. C. Croft, *Human Trafficking Prevention: A Brief Overview of our Primary Prevention Approach* (Raleigh: North Carolina Coalition Against Sexual Assault, 2020).

86. Michelle Alexander, *The New Jim Crow: Mass Incarceration in the Age of Colorblindness* (New York: The New Press, 2020), xxix.

87. Urie Bronfenbrenner, *The Ecology of Human Development: Experiments by Nature and Design* (Cambridge: Harvard University Press, 1979).

88. Michael Marmot, "Social Determinants of Health Inequalities," *Lancet* 365, no. 9464 (March 19, 2005), 1099–1104, doi:10.1016/s0140-6736(05)74234-3.

89. Link, "Social Conditions as Fundamental Causes of Disease," 80–94.

90. J. Biehl, *Vita: Life in a Zone of Abandonment* (Berkeley: University of California Press, 2005).

91. Seth M. Holmes, *Fresh Fruit, Broken Bodies: Migrant Farmworkers in the United States* (Berkeley: University of California Press, 2013).

92. Philippe Bourgois, "Homelessness, Addiction, and Politically Structured Violence," in *The Insecure American: How We Got Here and What We Should Do about It*, ed. Hugh Gusterson and Catherine Besteman (Berkeley: University of California Press, 2010), 238–254.

93. Klaus W. Lange, "Rudolf Virchow as a Pioneer of both Biomedicine and Social Medicine," *Scandinavian Journal of Public Health* 50, no. 7 (2022), 873–874, doi:10.1177/14034948211048289, https://doi.org/10.1177/14034948211048289. Howard Waitzkin, "One and a Half Centuries of Forgetting and Rediscovering: Virchow's Lasting Contributions to Social Medicine,"

Classics in Social Medicine 1, no. 1 (2006), 5-10, https://www.socialmedicine.info/index.php/socialmedicine/article/view/6.

94. Michael Marmot et al., "Health Inequalities among British Civil Servants: The Whitehall II Study," *Lancet* 337, no. 8754 (June 8, 1991), 1387–1393, doi:10.1016/0140-6736(91)93068-k.; World Health Organization, "Social Determinants of Health," accessed May 21, 2024, https://www.who.int/health-topics/social-determinants-of-health#tab=tab_1.

95. Mark L. Hatzenbuehler, Jo C. Phelan, and Bruce G. Link, "Stigma as a Fundamental Cause of Population Health Inequalities," *American Journal of Public Health* 103, no. 5 (May 2013), 813–821, doi:10.2105/AJPH.2012.301069.

96. Holmes, *Fresh Fruit, Broken Bodies.*

97. Johan Galtung, "Violence, Peace, and Peace Research," *Journal of Peace Research* 6, no. 3 (1969), 167–191.

98. Paul E. Farmer et al., "Structural Violence and Clinical Medicine," *PLOS Medicine* 3, no. 10 (October 24, 2006), e449, doi:10.1371/journal.pmed.0030449, https://journals.plos.org/plosmedicine/article?id=10.1371/journal.pmed.0030449.

99. Bourgois, "Homelessness, Addiction, and Politically Structured Violence," 238–254; Bourgois and Schonberg, *Righteous Dopefiend.*

100. James Quesada, Laurie Kain Hart, and Philippe Bourgois, "Structural Vulnerability and Health: Latino Migrant Laborers in the United States," *Medical Anthropology*, 30, no. 4 (2011), 339–362, http://dx.doi.org/10.1080/01459740.2011.576725.

101. Erin Denton, "Anatomy of Offending: Human Trafficking in the United States, 2006–2011," *Journal of Human Trafficking* 2, no. 1 (2016), 32, https://doi.org/10.1080/23322705.2016.1136540.

102. Peters, *Preventing Human Trafficking.*

103. Quesada et al., "Structural Vulnerability and Health," 2.

104. Christina Zarowsky, Slim Haddad, and Vinh-Kim Nguyen, "Beyond 'Vulnerable Groups': Contexts and Dynamics of Vulnerability," *Global Health Promotion* 20 (2012), 5, https://doi.org/10.1177/1757975912470062.

105. Zarowsky et al., "Beyond 'Vulnerable Groups'," 5–6.

106. Corinne Schwarz, "Theorizing Human Trafficking Through Slow Violence," *Feminist Theory* 24, no. 4 (2022), 7, https://doi.org/10.1177/14647001211062731.

107. Zarowsky et al., "Beyond 'Vulnerable Groups'," 3–9.

108. *The Power of Framing Human Trafficking as a Public Health Issue*, Office on Trafficking in Person, Administration for Children & Families, U.S. Department of Health and Human Services, last modified January 11, 2016, accessed August 8, 2023, https://www.acf.hhs.gov/otip/report/resource/publichealthlens.

109. U.S. Department of Health & Human Services, "Secretary Becerra Announces New HHS Task Force to Prevent Human Trafficking," Press Release, released January 31, 2022, accessed August 11, 2023, https://www.hhs.gov/about/news/2022/01/31/secretary-becerra-announces-new-hhs-task-force-to-prevent-human-trafficking.html.

110. See for example Jordan Greenbaum, "A Public Health Approach to Global Child Sex Trafficking," *Annual Review of Public Health* 41 (2020), 481, doi:10.1146/annurev-publhealth-040119-094335.

111. Mario N. Bronfman et al., "Mobile Populations and HIV/AIDS in Central America and Mexico: Research for Action," *AIDS* 16 (2002), S42–S49, https://doi.org/10.1097/00002030-200212003-00007.

112. Elaine J. Alpert and Sharon E. Chin, "Human Trafficking: Perspectives on Prevention," in *Human Trafficking is a Public Health Issue*, ed. Makini Chisolm-Straker and Hanni Stoklosa (Cham, Switzerland: Springer International, 2017), 379–400. http://link.springer.com/chapter/10.1007/978-3-319-47824-1_22.

One of the very few examples of primary human trafficking prevention currently taking place is the work of the Coalition of Immokalee Workers (CIW) and its Fair Food program that uses a market enforced agreement to hold farms to fair labor standards and supports fair compensation of farm workers, thereby preventing the possibility of exploitation and trafficking.

113. Q. A. Karim et al., "Reducing the Risk of HIV Infection among South African Sex Workers: Socioeconomic and Gender Barriers," *American Journal of Public Health* 85, no. 11 (1995), 1521–1525, https://doi.org/10.2105/AJPH.85.11.1521.

114. Bourgois and Schonberg, *Righteous Dopefiend*. Geeta Rao Gupta et al., "Structural Approaches to HIV Prevention," *The Lancet* 372, no. 9640 (2008), 764–775, doi:10.1016/S0140-6736(08)60887-9.

115. Brennan, *Life Interrupted*; Chapkis, "Trafficking, Migration, and the Law," 923–937; Lutnick, *Domestic Minor Sex Trafficking*; Showden, *Youth Who Trade Sex in the U.S.*

116. The project was approved by the University of New England's Institutional Review Board IRB #080316–004.

117. United States Census Bureau, "Race and Ethnicity in the United States: 2010 Census and 2020 Census."

118. Liam Sigaud, "The 'Two Maines' by the Numbers," *The Maine Wire*, July 23, 2023, https://www.themainewire.com/2019/07/the-two-maines-by-the-numbers/.

119. United States Census Bureau, "Maine," accessed May 22, 2024, https://data.census.gov/profile/Maine?g=040XX00US23; United States Census Bureau, "New Hampshire," accessed May 22, 2024, https://data.census.gov/profile/New_Hampshire?g=040XX00US33#education.

120. Michael Polizzotti, *New Hampshire's Numbers: Resource Inequities by County and Population Group in 2014–2018*, New Hampshire Fiscal Policy Institute, last modified February 7, 2020 accessed May 22, 2024, https://nhfpi.org/blog/new-hampshires-numbers-resource-inequities-by-county-and-population-group-in-2014-2018/.

121. Maine Department of Labor, *Maine Workforce Outlook 2012 to 2022* (Augusta) Center for Workforce Research and Information, 2014.

122. National Low Income Housing Coalition, "Housing Needs by State," (dataset) accessed May 22, 2024, https://nlihc.org/housing-needs-by-state. "NH among highest in country for housing need," *NH Business Review*, October 18, 2023, https://www.nhbr.com/nh-among-highest-in-country-for-housing-need/; Zara Norman, "Maine is Leading New England in Housing Production, but it Isn't Enough," *Bangor Daily News*, February 26, 2024, accessed May 22, 2024, http://www.bangordailynews.com/2024/02/26/state/state-housing/maine-leading-new-england-in-housing-production-joam40zk0w/.

123. Evan Popp, "Renewed Energy to Address Maine's 'Broken' Mental Health Care System in Upcoming Session," *Maine Morning Star*, November 15, 2023, https://mainemorningstar.com/2023/11/15/renewed-energy-to-address-maines-broken-mental-health-care-system-in-upcoming-session/; Annmarie Timmins, "'System is Broken': Mental Health Centers Seek $30 Million to Add Workers, Bolster Treatment" *New Hampshire Bulletin*, February 1, 2023, https://newhampshirebulletin.com/2023/02/01/system-is-broken-mental-health-centers-seek-30-million-to-add-workers-bolster-treatment/; Rose Lundy, "Amid Surge in Substance Use, 20 Beds are Available for Uninsured Mainers to Go Through Monitored Withdrawal," *Maine Monitor*, May 22, 2022, https://themainemonitor.org/amid-surge-in-substance-use-20-beds-are-available-for-uninsured-mainers-to-go-through-monitored-withdrawal/; Chris Costa, "Experts Say the Lack of Detox and Treatment Beds is Exacerbating Maine's Homelessness Crisis," *News Center Maine*, October 19, 2023, https://www.newscentermaine.com/article/news/local/housing/lack-of-detox-and-treatment-beds-exacerbating-maine-homelessness-crisis-experts-say-housing-portland-health-care/97-1806cb15-2642-4855-bb9e-2ea03e2e8d95.

124. Ben Jacobs, "The Politics of New Hampshire, America's Quirkiest State, Explained," *Vox*, October 13, 2022, https://www.vox.com/policy-and-politics/2022/10/13/23400859/politics

-new-hampshire-america-quirkiest-state-explained; Nora Flaherty, "Why is Maine so Politically Independent?" *Maine Public*, February 2, 2015. https://www.mainepublic.org/maine/2015-02-02/why-is-maine-so-politically-independent.

125. Maine adopted the Medicaid expansion through a ballot initiative in November 2017, and implemented it on January 10, 2019. After former Governor Paul LePage delayed implementation of the expansion for months, new Governor Janet Mills signed an executive order on her first day in office (January 3, 2019) directing the Maine Department of Health and Human Services to begin expansion implementation and to provide coverage to those eligible retroactively to July 2018. Kevin Miller, "LePage Says He'll Go to Jail before He Lets Maine Expand Medicaid without Funding," *Press Herald*, July 12, 2018. https://www.pressherald.com/2018/07/12/paul-lepage-says-hed-go-to-jail-before-he-expands-medicaid/; KFF, "Status of State Medicaid Expansion Decisions: Interactive Map (dataset), published May 8, 2024, https://www.kff.org/affordable-care-act/issue-brief/status-of-state-medicaid-expansion-decisions-interactive-map/.

126. In Maine, victim services funding was distributed through the Department of Justice Office for Victims of Crime to a victim services agency. On the law enforcement side, in addition to agency funding, the District of Maine was designated as a participant in the Anti-Trafficking Coordination Team (ACTeam) Initiative, an interagency federal law enforcement initiative aimed at streamlining the investigation and prosecution of federal human trafficking offenses. United States Attorney's Office, District of Main, "District of Maine Selected as Phase II Anti-Trafficking Coordination Team," Press Release, December 18, 2015, accessed August 14, 2023, https://www.justice.gov/usao-me/pr/district-maine-selected-phase-ii-anti-trafficking-coordination-team.

New Hampshire's antitrafficking response was funded by a Department of Justice Office for Victims of Crime Enhanced Collaborative Model Task Force grant. Office for Victims of Crimes, Department of Justice, "OVC FY 2023 Enhanced Collaborative Model (ECM) Task Force to Combat Human Trafficking," posted March 10, 2023, accessed August 14, 2023, https://ovc.ojp.gov/funding/opportunities/o-ovc-2023-171656.

127. Peters, *Responding to Human Trafficking*; Lutnick, *Domestic Minor Sex Trafficking.*

128. United Nations Office on Drugs, and Crime, Forum on Crime and Society, Special Issue, *Researching Hidden Populations: Approaches to and Methodologies for Generating Data on Trafficking in Persons* Volume 8 (Havertown: United Nations, 2015). Peter Andreas and Kelly M. Greenhill, ed., *Sex, Drugs, and Body Counts: The Politics of Numbers in Global Crime and Conflict* (Ithaca: Cornell University Press, 2010). David A. Feingold, "Trafficking in Numbers: The Social Construction of Human Trafficking Data," in *Sex, Drugs, and Body Counts*, ed. Peter Andreas and Kelly M. Greenhill (Ithaca: Cornell University Press, 2010), 46–74.

129. Hornby Zeller Associates, Inc., *Maine Human Trafficking Needs Assessment* (South Portland: Maine Coalition Against Sexual Assault (MECASA), 2015).

130. Stephanie Halter, *New Hampshire Human Trafficking Collaborative Task Force End of the Year Report, 2017* (New Hampshire Human Trafficking Collaborative Task Force, 2018); Stephanie Halter and Scott Meyer, *New Hampshire Human Trafficking Collaborative Task Force 2018 Annual Report* (New Hampshire Human Trafficking Collaborative Task Force, 2019).

131. One survivor elected to share her story through her case workers rather than participating directly.

132. Elżbieta Goździak and Elizabeth A. Collet, "Research on Human Trafficking in North America: A Review of Literature," *International Migration* 43, no. 1–2 (2005), 99–127.

133. Anette Brunovskis and Rebecca Surtees, "Untold Stories: Biases and Selection Effects in Research with Victims of Trafficking for Sexual Exploitation," *International Migration* 48, no. 4 (2010), 1–37.

134. Lutnick, *Domestic Minor Sex Trafficking.*

135. Peters, *Responding to Human Trafficking*; Martinez, "Sex Trafficking of LGBT Individuals," 1–6.

136. Denise Brennan, "Methodological Challenges in Research with Trafficked Persons: Tales from the Field," *International Migration* 43, no. 1 (2005), 35–54. Nancy Scheper-Hughes, "Ire in Ireland," *Ethnography* 1, no. 1 (2000), 117–140.

137. For a discussion of "white slavery" and the "traffic in women," see Walkowitz, "The Maiden Tribute of Modern Babylon," 81–120; Doezema, "Loose Women or Lost Women?" 23–50.

138. *Victims of Trafficking and Violence Protection Act of 2000, Public Law 106–386, 22 U.S.C. 7101 Et Seq.*

139. Weitzer, "The Social Construction of Sex Trafficking," 447–475; Bernstein, "The Sexual Politics of the 'New Abolitionism'," 128–151.

140. Peters, *Responding to Human Trafficking.*

141. Maine state law includes "aggravated sex trafficking" that roughly correlates with the federal law's severe forms of trafficking and "sex trafficking," which until 2014 was known as "promotion of prostitution." *Title 17-A, §853: Sex Trafficking* (2013b) https://www.mainelegislature.org/legis/statutes/17-a/title17-Asec853.html.; *Title 17-A, §852: Aggravated Sex Trafficking* (2013a): https://www.mainelegislature.org/legis/statutes/17-a/title17-Asec852.html.

Chapter 2

1. Alicia W. Peters, *Responding to Human Trafficking: Sex, Gender, and Culture in the Law* (Philadelphia: University of Pennsylvania Press, 2015).

2. Julia O'Connell Davidson, "Will the Real Sex Slave Please Stand Up?" *Feminist Review* 83, no. 1 (2006), 4–22, https://doi.org/10.1057/palgrave.fr.9400278; Amy Farrell and Rebecca Pfeffer, "Policing Human Trafficking: Cultural Blinders and Organizational Barriers," *Annals of the American Academy of Political and Social Sciences* 653 (2014), 46–64.

3. Peters, *Responding to Human Trafficking*; Emily H. Novak, *Vagrants, Vixens, and Victims: Exploring the Limitations of Human Trafficking Victim Recognition Criteria in Texas* (Denton: Texas Woman's University, 2016); Amy Farrell, Rebecca Pfeffer, and Katherine Bright, "Police Perceptions of Human Trafficking," 38, no. 3 (2015), 1–19, doi:10.1080/0735648X.2014.995412, http://www.tandfonline.com/doi/abs/10.1080/0735648X.2014.995412?journalCode=rjcj20.

4. The U.S. Trafficking Victims Protection Act created a bifurcated definition that distinguishes between severe forms of sex and non-sex trafficking, which are typically described in shorthand as "sex" and "labor" trafficking. See Peters, *Responding to Human Trafficking,* for a more complete explanation of how this bifurcation affects implementation of antitrafficking policy.

5. For a discussion of how these issues arise in the lives of foreign born labor trafficking survivors, see Denise Brennan, *Life Interrupted: Trafficking into Forced Labor in the United States* (Durham: Duke University Press, 2014).

6. Corinne Schwarz et al., "The Trafficking Continuum: Service Providers' Perspectives on Vulnerability, Exploitation, and Trafficking," *Feminist Inquiry in Social Work* 34, no. 1 (2019), 116–132, https://doi.org/10.1177/0886109918803648.

Chapter 3

Epigraph: Seth Holmes, *Fresh Fruit, Broken Bodies: Migrant Farmworkers in the United States* (Berkeley: University of California Press, 2013), 26.

1. Richard G. Wilkinson and Michael Marmot, *The Solid Facts: Social Determinants of Health* (Copenhagen: WHO Regional Office for Europe, 1998); Loren Saulsberry et al., "The Social Vulnerability Metric (SVM) as a New Tool for Public Health," *Health Services Research* 58, no. 4 (2023), 873–881, https://doi.org/10.1111/1475-6773.14102; Michael Marmot, "Social Determinants of Health Inequalities," *Lancet* 365, no. 9464 (March 19, 2005), 1099–1104, doi:10.1016/s0140-6736(05)74234-3.

2. Johan Galtung, "Violence, Peace, and Peace Research," *Journal of Peace Research* 6, no. 3 (1969), 167–191; Paul Farmer, *Infections and Inequalities* (Berkeley: University of California Press, 2001); Paul Farmer, "On Suffering and Structural Violence: A View from Below," *Daedalus* 125, no. 1 (1996), 261–283, http://www.jstor.org/stable/20027362.

3. Clare Herrick and Kirsten Bell, "Concepts, Disciplines and Politics: On 'Structural Violence' and the 'Social Determinants of Health'," *Critical Public Health* 32, no. 3 (August 25, 2020), 295–308, https://doi.org/10.1080/09581596.2020.1810637.

4. Geordan D. Shannon et al., "¿Somos Iguales? Using a Structural Violence Framework to Understand Gender and Health Inequities from an Intersectional Perspective in the Peruvian Amazon," *Global Health Action* 10, no. sup2 (2017), 43-54, doi:10.1080/16549716.2017.1330458.

5. Sabrina Thulander and Caren Benjamin, *In Harm's Way: How Systems Fail Human Trafficking Survivors: Survey Results from the First National Survivor Study* (Washington, D.C.: Polaris, 2023).

6. Jennifer Middleton et al., "Adverse Childhood Experiences (ACEs) and Homelessness: A Critical Examination of the Association between Specific ACEs and Sex Trafficking among Homeless Youth in Kentuckiana," *Journal of Human Trafficking* (February 10, 2022), 1–14. doi:10.1080/23322705.2021.2020061; T. K. Logan, *Human Trafficking in Kentucky* (Lexington: University of Kentucky, 2007). http://cdar.uky.edu/VAW/docs/Human%20Trafficking%20in%20Kentucky.pdf; Joan A. Reid et al., "Human Trafficking of Minors and Childhood Adversity in Florida," *American Journal of Public Health* 107, no. 2 (February 1, 2017), 306–311. doi:10.2105/AJPH.2016.303564. https://www.ncbi.nlm.nih.gov/pmc/articles/PMC5227932/.

7. In both Maine and New Hampshire "DHHS" is the acronym for the Department of Health and Human Services, the state agency that provides child protective services and oversees foster care placements.

8. Corinne Schwarz et al., "The Trafficking Continuum: Service Providers," *Perspectives on Vulnerability, Exploitation, and Trafficking*, 34, no. 1 (2019), 116–132. https://doi.org/10.1177/0886109918803648.

9. Jane Stevens, "Adding Layers to the ACEs Pyramid—What Do You Think?" PACEsConnection, April 7, 2015, https://www.pacesconnection.com/blog/adding-layers-to-the-aces-pyramid-what-do-you-think.

10. Elaine J. Alpert and Sharon E. Chin, "Human Trafficking: Perspectives on Prevention," in *Human Trafficking Is a Public Health Issue*, ed. Makini Chisolm-Straker and Hanni Stoklosa (Cham, Switzerland: Springer International, 2017), 379–400, http://link.springer.com/chapter/10.1007/978-3-319-47824-1_22.

11. "Drug Overdose Mortality by State," CDC National Center for Health Statistics, last modified March 1, 2022, https://www.cdc.gov/nchs/pressroom/sosmap/drug_poisoning_mortality/drug_poisoning.htm; Joe Lawlor, "Drug Overdose Deaths in Maine Continue to Decline After Plummeting in 2023," *Portland Press Herald*, July 22, 2024, https://www.pressherald.com/2024/07/22/drug-overdose-deaths-continue-to-decline-in-maine/; Brian Mann, "U.S. Overdose Deaths Plummet, Saving Thousands of Lives," *NPR*, September 18, 2024, https://www.npr.org/2024/09/18/nx-s1-5107417/overdose-fatal-fentanyl-death-opioid.

12. For additional discussion, see Erica Koegler et al., "Traffickers' Use of Substances to Recruit and Control Victims of Domestic Trafficking for Sexual Exploitation in the American Midwest," *Anti-Trafficking Review* 18 (April 2022), 103–20, https://doi.org/10.14197/atr.201222187.

13. Laura T. Murphy, *Labor and Sex Trafficking Among Homeless Youth* (Loyola University New Orleans and Modern Slavery Project, 2016), 5, https://static1.squarespace.com/static/5887a2a61b631bfbbc1ad83a/t/5a7490fdc8302508d6b76f1c/1517588734590/Labor+and+Sex+Trafficking+Among+Homeless+Youth.pdf. Survival sex refers to when individuals engage in sexual activity in exchange for basic living necessities such as food and shelter. It can be voluntary (adults 18+), exploitative, or meet the definition of trafficking if force, fraud, or coercion is pre-

sent or the person is under the age of 18. Marginalized populations frequently experience housing insecurity as a result of family conflict and discrimination, making them vulnerable to exploitation and trafficking. This is especially true among LGBTQIA+ youth. LGBTQIA+ homeless youth are three to seven times more likely to enter the street economy and engage in the sex trades to meet basic needs than their non-LGBTQIA+ peers. Traffickers may exploit LGBTQIA+ individuals' housing insecurity and need for family support, or threaten to "out" them to loved ones as methods of control. National Coalition for the Homeless, https://nationalhomeless.org/lgbtq-homelessness/; Thulander and Benjamin, *In Harm's Way.*

14. Murphy, *Labor and Sex Trafficking among Homeless Youth*, 4, 30.

15. Beth Jacobs and Stephanie Richard, *National Survivor Network Members Survey: Impact of Criminal Arrest and Detention on Survivors of Human Trafficking* (National Survivor Network, [2016]).

16. Leigh Goodmark, *Imperfect Victims: Criminalized Survivors and the Promise of Abolition Feminism* (Oakland: University of California Press, 2023), 12–13.

17. Equal Justice Works, https://www.equaljusticeworks.org/news/preventing-human-trafficking-through-systems-reformation/.

18. Global Network of Sex Work Projects. *Policy Brief: The Impact of Criminalization on Sex Workers' Vulnerability to HIV and Violence* (Edinburgh: Global Network of Sex Work Projects, 2017).

19. Justine A. Hill and Kelsey J. Mullins, *A Threat to Healing and a Barrier to Recovery: An Assessment of Health Impacts of Criminalization through the Stages of Domestic Sex Trafficking* (University of Wisconsin—Madison: UNESCO Working Paper Series 005-06-2022,[2022]). https://minds.wisconsin.edu/handle/1793/83657. The same is true for those engaged in the sex trades by choice and makes it difficult for them to move into the legal work sector.

20. Alexandra Lutnick, *Domestic Minor Sex Trafficking: Beyond Victims and Villains* (New York: Columbia University Press, 2016).

21. Research suggests that a large gap exists nationwide between treatment need and treatment capacity. Christopher M. Jones et al., "National and State Treatment Need and Capacity for Opioid Agonist Medication-Assisted Treatment," *American Journal of Public Health* 105, no. 8 (August 2015), 55, doi:10.2105/AJPH.2015.302664.

22. For a discussion of how those with substance use disorder put physiological need for heroin above all else, see Philippe Bourgois and Jeff Schonberg, *Righteous Dopefiend* (Berkeley: University of California Press, 2009).

23. For a discussion of individual choice within the context of incarceration, see Nicole Coffey Kellett and Cathleen Elizabeth Willging, "Pedagogy of Individual Choice and Female Inmate Reentry in the U.S. Southwest," *International Journal of Law and Psychiatry* 34, no. 4 (July–August, 2011), 256–263.

24. For further discussion of the need for follow-up services that address structural problems after detox, see Bourgois and Schonberg, *Righteous Dopefiend*, 272–280.

25. Richard P. Mattick et al., "Methadone Maintenance Therapy Versus no Opioid Replacement Therapy for Opioid Dependence," *The Cochrane Database of Systematic Reviews* 2009, no. 3 (July 2009), CD002209, doi:10.1002/14651858.CD002209.pub2, https://www.ncbi.nlm.nih.gov/pmc/articles/PMC7097731/; Carmen E. Albizu-García and Oscar Miranda Miller, *Vulnerability in Persons with Addiction Disorders in Puerto Rico and its Relationship with Human Trafficking* (Puerto Rico: Center for Sociomedical Research and Evaluation, University of Puerto Rico, n.d.).

26. Koegler, "Traffickers' use of Substances to Recruit and Control Victims of Domestic Trafficking for Sexual Exploitation in the American Midwest," 103–120.

27. A Polaris Survivor Survey similarly found that 64 percent of respondents reported being homeless or experiencing unstable housing at the time of recruitment and 64 percent reported

that lack of affordable housing was a barrier to leaving their trafficking situations. *On-Ramps, Intersections, and Exit Routes: A Roadmap for Systems and Industries to Prevent and Disrupt Human Trafficking* (Washington, D.C.: Polaris, 2018).

28. See Lynda M. Baker, Rochelle L. Dalla, and Celia Williamson, "Exiting Prostitution: An Integrated Model," *Violence Against Women* 16, no. 5 (2010), 579–600. https://doi.org/10.1177/107780121036764; Victoria H. Chen et al., "Sex Trafficking in New York City and Vulnerabilities to Re-Trafficking," *Journal of Interpersonal Violence* 38 (July 8, 2023): 21–22. https://doi.org/10.1177/08862605231183452.

29. Schwarz, "The Trafficking Continuum," 116–132.

30. "The Vital Role of Case Management & Service Planning," accessed September 14, 2023, https://www.ovcttac.gov/taskforceguide/eguide/4-supporting-victims/43-the-vital-role-of-case-management-service-planning/.

31. Some organizations may make internal referrals for services such as shelter or counseling.

32. Jo Doezema, "Loose Women or Lost Women? The Re-Emergence of the Myth of 'White Slavery' in Contemporary Discourses on 'Trafficking in Women'," *Gender Issues* 18, no. 1 (1999), 23–50.

33. "Human Trafficking Data Collection Activities, 2023," accessed December 15, 2023, https://bjs.ojp.gov/document/htdca23.pdf.

34. Michelle Alexander, *The New Jim Crow: Mass Incarceration in the Age of Colorblindness* (New York: The New Press, 2020).

35. Alexander, *The New Jim Crow*; Elizabeth Bernstein, *Brokered Subjects: Sex, Trafficking, and the Politics of Freedom* (Chicago: University of Chicago Press, 2019).

36. Julia O'Connell Davidson, *Prostitution, Power and Freedom* (Ann Arbor: University of Michigan Press, 1998).

37. Philippe Bourgois, *In Search of Respect: Selling Crack in El Barrio* (Cambridge: Cambridge University Press, 1995).

38. Jody Raphael and Brenda Myers-Powell, *From Victims to Victimizers: Interviews with 25 Ex-Pimps in Chicago* (Minneapolis: DePaul College of Law, 2010).

Chapter 4

Epigraph: Aubrey Lloyd, "What Does Real Healing Look Like for Trafficking Survivors?," *openDemocracy*, June 5, 2025, https://www.opendemocracy.net/en/beyond-trafficking-and-slavery/real-healing-survivors-of-trafficking-engagement/.

1. "3Ps: Prosecution, Protection, and Prevention," accessed September 20, 2023, https://www.state.gov/3ps-prosecution-protection-and-prevention/. The U.S. government's strategy at times includes a fourth P—partnership.

2. *Combatting Human Trafficking: A Budget for America's Future*, (Office of Management and Budget, 2020), https://www.novoco.com/sites/default/files/atoms/files/fy21_fact_sheet_human_trafficking_021020.pdf; https://trumpwhitehouse.archives.gov/wp-content/uploads/2020/02/budget_fy21.pdf.

3. "Combatting Human Trafficking;" "OVC FY 2022 Enhanced Collaborative Model Task Force to Combat Human Trafficking," accessed September 20, 2023, https://ovc.ojp.gov/funding/opportunities/o-ovc-2022-171264.

4. "Human Trafficking Data Collection Project," accessed September 20, 2023, https://www.acf.hhs.gov/otip/research-policy/data-collection.; "Combatting Human Trafficking." "Human Trafficking Youth Prevention Education (HTYPE) Demonstration Program: Year 1 Reflections," accessed September 20, 2023, https://www.acf.hhs.gov/opre/report/human-trafficking-youth-prevention-education-htype-demonstration-program-year-1; "Combatting Human Trafficking."

5. "Look Beneath the Surface Public Awareness Materials," accessed September 20, 2023, https://www.acf.hhs.gov/otip/outreach-material/lbs-public-awareness-materials. Elena Shih and Joel Quirk, "Introduction: do the hidden costs outweigh the practical benefits of human trafficking awareness campaigns?," openDemocracy, June 20, 2019, https://www.opendemocracy.net/en/beyond-trafficking-and-slavery/introduction-do-hidden-costs-outweigh-practical-benefits-of-huma/.

6. Maine shifted its response in 2023 by passing partial decriminalization legislation, though it is still too soon to assess the effects Alexandra Heal, "Maine Becomes First State to Decriminalize Selling Sex," *The Washington Post*, June 30, 2023, https://www.washingtonpost.com/politics/2023/06/30/maine-sex-work-decrimilization/.

7. Barbara Stolz, "Educating Policymakers and Setting the Criminal Justice Policymaking Agenda: Interest Groups and the 'Victims of Trafficking and Violence Act of 2000'," *Criminal Justice* 5, no. 4 (2005), 407–430.

8. Kathleen Barry, *The Prostitution of Sexuality: The Global Exploitation of Women* (New York: New York University Press, 1995), 371. Kathleen Barry, *Female Sexual Slavery* (Englewood Cliffs, NJ: Prentice-Hall, 1979).

9. Stolz, "Educating Policymakers and Setting the Criminal Justice Policymaking Agenda," 407–430; Alicia W. Peters, *Responding to Human Trafficking: Sex, Gender, and Culture in the Law* (Philadelphia: University of Pennsylvania Press, 2015).

10. Erin Albright and Kate D'Adamo, "Decreasing Human Trafficking through Sex Work Decriminalization," *AMA Journal of Ethics* 19, no. 1 (January 1, 2017), 122–126, doi:10.1001/journalofethics.2017.19.1.sect2-1701.

11. U.S. Department of State. *2023 Trafficking in Persons Report: United States* (Washington, D.C.: Office to Monitor and Combat Trafficking in Persons 2023), https://www.state.gov/reports/2023-trafficking-in-persons-report/united-states/.

12. Michele R. Decker et al., "Human Rights Violations Against Sex Workers: Burden and Effect on HIV," *Lancet* 385, no. 9963 (January 10, 2015), 186–199, doi:10.1016/S0140-6736(14)60800-X.

13. *Human Trafficking and Sex Workers' Rights* (Washington, D.C.: Freedom Network USA, 2015).

14. "Organizations that Support the Decriminalization of Prostitution," Decriminalize Sex Work, accessed September 21, 2023, https://decriminalizesex.work/why-decriminalization/organizations-endorsing-decriminalization; "GAATW-IS Statement on Attack on UN Research Calling for the Decriminalization of Sex Work," Global Alliance against Traffic in Women (GAATW), October, 2013, https://www.gaatw.org/component/content/article; "Why Sex Work Should Be Decriminalized," last modified August 7, https://www.hrw.org/news/2019/08/07/why-sex-work-should-be-decriminalized; openDemocracy, Joanna Ewart-James, "Why Freedom United Supports the Decriminalization of Sex Work," August 23, 2021, https://www.opendemocracy.net/en/beyond-trafficking-and-slavery/why-freedom-united-supports-decriminalisation-sex-work/; "Amnesty International Policy on State Obligations to Respect, Protect and Fulfil the Human Rights of Sex Workers," last modified May 26, https://www.amnesty.org/en/documents/pol30/4062/2016/en/; Reason.com, Elizabeth Nolan Brown, "Science-Based Policy Means Decriminalizing Sex Work, Say Hundreds of Researchers," March 3, 2021, https://reason.com/2021/03/03/science-based-policy-means-decriminalizing-sex-work-say-hundreds-of-researchers/.

15. New Hampshire's human trafficking law closely overlaps with the definition of trafficking included in the federal Trafficking Victims Protection Act in that both require force, fraud, or coercion, while Maine state law includes both "aggravated sex trafficking" and "sex trafficking." The former roughly corresponds to the federal definition, however the latter refers to promotion of prostitution, thereby defining instances of voluntary sex work as trafficking and

opening up opportunities for local investigators to focus on prostitution under the guise of "trafficking."

16. See also Alexandra Lutnick, *Domestic Minor Sex Trafficking: Beyond Victims and Villains* (New York: Columbia University Press, 2016); Jennifer Musto, *Control and Protect: Collaboration, Carceral Protection, and Domestic Sex Trafficking in the United States* (Berkeley: University of California Press, 2016); Denise Brennan, "Fighting Human Trafficking Today: Moral Panics, Zombie Data, and the Seduction of Rescue," *Wake Forest Law Review* 52 (2017), 477–496, http://heinonline.org/HOL/Page?handle=hein.journals/wflr52&id=493&div=&collection=.

17. See also, for example, Annie Gilbertson et al., "Collateral Damage: How LA's Fight Against Sex Trafficking is Actually Hurting vulnerable Women," *LAist*, August 7, 2019, https://projects.laist.com/2019/collateral-damage/index.html.

18. For example, Jeffery P. Dennis, "Women Are Victims, Men Make Choices: The Invisibility of Men and Boys in the Global Sex Trade," *Gender Issues* 25 (2008), 11–25.

19. Musto, *Control and Protect.*

20. *Victims of Trafficking and Violence Protection Act of 2000, Public Law 106-386, 22 U.S.C. 7101 Et Seq*, 2000.

21. Suzannah Phillips et al., *Clearing the Slate: Seeking Effective Remedies for Criminalized Trafficking Victims* (New York: IWHRC, 2014); *Policy Brief: The Impact of Criminalization on Sex Workers' Vulnerability to HIV and Violence* (Edinburgh: Global Network of Sex Work Projects, 2017).

22. The Ban the Box Campaign advocates for landlords and employers to eliminate questions on applications that force formerly incarcerated people to reveal their criminal histories "Take the Fair Chance Pledge!", Ban the Box Campaign, accessed September 21, 2023, https://bantheboxcampaign.org/.

23. Sebastian Kohn, "The False Promises of 'End Demand' Laws," Open Society Foundations, accessed January 5, 2018, https://www.opensocietyfoundations.org/voices/false-promise-end-demand-laws; "End Demand Tactics Harm all People in the Sex Trades, Including Survivors of Trafficking," National Survivor Network, accessed September 21, 2023, https://nationalsurvivornetwork.org/enddemandstatement/; Bridget Anderson and Julia O'Connell Davidson, *Trafficking—a Demand Led Problem? A Multi-Country Pilot Study* (Stockholm: Save the Children, 2002), https://documentation.lastradainternational.org/lsidocs/11%20Trafficking%20-%20a%20demand%20led%20problem.pdf; Bronwyn McBride et al., "Harms of Third Party Criminalisation Under End-Demand Legislation: Undermining Sex Workers' Safety and Rights," *Culture, Health & Sexuality* 23, no. 9 (September 1, 2021), 1165–1181, doi:10.1080/13691058.2020.1767305. https://www.ncbi.nlm.nih.gov/pmc/articles/PMC7855821/; Jennifer McDermid et al., "How Client Criminalisation Under End-Demand Sex Work Laws Shapes the Occupational Health and Safety of Sex Workers in Metro Vancouver, Canada: A Qualitative Study," *BMJ Open* 12, no. 11 (November 22, 2022), e061729. doi:10.1136/bmjopen-2022-061729, https://www.ncbi.nlm.nih.gov/pmc/articles/PMC9685237/.

24. Joy Ngozi Ezeilo, *Report of the Special Rapporteur on Trafficking in Persons, Especially Women and Children* (Geneva: United Nations, 2014).

25. Peters, *Responding to Human Trafficking.*

26. Peters, *Responding to Human Trafficking.*

27. In Maine, in addition to "aggravated sex trafficking"—roughly corresponding to the TVPA's definition of severe forms of trafficking—investigators may also pursue cases involving "sex trafficking." The Maine statute specifies that a person is guilty of sex trafficking, which does not include any elements of coercion or force, if: "A. The person knowingly promotes prostitution. Violation of this paragraph is a Class D crime; or [PL 2013, c. 407, §3 (NEW).] B. The person violates paragraph A and has 2 or more prior convictions in this State for any combination of the

Maine offenses listed in this paragraph or for engaging in substantially similar conduct to that of the Maine offenses listed in this paragraph in another jurisdiction. The Maine offenses are any violation of this section or section 852, 853-A, 853-B or 855 or attempts to commit any of these crimes." *Title 17-A, §853: Sex Trafficking,* Public Law Chapter 35, (2015), https://legislature.maine.gov/statutes/17-A/title17-Asec853.html.

28. Sandie Morgan, host, *Human Trafficking and Public Health,* "Susie Baldwin," podcast, 2020.

Chapter 5

Epigraphs: Alexandra Lutnick, *Domestic Minor Sex Trafficking: Beyond Victims and Villains* (New York: Columbia University Press, 2016), 46; Michelle Alexander, *The New Jim Crow: Mass Incarceration in the Age of Colorblindness* 10th anniversary edition (New York: New Press, 2020), xxi.

1. Kamala Kempadoo, "The Modern-Day White (Wo)Man's Burden: Trends in Anti-Trafficking and Anti-Slavery Campaigns," *Journal of Human Trafficking* 1, no. 1 (2015), 8–20, https://doi.org/10.1080/23322705.2015.1006120; Carisa Renae Showden and Samantha Majic, *Youth Who Trade Sex in the U.S.: Intersectionality, Agency, and Vulnerability* (Philadelphia: Temple University Press, 2018).

2. Elizabeth Bernstein, *Brokered Subjects: Sex, Trafficking, and the Politics of Freedom* (Chicago: University of Chicago Press, 2019); A. Terwiel, "What is Carceral Feminism?" *Political Theory* 48, no. 4 (2020), 421–442, doi:10.1177/0090591719889946.

3. Carole Vance, "States of Contradiction: Twelve Ways to Do Nothing About Trafficking While Pretending To," *Social Research* 78, no. 3 (2011), 933–948.

4. *Victims of Trafficking and Violence Protection Act of 2000, Public Law 106–386, 22 U.S.C. 7101 Et Seq*, 2000. Amy Farrell and Stephanie Fahy, "The Problem of Human Trafficking in the U.S.: Public Frames and Policy Responses," *Journal of Criminal Justice* 37, no. 6 (2009), 617–626, https://www.sciencedirect.com/science/article/abs/pii/S0047235209001159.

5. Amy Farrell and Rebecca Pfeffer, "Policing Human Trafficking: Cultural Blinders and Organizational Barriers," *Annals of the American Academy of Political and Social Sciences* 653 (2014), 46–64.

6. "The National Action Plan to Combat Human Trafficking (NAP)," (The White House, 2021), last modified December 3, 2021, accessed September 28, 2023, https://www.whitehouse.gov/wp-content/uploads/2021/12/National-Action-Plan-to-Combat-Human-Trafficking.pdf.

7. *The National Action Plan to Combat Human Trafficking (NAP).*

8. "American Rescue Plan," (The White House, n.d.), accessed September 28, 2023, https://www.whitehouse.gov/american-rescue-plan/.

9. Tina Vasquez, "Human trafficking or a guest worker program? H-2A's systemic issues result in ratastrophic [*sic*] violations," *Futuro Unidad Hinojosa,* April 14, 2023, https://futuroinvestigates.org/investigative-stories/head-down/human-trafficking-or-a-guest-worker-program-h-2as-systemic-issues-result-in-catastrophic-violations/. Melissa Hope Ditmore, *Unbroken Chains* (Boston: Beacon Press, 2023).

10. Kelsey Peden, "After the Rescue: California's Legal Methods to Prevent Re-Trafficking," *SSRN,* December 15, 2020, https://papers.ssrn.com/sol3/papers.cfm?abstract_id=3835365.; Corinne Schwarz et al., "The Trafficking Continuum: Service Providers' Perspectives on Vulnerability, Exploitation, and Trafficking," *Affilia* (2018). https://doi.org/10.1177/0886109918803648. Marietta Baba et al., "Understanding Re-Trafficking in the United States: Why do we have a Revolving Door?" in *Human Trafficking: A Global Health Emergency,* ed. M. de Chesnay and D. Sabella (Cham, Switzerland: Springer, 2023).

11. Polaris, *On-Ramps, Intersections, and Exit Routes: A Roadmap for Systems and Industries to Prevent and Disrupt Human Trafficking* (Washington D.C.: Polaris, 2018).

12. *Federal Housing and Homelessness Programs for Survivors of Human Trafficking* (Washington, D.C.: U.S. Administration for Children and Families Office for Trafficking in Persons, 2020).

13. Freedom Network Training Institute, *Housing First: Improving Access to Housing for Youth Survivors* (Freedom Network USA, 2021).

14. "Medications for Substance use Disorders," Substance Abuse and Mental Health Services Administration, last modified April 11, 2024, https://www.samhsa.gov/medications-substance-use-disorders.

15. "Harm Reduction," last modified February 22, 2023, accessed September 28, 2023, https://www.samhsa.gov/find-help/harm-reduction; "Harm Reduction," last modified October 26, 2023, accessed September 28, 2023, https://nida.nih.gov/research-topics/harm-reduction.

16. *Approaches to Decriminalizing Drug Use & Possession* (Drug Policy Alliance, 2015), https://www.unodc.org/documents/ungass2016/Contributions/Civil/DrugPolicyAlliance/DPA_Fact_Sheet_Approaches_to_Decriminalization_Feb2015_1.pdf.

17. Nicholas C. Coombs et al., "Barriers to Healthcare Access among U.S. Adults with Mental Health Challenges: A Population-Based Study," *SSM—Population Health* 15 (2021), 100847doi:10.1016/j.ssmph.2021.100847, https://www.sciencedirect.com/science/article/pii/S2352827321001221; Mary E. Northridge, Anjali Kumar, and Raghbir Kaur, "Disparities in Access to Oral Health Care," *Annual Review of Public Health* 41, no. 1 (2020), 513–535, https://doi.org/10.1146/annurev-publhealth-040119-094318; "Health Care Access and Quality," accessed September 21, 2023, https://health.gov/healthypeople/objectives-and-data/browse-objectives/health-care-access-and-quality.

18. Hermangi Modi et al., "Exploring Barriers to Mental Health Care in the U.S." last modified October 10, 2022, accessed September 21, 2023, https://www.aamcresearchinstitute.org/our-work/issue-brief/exploring-barriers-mental-health-care-us.

19. Elaine M. Maccio and Kristin M. Ferguson, "Services to LGBTQ Runaway and Homeless Youth: Gaps and Recommendations," *Children and Youth Services Review* 63 (2016), 47–57, doi:10.1016/j.childyouth.2016.02.008, https://www.sciencedirect.com/science/article/pii/S0190740916300317; Family & Youth Service Bureau, *Issue Brief: Human Trafficking Prevention—Strategies for Runaway and Homeless Youth Settings*, Washington, D.C.: Administration for Children and Families, 2020; *LGBTQIA+ Youth and Experiences of Human Trafficking: A Healing Centered Approach*, (National LGBTQIA+ Health Education Center, Futures Without Violence and Health Partners on IPV + Exploration, 2021). Yaren Bilge Kaya et al., "Improving Access to Housing and Supportive Services for Runaway and Homeless Youth: Reducing Vulnerability to Human Trafficking in New York City," *IISE Transactions* 56, no. 3 (2022): 296–310, https://doi.org/10.1080/24725854.2022.2120223.

20. Laura T. Murphy, "Labor and Sex Trafficking among Homeless Youth," (2016); "Sex Work & Harm Reduction," National Harm Reduction Coalition, accessed September 28, 2023, https://harmreduction.org/issues/sex-work/harm-reduction-facts/.

21. National Conference of State Legislatures, *Disproportionality and Race Equity in Child Welfare* (Washington, D.C.: NCSL 2021), https://www.ncsl.org/human-services/disproportionality-and-race-equity-in-child-welfare.

22. "Florida's Child Welfare System is found to be Complicit in Sex Trafficking," accessed September 28, 2023, https://jezebel.com/floridas-child-welfare-system-is-found-to-be-complicit-1849827559; National Conference of State Legislatures, *Disproportionality and Race Equity in Child Welfare*; Madeline Hannan et al., "Children at Risk: Foster Care and Human Trafficking," in *Human Trafficking is a Public Health Issue: A Paradigm Expansion in the United States*, ed. Makini Chisolm-Straker and Hanni Stoklosa, 105–121 (Cham, Switzerland: Springer, 2017).

23. "Family Support Services," accessed September 28, 2023, https://www.childwelfare.gov/topics/supporting/support-services/; Sarah Griffen, *The Two-Generation Approach: Recommendations for Bridging Practice and Policy in Maine* (Portland, ME: John T. Gorman Foundation, 2020).

24. National Center for Education Evaluation and Regional Assistance, *Do Disadvantaged Students Get Less Effective Teaching? Key Findings from Recent Institute of Education Sciences Studies* (2014).

25. International Women's Human Rights Clinic, City University of New York Law School Trafficking Victims Advocacy Project and Legal Aid Society of New York, *Criminalization of Trafficking Victims: Submission to the United Nations Universal Periodic Review of United States of America* (2015); Gregory Mitchell, *Panics without Borders: How Global Sporting Events Drive Myths about Sex Trafficking* (Oakland: University of California Press, 2022); Jennifer Musto, "Domestic Minor Sex Trafficking and the Detention-to-Protection Pipeline," *Dialectical Anthropology* 37, no. 2 (2013), 257–276, https://doi.org/10.1007/s10624-013-9295-0; Hannah Garry and Maura Reinbrecht, *Over-Policing Sex Trafficking: How U.S. Law Enforcement Should Reform Operations* (International Human Rights Law Clinic USC Gould School of Law 2021), https://humanrightsclinic.usc.edu/2021/11/15/over-policing-sex-trafficking-how-u-s-law-enforcement-should-reform-operations/.

26. Freedom network USA, November 10, 2021, http://freedomnetworkusa.org/2021/11/10/impact-of-arrest-and-conviction-histories-on-trafficking-survivors/; The Survivor Reentry Project, *Workable Solutions for Criminal Record Relief: Recommendations for Prosecutors Serving Victims of Human Trafficking* American Bar Association Commission on Domestic & Sexual Violence, 2019; Polaris, *Criminal Record Relief for Trafficking Survivors Updating Grades and Rubric to Reflect Current Improvements and Changes* (Polaris, 2019); Ashleigh Pelto, "Criminal Record Relief for Human Trafficking Survivors: Analysis of Current State Statutes and the Need for a Federal Model Statute," *Michigan Journal of Gender & Law* 27, no. 2 (2021), 473, https://repository.law.umich.edu/mjgl/vol27/iss2/6?utm_source=repository.law.umich.edu%2Fmjgl%2Fvol27%2Fiss2%2F6&utm_medium=PDF&utm_campaign=PDFCoverPages.

27. "Amnesty International Policy on State Obligations to Respect, Protect and Fulfil the Human Rights of Sex Workers," last modified May 26, 2016, https://www.amnesty.org/en/documents/pol30/4062/2016/en/; "Partial Decriminalization of Sex Work could Cause More Harm than Good," last modified April 15, 2021, accessed September 28, 2023, https://www.urban.org/urban-wire/partial-decriminalization-sex-work-could-cause-more-harm-good; Belinda Brooks-Gordon, Max Morris, and Teela Sanders, "Harm Reduction and Decriminalization of Sex Work: Introduction to the Special Section," *Sexuality Research and Social Policy* 18, no. 4 (2021), 809–818, https://doi.org/10.1007/s13178-021-00636-0.

28. Erin Albright and Kate D'Adamo, "Decreasing Human Trafficking through Sex Work Decriminalization," *AMA Journal of Ethics* 19, no. 1 (January 1, 2017), 122–126, doi:10.1001/journalofethics.2017.19.1.sect2-1701. Andrea Krüsi, Kate D'Adamo, and Ariel Sernick, "Criminalised Interactions with Law Enforcement and Impacts on Health and Safety in the Context of Different Legislative Frameworks Governing Sex Work Globally," in *Sex Work, Health, and Human Rights: Global Inequities, Challenges, and Opportunities for Action*, ed. Shira M. Goldenberg et al., 121–140 (Cham: Springer International, 2021), 121–140, https://doi.org/10.1007/978-3-030-64171-9_7.

29. Families Against Mandatory Minimums, *Alternatives to Incarceration in a Nutshell* (Washington, D.C., n.d.).

30. Etan Newman, *No Way to Treat a Guest: Why the H2-A Agricultural Visa Program Fails U.S. and Foreign Workers* (Washington, D.C.: Farmworker Justice, n.d.); Ximena Bustillo, "A Human-Trafficking Case Exposed Farmworker Abuses. the Government is Promising

Change," *NPR*, May 27, 2022, https://www.npr.org/2022/05/27/1101741366/human-trafficking-farmworker-abuse-georgia.

31. "National Survivor Network," accessed September 28, 2023, https://nationalsurvivornetwork.org/; "U.S. Advisory Council on Human Trafficking," accessed September 28, 2023, https://www.state.gov/u-s-advisory-council-on-human-trafficking/.

32. Hanna Love et al., *Justice in their Own Words Perceptions and Experiences of (in)Justice among Human Trafficking Survivors* (Washington, D.C.: Urban Institute, 2018).

33. Michael McLaughlin et al., *The Economic Burden of Incarceration in the United States* (Institute for Justice Research and Development at Florida State University, 2016). https://ijrd.csw.fsu.edu/sites/g/files/upcbnu1766/files/media/images/publication_pdfs/Economic_Burden_of_Incarceration_IJRD072016_0_0.pdf

34. Maine is expected to receive $235 million and New Hampshire $310 million over the next eighteen years. Emily Bader, "Maine Will Receive at Least $235 Million in Settlements from Companies Accused of Fueling the Opioid Crisis," *Portland Press Herald*, June 20, 2023, https://www.pressherald.com/2023/06/20/maine-will-receive-at-least-235-million-in-settlements-from-companies-accused-of-fueling-the-opioid-crisis/; Paul Cuno-Booth, "How NH Is Using Its Opioid Lawsuit Payouts: 'That Money Has to Go Back to Helping Those People Hit the Hardest'," *nhpr*, April 19, 2023, https://www.nhpr.org/nh-news/2023-04-19/new-hampshire-opioid-lawsuits-money-settlements-treatment-recovery-enforcement.

BIBLIOGRAPHY

2023 Trafficking in Persons Report: United States. U.S. Department of State, Office to Monitor and Combat Trafficking in Persons, 2023.

Agustin, Laura Maria. *Sex at the Margins: Migration, Labour Markets and the Rescue Industry.* New York: Zed Books, 2007.

Albizu-García, Carmen E. and Oscar Miranda Miller. *Vulnerability in Persons with Addiction Disorders in Puerto Rico and its Relationship with Human Trafficking.* San Juan, PR: Center for Sociomedical Research and Evaluation, Medical Sciences Campus, University of Puerto Rico, n.d.

Albright, Erin, and Kate D'Adamo. "The Media and Human Trafficking: A Discussion and Critique of the Dominant Narrative." In *Human Trafficking Is a Public Health Issue*, ed. Makini Chisolm-Straker and Hanni Stoklosa. Cham, Switzerland: Springer International, 2017.

Albright, Erin and Kate D'Adamo. "Decreasing Human Trafficking through Sex Work Decriminalization." *AMA Journal of Ethics* 19, no. 1 (January 1, 2017): 122–126. doi:10.1001/journalofethics.2017.19.1.sect2-1701.

Alexander, Michelle. *The New Jim Crow: Mass Incarceration in the Age of Colorblindness.* New York: The New Press, 2020.

Alpert, Elaine J. and Sharon E. Chin. "Human Trafficking: Perspectives on Prevention." In *Human Trafficking is a Public Health Issue*, ed. Makini Chisolm-Straker and Hanni Stoklosa, Cham, Switzerland: Springer International, 2017.

American Public Health Association. "Expanding and Coordinating Human Trafficking-Related Public Health Research, Evaluation, Education, and Prevention." Accessed August 8, 2023. https://www.apha.org/policies-and-advocacy/public-health-policy-statements/policy-database/2016/01/26/14/28/expanding-and-coordinating-human-trafficking-related-public-health-activities.

Amnesty International. "Amnesty International Policy on State Obligations to Respect, Protect and Fulfil the Human Rights of Sex Workers." https://www.amnesty.org/en/documents/pol30/4062/2016/en/.

Anderson, Bridget and Julia O'Connell Davidson. *Trafficking—a Demand Led Problem? A Multi-Country Pilot Study.* Stockholm: Save the Children, 2002. https://documentation.lastradainternational.org/lsidocs/11%20Trafficking%20-%20a%20demand%20led%20problem.pdf.

Andreas, Peter and Kelly M. Greenhill. *Sex, Drugs, and Body Counts: The Politics of Numbers in Global Crime and Conflict.* Ithaca, NY: Cornell University Press, 2010.

Andrijasevic, R. *Migration, Agency and Citizenship in Sex Trafficking.* London: Palgrave Macmillan, 2010.

Approaches to Decriminalizing Drug Use & Possession. Drug Policy Alliance, 2015. https://www.unodc.org/documents/ungass2016/Contributions/Civil/DrugPolicyAlliance/DPA_Fact_Sheet_Approaches_to_Decriminalization_Feb2015_1.pdf

Baba, Marietta, et al. "Understanding Re-Trafficking in the United States: Why do we have a Revolving Door?" In *Human Trafficking: A Global Health Emergency*, ed. M. de Chesnay and D. Sabella. Cham, Switzerland: Springer, 2023.

Bader, Emily. "Maine Will Receive at Least $235 Million in Settlements from Companies Accused of Fueling the Opioid Crisis." *Portland Press Herald.* June 20, 2023. https://www.pressherald.com/2023/06/20/maine-will-receive-at-least-235-million-in-settlements-from-companies-accused-of-fueling-the-opioid-crisis/.

Baker, Carrie N. "Racialized Rescue Narratives in Public Discourses on Youth Prostitution and Sex Trafficking in the United States." *Politics & Gender*, 15, no. 4 (2018): 773–800. https://doi.org/10.1017/S1743923X18000661.

Baker, Lynda M., Rochelle L. Dalla, and Celia Williamson. "Exiting Prostitution: An Integrated Model." *Violence Against Women* 16, no. 5 (2010): 579–600. https://doi.org/10.1177/1077801210367643.

Banks, Duren and Tracey Kyckelhahn. *Characteristics of Suspected Human Trafficking Incidents, 2008–2010* Washington, D.C.: Bureau of Justice Statistics, 2011.

Barry, Kathleen. *Female Sexual Slavery.* Englewood Cliffs: Prentice-Hall, 1979.

———. *The Prostitution of Sexuality: The Global Exploitation of Women.* New York: New York University Press, 1995.

Berman, Jacqueline. "The Left, the Right, and the Prostitute: The Making of U.S. Antitrafficking in Persons Policy." *Tulane Journal of International and Comparative Law* 14, (2006): 269–293.

Bernstein, Elizabeth. *Brokered Subjects: Sex, Trafficking, and the Politics of Freedom.* Chicago: University of Chicago Press, 2019.

———. "Carceral Politics as Gender Justice? The 'Traffic in Women' and Neoliberal Circuits of Crime, Sex, and Rights." *Theory and Society* 41, no. 3 (2012): 233–259.

———. "Militarized Humanitarianism Meets Carceral Feminism: The Politics of Sex, Rights, and Freedom in Contemporary Anti-Trafficking Campaigns." *Signs* 35, no. 1 (2010): 45–71.

———. "The Sexual Politics of the 'New Abolitionism.'" *Differences* 18, no. 3 (2007): 128–151.

Biehl, João. *Vita: Life in a Zone of Abandonment.* Berkeley: University of California Press, 2005.

Bose, Diya. "'There are no Victims here': Ethnography of a Reintegration Shelter for Survivors of Trafficking in Bangladesh." *Anti-Trafficking Review* 10 (2018): 139–154. doi:10.14197/atr.201218109. http://www.antitraffickingreview.org/index.php/atrjournal/article/view/326.

Bourgois, Philippe. "Homelessness, Addiction, and Politically Structured Violence." In *The Insecure American: How We Got Here and What We Should Do about It*, ed. Hugh Gusterson and Catherine Besteman. Berkeley: University of California Press, 2010.

———. *In Search of Respect: Selling Crack in El Barrio.* Cambridge: Cambridge University Press, 1995.

Bourgois, Philippe and Jeff Schonberg. *Righteous Dopefiend.* Berkeley: University of California Press, 2009.

Brennan, Denise. "Fighting Human Trafficking Today: Moral Panics, Zombie Data, and the Seduction of Rescue." *Wake Forest Law Review* 52, (2017): 477–496. http://heinonline.org/HOL/Page?handle=hein.journals/wflr52&id=493&div=&collection=.

———. *Life Interrupted: Trafficking into Forced Labor in the United States.* Durham: Duke University Press, 2014.

———. "Methodological Challenges in Research with Trafficked Persons: Tales from the Field." *International Migration* 43, no. 1 (2005): 35–54.

———. *What's Love Got to do with it? Transnational Desires and Sex Tourism in the Dominican Republic.* Durham: Duke University Press, 2004.

Briand, Paul. "NH among Highest in Country for Housing Need." *NH Business Review.* October 18, 2023. https://www.nhbr.com/nh-among-highest-in-country-for-housing-need/.

Bronfenbrenner, Urie. *The Ecology of Human Development: Experiments by Nature and Design.* Cambridge: Harvard University Press, 1979.

Bronfman, Mario N. et al. "Mobile Populations and HIV/AIDS in Central America and Mexico: Research for Action." *AIDS* 16 Suppl. 3 (December 16, 2002): 42–49. doi:10.1097/00002030-200212003-00007.

Brooks-Gordon, Belinda, Max Morris, and Teela Sanders. "Harm Reduction and Decriminalization of Sex Work: Introduction to the Special Section." *Sexuality Research and Social Policy* 18, no. 4 (2021): 809–818. https://doi.org/10.1007/s13178-021-00636-0.

Brown, Elizabeth Nolan. *Science-Based Policy Means Decriminalizing Sex Work, Say Hundreds of Researchers.* Reason.Com. 2021. https://reason.com/2021/03/03/science-based-policy-means-decriminalizing-sex-work-say-hundreds-of-researchers/.

Brunovskis, Anette and Rebecca Surtees. "Untold Stories: Biases and Selection Effects in Research with Victims of Trafficking for Sexual Exploitation." *International Migration* 48, no. 4 (2010): 1–37.

Bryant, Erica. "Why We Say 'Criminal Legal System,' Not 'Criminal Justice System.'" Vera. December 1, 2021. Accessed May 29, 2024. https://www.vera.org/news/why-we-say-criminal-legal-system-not-criminal-justice-system.

Budman, Scott. "Hayward Woman Suspected of Human Trafficking Accuses American Airlines of Racial Profiling." *NBC Bay Area.* March 28, 2019. https://www.nbcbayarea.com/news/local/hayward-woman-accuses-american-airlines-of-racial-profiling/159441/.

Bustillo, Ximena. "A Human-Trafficking Case Exposed Farmworker Abuses. The Government is Promising Change." *NPR*, May 27, 2022. https://www.npr.org/2022/05/27/1101741366/human-trafficking-farmworker-abuse-georgia.

Butler, Cheryl Nelson. "The Racial Roots of Human Trafficking." *UCLA Law Review* 62 (September 1, 2015): 1464–1514. https://www.uclalawreview.org/racial-roots-human-trafficking/.

Chapkis, Wendy. "Soft Glove, Punishing Fist: The Trafficking Victims Protection Act of 2000." In *Regulating Sex: The Politics of Intimacy and Identity*, ed. Elizabeth Bernstein and L. Schaffner. New York: Routledge, 2005.

———. "Trafficking, Migration, and the Law: Protecting Innocents, Punishing Immigrants." *Gender & Society* 17, no. 6 (December 2003): 923–937.

Chen, Victoria H., et al. "Sex Trafficking in New York City and Vulnerabilities to Re-Trafficking." *Journal of Interpersonal Violence* 38, no. 21–22 (July 8, 2023): 11501–11519. https://doi.org/10.1177/08862605231183452.

Cheng, Sealing. *On the Move for Love: Migrant Entertainers and the U.S. Military in South Korea.* Philadelphia: University of Pennsylvania Press, 2010.

Chisolm-Straker, Makini and Hanni Stoklosa, eds. *Human Trafficking is a Public Health Issue: A Paradigm Expansion in the United States.* Cham, Switzerland: Springer International, 2017.

Christie, Nils. "The Ideal Victim." In *From Crime Policy to Victim Policy: Reorienting the Justice System*, ed. Ezzat A. Fattah. London: Macmillan, 1986.

Chuang, Janie A. "Exploitation Creep and the Unmaking of Human Trafficking Law." *American Journal of International Law* 108, no. 4 (2014): 609–649.

———. "Rescuing Trafficking from Ideological Capture: Prostitution Reform and Anti-Trafficking Law and Policy." *University of Pennsylvania Law Review* 158, (2010): 1655–1728.

Combatting Human Trafficking: A Budget for America's Future. Office of Management and Budget, 2020. https://www.novoco.com/sites/default/files/atoms/files/fy21_fact_sheet_human_trafficking_021020.pdf;

https://trumpwhitehouse.archives.gov/wp-content/uploads/2020/02/budget_fy21.pdf

Coombs, Nicholas C., et al. "Barriers to Healthcare Access among U.S. Adults with Mental Health Challenges: A Population-Based Study." *SSM—Population Health* 15, (2021): 100847. doi:10.1016/j.ssmph.2021.100847.

Costa, Chris. "Experts Say the Lack of Detox and Treatment Beds is Exacerbating Maine's Homelessness Crisis." *News Center Maine*, October 19, 2023. https://www.newscentermaine.com/article/news/local/housing/lack-of-detox-and-treatment-beds-exacerbating-maine-homelessness-crisis-experts-say-housing-portland-health-care/97-1806cb15-2642-4855-bb9e-2ea03e2e8d95.

Crenshaw, Kimberle. "Mapping the Margins: Intersectionality, Identity Politics, and Violence Against Women of Color." *Stanford Law Review* 43, no. 6 (1991): 1241–1299. doi:10.2307/1229039.

Criminal Record Relief for Trafficking Survivors Updating Grades and Rubric to Reflect Current Improvements and Changes. Polaris, 2019.

Criminalization of Trafficking Victims: Submission to the United Nations Universal Periodic Review of United States of America. International Women's Human Rights Clinic, City University of New York Law School Trafficking Victims Advocacy Project and Legal Aid Society of New York, 2015.

Croft, C. *Human Trafficking Prevention: A Brief Overview of our Primary Prevention Approach*. Raleigh: North Carolina Coalition Against Sexual Assault, 2020.

Cuno-Booth, Paul. "How NH is using its Opioid Lawsuit Payouts: 'That Money has to Go Back to Helping those People Hit the Hardest'." *nhpr*, April 19, 2023. https://www.nhpr.org/nh-news/2023-04-19/new-hampshire-opioid-lawsuits-money-settlements-treatment-recovery-enforcement.

Davis, Angela Y. *Are Prisons Obsolete?* New York: Seven Stories Press, 2003.

Decker, Michele R., et al. "Human Rights Violations Against Sex Workers: Burden and Effect on HIV." *Lancet* 385, no. 9963 (January 10, 2015): 186–199. doi:10.1016/S0140-6736(14)60800-X.

Dennis, Jeffery P. "Women are Victims, Men make Choices: The Invisibility of Men and Boys in the Global Sex Trade." *Gender Issues* 25, (2008): 11–25.

Denton, Erin. "Anatomy of Offending: Human Trafficking in the United States, 2006–2011." *Journal of Human Trafficking* 2, no. 1 (2016): 32. doi:10.1080/23322705.2016.1136540.

Dewey, Susan. *Hollow Bodies: Institutional Responses to Sex Trafficking in Armenia, Bosnia, and India*. Sterling: Kumarian Press, 2008.

Dewey, Susan, and Tonia St. Germain. *Women of the Street: How the Criminal Justice-Social Services Alliance Fails Women*. New York: New York University Press, 2017.

Diagnostic and Statistical Manual of Mental Disorders. 5th ed. Text Revision. American Psychiatric Association, 2022.

Ditmore, Melissa Hope. *Unbroken Chains*. Boston: Beacon Press, 2023.

Doezema, Jo. "Loose Women or Lost Women? The Re-Emergence of the Myth of 'White Slavery' in Contemporary Discourses on 'Trafficking in Women'." *Gender Issues* 18, no. 1 (1999): 23–50.

Erin O'Brien. *Challenging the Human Trafficking Narrative: Victims, Villains, and Heroes*. London: Routledge, 2019.

Ewart-James, Joanna. *Why Freedom United Supports the Decriminalisation of Sex Work*. openDemocracy. 2021. https://www.opendemocracy.net/en/beyond-trafficking-and-slavery/why-freedom-united-supports-decriminalisation-sex-work/.

Ezeilo, Joy Ngozi. *Report of the Special Rapporteur on Trafficking in Persons, especially Women and Children*. Geneva: United Nations, 2014.

Fair Girls. *Amplified Risk Factors to Human Trafficking Experienced by the LGBTQIA+ Community*. Washington, D.C.: Fair Girls, 2020.

Families Against Mandatory Minimums. *Alternatives to Incarceration in a Nutshell*. Washington, D.C.: FAMM, n.d.

Family & Youth Service Bureau. *Issue Brief: Human Trafficking Prevention—Strategies for Runaway and Homeless Youth Settings*. Washington, D.C.: Administration for Children and Families, 2020.

Farmer, Paul. *Infections and Inequalities*. Berkeley: University of California Press, 2001.

———. "On Suffering and Structural Violence: A View from Below." *Daedalus* 125, no. 1 (1996): 261–283.

Farmer, Paul E., et al. "Structural Violence and Clinical Medicine." *PLOS Medicine* 3, no. 10 (October 24, 2006): e449. doi:10.1371/journal.pmed.0030449. https://journals.plos.org/plosmedicine/article?id=10.1371/journal.pmed.0030449.

Farrell, Amy, Vanessa Bouché, and Dana Wolfe. "Assessing the Impact of State Human Trafficking Legislation on Criminal Justice System Outcomes." *Law & Policy* 41, no. 2 (2019): 174–197. doi:10.1111/lapo.12124.

Farrell, Amy, et al. "Failing Victims? Challenges of the Police Response to Human Trafficking." *Criminology & Public Policy* 18, no. 3 (2019): 649–673. https://doi-org.une.idm.oclc.org/10.1111/1745-9133.12456.

Farrell, Amy and Stephanie Fahy. "The Problem of Human Trafficking in the U.S.: Public Frames and Policy Responses." *Journal of Criminal Justice* 37, no. 6 (2009): 617–626. https://www.sciencedirect.com/science/article/abs/pii/S0047235209001159.

Farrell, Amy and Rebecca Pfeffer. "Policing Human Trafficking: Cultural Blinders and Organizational Barriers." *Annals of the American Academy of Political and Social Sciences* 653, (2014): 46–64.

Farrell, Amy, Rebecca Pfeffer, and Katherine Bright. "Police Perceptions of Human Trafficking." *Journal of Crime & Justice* 38, no. 3 (2015): 1–19. doi:10.1080/0735648X.2014.995412. http://www.tandfonline.com/doi/abs/10.1080/0735648X.2014.995412?journalCode=rjcj20.

Federal Housing and Homelessness Programs for Survivors of Human Trafficking. U.S. Administration for Children and Families Office for Trafficking in Persons, 2020.

Federal Prosecution of Human Trafficking Cases, 2015. U.S. Department of Justice, 2018.

Feingold, David A. "Trafficking in Numbers: The Social Construction of Human Trafficking Data." In *Sex, Drugs, and Body Counts*, ed. Peter Andreas and Kelly M. Greenhill. Ithaca: Cornell University Press, 2010.

Flaherty, Nora. "Why is Maine so Politically Independent?" *Maine Public*, February 2, 2015. https://www.mainepublic.org/maine/2015-02-02/why-is-maine-so-politically-independent.

Forum on Crime and Society: Special Issue—Researching Hidden Populations: Approaches to and Methodologies for Generating Data on Trafficking in Persons Volume 8. United Nations Office on Drugs, and Crime, 2015.

Freedom Network Training Institute. *Housing First: Improving Access to Housing for Youth Survivors*. Washington, D.C.: Freedom Network USA, 2021.

Galtung, Johan. "Violence, Peace, and Peace Research." *Journal of Peace Research* 6, no. 3 (1969): 167–191.

Garry, Hannah and Maura Reinbrecht. *Over-Policing Sex Trafficking: How U.S. Law Enforcement should Reform Operations*. Los Angeles: USC Gould School of Law International Human Rights Clinic, 2021.

Gerassi, Lara and Andrea Nichols. "Social Work Education that Addresses Trafficking for Sexual Exploitation: An Intersectional, Anti-Oppressive Practice Framework." *Anti-Trafficking Review* no. 17 (2021): 20–37. doi:10.14197/atr.201221172. https://antitraffickingreview.org/index.php/atrjournal/article/view/574.

Gilbertson, Annie, Aaron Mendelson, and Angela Caputo. "LA's Fight Against Sex Trafficking is Actually Hurting the Women It's Supposed to Help." *Collateral Damage* (blog). LAist.Com, August 7, 2019.

Global Alliance Against Traffic in Women. *GAATW-IS Statement on Attack on UN Research Calling for the Decriminalisation of Sex Work*. Global Alliance Against Traffic in Women (GAATW). 2013.

Global Network of Sex Work Projects. *The Impact of Criminalization on Sex Workers' Vulnerability to HIV and Violence*. Edinburgh: Global Network of Sex Work Projects, 2017.

Gonzalez, Cassandra Mary Frances. "'I Went from being Held Captive to Captivity again': How the Criminal Legal System Fails Black Women and Girl Survivors of Sex Trafficking." *Qualitative Criminology* 11, no. 3 (2022): 293–327.

Goodmark, Leigh. *Imperfect Victims: Criminalized Survivors and the Promise of Abolition Feminism*. Oakland: University of California Press, 2023.

Goździak, Elżbieta M. *Trafficked Children and Youth in the United States: Reimagining Survivors*. New Brunswick: Rutgers University Press, 2016.

Goździak, Elżbieta M. and Micah N. Bump. *Data and Research on Human Trafficking: Bibliography of Research-Based Literature*. Washington, D.C.: Institute for the Study of International Migration, 2008.

Goździak, Elżbieta, M. and Elizabeth A. Collet. "Research on Human Trafficking in North America: A Review of Literature." *International Migration* 43, no. 1–2 (2005): 99–127.

Greenbaum, Jordan. "A Public Health Approach to Global Child Sex Trafficking." *Annual Review of Public Health* 41, (2020): 481. doi:10.1146/annurev-publhealth-040119-094335.

Griffen, Sarah. *The Two-Generation Approach: Recommendations for Bridging Practice and Policy in Maine*. Portland: John T. Gorman Foundation, 2020.

Gulati, J. "News Frames and Story Triggers in the Media's Coverage of Human Trafficking." *Human Rights Review* 12 (2011): 363–379.

Gupta, Geeta Rao, et al. "Structural Approaches to HIV Prevention." *The Lancet* 372, no. 9640 (2008): 764–775. doi:10.1016/S0140-6736(08)60887-9.

Halter, Stephanie. *New Hampshire Human Trafficking Collaborative Task Force End of the Year Report, 2017.* New Hampshire Human Trafficking Collaborative Task Force, 2018.

Halter, Stephanie and Scott Meyer. *New Hampshire Human Trafficking Collaborative Task Force 2018 Annual Report*. New Hampshire Human Trafficking Collaborative Task Force, 2019.

Hamilton, D., K. Hodgson, and J. Quirk. *Slavery, Memory and Identity: National Representations and Global Legacies*. New York: Routledge, 2015.

Hamilton-Jiang, Sarah. *Racially Marginalized Migrant Women: Human Rights Abuses at the Intersection of Race, Gender, and Migration*. New York: UN Women, n.d.

Hannan, Madeline, et al. "Children at Risk: Foster Care and Human Trafficking." In *Human Trafficking is a Public Health Issue: A Paradigm Expansion in the United States*, ed. Chisolm-Straker, Makini and Hanni Stoklosa, 105–121. Cham: Springer International, 2017.

"Harm Reduction." National Institutes of Health National Institute on Drug Abuse. Accessed September 28, 2023. https://nida.nih.gov/research-topics/harm-reduction.

Harm Reduction. Substance Abuse and Mental Health Services Administration, Last modified October 29, 2024. https://www.samhsa.gov/find-help/harm-reduction.

Hatzenbuehler, Mark L., Jo C. Phelan, and Bruce G. Link. "Stigma as a Fundamental Cause of Population Health Inequalities." *American Journal of Public Health* 103, no. 5 (May, 2013): 813–821. Doi:10.2105/AJPH.2012.301069.

Haynes, Dina Francesca. "Good Intentions are Not enough: Four Recommendations for Implementing the Trafficking Victims Protection Act." *University of St. Thomas Law Journal* 6, no. 1 (2009): 77–95.

Heal, Alexandra. "Maine Becomes First State to Decriminalize Selling Sex." *The Washington Post*, June 30, 2023. https://www.washingtonpost.com/politics/2023/06/30/maine-sex-work-decrimilization/.

Healthy People 2030. "Health Care Access and Quality." Accessed September 21, 2023. https://health.gov/healthypeople/objectives-and-data/browse-objectives/health-care-access-and-quality.

Herrick, Clare and Kirsten Bell. "Concepts, Disciplines, and Politics: On 'Structural Violence' and the 'Social Determinants of Health'." *Critical Public Health* 32, no. 3 (August 25, 2020): 295–308. https://doi.org/10.1080/09581596.2020.1810637.

Hill, Justine A. and Kelsey J. Mullins. "A Threat to Healing and a Barrier to Recovery: An Assessment of Health Impacts of Criminalization through the Stages of Domestic Sex Trafficking." UNESCO Working Paper Series. University of Wisconsin, Madison. May 6, 2022. https://minds.wisconsin.edu/handle/1793/83657.

Hoang, Kimberly Kay. *Dealing in Desire: Asian Ascendancy, Western Decline, and the Hidden Currencies of Global Sex Work*. Oakland: University of California Press, 2015.

Holmes, Seth M. *Fresh Fruit, Broken Bodies: Migrant Farmworkers in the United States*. Berkeley: University of California Press, 2013.

Homelessness among the LGBTQ Community. National Coalition for the Homeless, 2022.

Hornby Zeller Associates, Inc. *Maine Human Trafficking Needs Assessment*. South Portland: Maine Coalition Against Sexual Assault (MECASA), 2015.

Horning, Amber and Anthony Marcus. "Introduction: In Search of Pimps and Other Varieties." In *Third Party Sex Work and Pimps in the Age of Anti-Trafficking*, ed. Amber Horning and Anthony Marcus. Cham, Switzerland: Springer International, 2017.

Huckerby, Jane. "United States of America (USA)." In *Collateral Damage: The Impact of Anti-Trafficking Measures on Human Rights Around the World*, ed. Bandana Pattanaik. Bangkok: Global Alliance Against Traffic in Women, 2007.

Human Trafficking and Sex Workers' Rights. Washington, D.C.: or USA, 2015.

Human Trafficking Data Collection Activities, 2021. Bureau of Justice Statistics, October 2021. Accessed August 9, 2023. https://bjs.ojp.gov/library/publications/human-trafficking-data-collection-activities-2021.

Human Trafficking Data Collection Activities, 2023. Bureau of Justice Statistics, 2023. Accessed December 15, 2023. https://bjs.ojp.gov/document/htdca23.pdf.

Human Trafficking Data Collection Project. U.S. Department of Health and Human Services, 2019. Accessed September 20, 2023. https://www.acf.hhs.gov/otip/research-policy/data-collection.

Jacobs, Ben. "The Politics of New Hampshire, America's Quirkiest State, Explained." *Vox*, October 13, 2022, https://www.vox.com/policy-and-politics/2022/10/13/23400859/politics-new-hampshire-america-quirkiest-state-explained.

Jacobs, Beth and Stephanie Richard. *National Survivor Network Members Survey: Impact of Criminal Arrest and Detention on Survivors of Human Trafficking*. Washington, D.C.: National Survivor Network, 2016.

Jeanette Hussemann, et al. *Bending Towards Justice: Perceptions of Justice among Human Trafficking Survivors*. Washington D.C.: Urban Institute, 2018.

Johnston, A., B. Friedman, and M. Sobel. "Framing an Emerging Issue: How U.S. Print and Broadcast News Media Covered Sex Trafficking, 2008–2012." *Journal of Human Trafficking* 1, no. 3 (2015): 235–254.

Jones, Christopher M., et al. "National and State Treatment Need and Capacity for Opioid Agonist Medication-Assisted Treatment." *American Journal of Public Health* 105, no. 8 (August 2015): 55. Doi:10.2105/AJPH.2015.302664.

Jordan, Ann D. "Human Rights or Wrongs? The Struggle for a Rights-Based Approach to Trafficking in Human Beings." *Gender and Development* 10, no. 1 (2002): 28–37.

———. *When Will Governments Get Serious about Addressing the Root Causes of Human Trafficking and Forced Labor?* Washington D.C.: Rightswork, 2011.

Karim, Q. A., et al. "Reducing the Risk of HIV Infection among South African Sex Workers: Socioeconomic and Gender Barriers." *American Journal of Public Health* 85, no. 11 (1995): 1521–1525. https://doi.org/10.2105/AJPH.85.11.1521.

Kaya, Yaren Bilge, et al. "Improving Access to Housing and Supportive Services for Runaway and Homeless Youth: Reducing Vulnerability to Human Trafficking in New York City." *IISE Transactions* 56, no. 3 (October 12, 2022): 296–310. https://doi.org/10.1080/24725854.2022.2120223.

Kaye, Julie, et al. "Beyond Criminal Justice: A Case Study of Responding to Human Trafficking in Canada." *Canadian Journal of Criminology and Criminal Justice* 56, no. 1 (2014): 23–48.

Kaye, Kerwin. "The Gender of Trafficking, Or Why Can't Men be Sex Slaves?" In *Understanding Sex for Sale: Meanings and Moralities of Sexual Commerce*, ed. May-Len Skilbrei and Marlene Spanger. New York: Routledge, 2018.

Kellett, Nicole Coffey and Cathleen Elizabeth Willging. "Pedagogy of Individual Choice and Female Inmate Reentry in the U.S. Southwest." *International Journal of Law and Psychiatry* 34, no. 4 (July–August 2011): 256–263. https://doi.org/10.1016/j.ijlp.2011.07.003.

Kempadoo, Kamala. "The Modern-Day White (Wo)Man's Burden: Trends in Anti-Trafficking and Anti-Slavery Campaigns." *Journal of Human Trafficking* 1, no. 1 (2015): 8–20. https://doi.org/10.1080/23322705.2015.1006120.

Kempadoo, Kamala and Elena Shih. *White Supremacy, Racism and the Coloniality of Anti-Trafficking*. New York: Routledge, 2022.

KFF. *Status of State Medicaid Expansion Decisions: Interactive Map*. KFF. May 8, 2024. https://www.kff.org/affordable-care-act/issue-brief/status-of-state-medicaid-expansion-decisions-interactive-map/.

Kidder, Tracy. *Mountains Beyond Mountains: The Quest of Dr. Paul Farmer, a Man Who Would Cure the World*. New York: Random House, 2003.

Kitson, Jessica and Kate Mogulescu. *Workable Solutions for Criminal Record Relief: Recommendations for Prosecutors Serving Victims of Human Trafficking*. The Survivor Reentry Project, American Bar Association Commission on Domestic & Sexual Violence, n.d.

Kleinman, Arthur and Joan Kleinman. "The Appeal of Experience; the Dismay of Images: Cultural Appropriations of Suffering in our Times." In *Social Suffering*, ed. Arthur Kleinman, Veena Das, and Margaret Lock. Berkeley: University of California Press, 1997.

Knight, Kelly Ray. *Addicted. Pregnant. Poor.* Durham: Duke University Press, 2015.

Koegler, Erica, et al. "Traffickers' Use of Substances to Recruit and Control Victims of Domestic Trafficking for Sexual Exploitation in the American Midwest." *Anti-Trafficking Review* 18 (April 2022): 103–20. https://doi.org/10.14197/atr.201222187.

Kohn, Sebastian. "The False Promise of 'End Demand' Laws." Open Society Foundations, Accessed January 5, 2018. https://www.opensocietyfoundations.org/voices/false-promise-end-demand-laws.

Krüsi, Andrea, Kate D'Adamo, and Ariel Sernick. "Criminalised Interactions with Law Enforcement and Impacts on Health and Safety in the Context of Different Legislative Frameworks Governing Sex Work Globally." In *Sex Work, Health, and Human Rights: Global Inequities, Challenges, and Opportunities for Action*, ed. Shira Goldenberg, et al. Cham, Switzerland: Springer International, 2021. https://doi.org/10.1007/978-3-030-64171-9_7.

Lange, Klaus W. "Rudolf Virchow as a Pioneer of both Biomedicine and Social Medicine." *Scandinavian Journal of Public Health* 50, no. 7 (2022): 873–874. https://doi.org/10.1177/14034948211048289.

Larsen, Peter Billie, et al. "Repositioning Engaged Anthropology: Critical Reflexivity and Overcoming Dichotomies." *Tsantsa* 27 (2022): 4–15. https://www.redalyc.org/journal/6647/664772596002/html/.

Lauger, Amy D. and Matthew R. Durose, *Human Trafficking Data Collection Activities, 2021*. Bureau of Justice Statistics, Department of Justice, October 2021. https://bjs.ojp.gov/library/publications/human-trafficking-data-collection-activities-2021.

Lawlor, Joe. "Drug Overdose Deaths in Maine Continue to Decline After Plummeting in 2023." *Portland Press Herald*, July 22, 2024. https://www.pressherald.com/2024/07/22/drug-overdose-deaths-continue-to-decline-in-maine/

Leff, Gary. "American Airlines Flight Attendants Calls Cops on Dad, Falsely Report Him as a Sex Trafficker." *View from the Wing*, May 13, 2023.

Leibert, Emily. "Florida's Child Welfare System is found to be Complicit in Sex Trafficking." *Jezebel*, November 28, 2022.

LGBTQIA+ Youth and Experiences of Human Trafficking: A Healing Centered Approach. National LGBTQIA+ Health Education Center, Futures Without Violence, and Health Partners on IPV + Exploration, 2021.

Link, Bruce and Jo Phelan. "Social Conditions as Fundamental Causes of Disease." *Journal of Health and Social Behavior* (1995): 80–94.

Lloyd, Aubrey. "What Does Real Healing Look Like for Trafficking Survivors?," *openDemocracy* June 5, 2025. https://www.opendemocracy.net/en/beyond-trafficking-and-slavery/real-healing-survivors-of-trafficking-engagement/.

Logan, T. K. *Human Trafficking in Kentucky*. Lexington: University of Kentucky, 2007. http://cdar.uky.edu/VAW/docs/Human%20Trafficking%20in%20Kentucky.pdf.

Look Beneath the Surface Public Awareness Materials. U.S. Department of Health and Human Services, 2019. Accessed September 20, 2023. https://www.acf.hhs.gov/otip/outreach-material/lbs-public-awareness-materials.

Lopez, Marlihan. "Opinion: Prison Abolition Is a Feminist Struggle." Opinion. *CBC*. November 23, 2020. https://www.cbc.ca/news/canada/montreal/prison-abolition-defund-the-police-violence-against-women-feminism-1.5809912.

Love, Hanna, et al. *Justice in their Own Words Perceptions and Experiences of (in)Justice among Human Trafficking Survivors*. Washington, D.C.: Urban Institute, 2018.

Lovejoy, Michaela and Ashleigh Pelto. *Preventing Human Trafficking through Systems Reformation*. Equal Justice Works, January 11, 2022. https://www.equaljusticeworks.org/news/preventing-human-trafficking-through-systems-reformation/.

Lundy, Rose. "Amid Surge in Substance use, 20 Beds are Available for Uninsured Mainers to Go through Monitored Withdrawal." *The Maine Monitor*, May 22, 2022. https://themainemonitor.org/amid-surge-in-substance-use-20-beds-are-available-for-uninsured-mainers-to-go-through-monitored-withdrawal/.

Lutnick, Alexandra. *Domestic Minor Sex Trafficking: Beyond Victims and Villains*. New York: Columbia University Press, 2016.

Maccio, Elaine M. and Kristin M. Ferguson. "Services to LGBTQ Runaway and Homeless Youth: Gaps and Recommendations." *Children and Youth Services Review* 63, (2016): 47–57. Doi:10.1016/j.childyouth.2016.02.008. https://www.sciencedirect.com/science/article/pii/S0190740916300317.

Mahdavi, Pardis. *Gridlock: Labor, Migration, and Human Trafficking in Dubai*. Palo Alto: Stanford University Press, 2011.

Maine Department of Labor. *Maine Workforce Outlook 2012 to 2022*. Augusta: Center for Workforce Research and Information, 2014.

Mann, Brian. "U.S. Overdose Deaths Plummet, Saving Thousands of Lives." *NPR*, September 18, 2024. https://www.npr.org/2024/09/18/nx-s1-5107417/overdose-fatal-fentanyl-death-opioid.

Mapp, Susan, et al. "Local Law Enforcement Officers' Knowledge of Human Trafficking: Ability to Define, Identify, and Assist." *Journal of Human Trafficking* 2, no. 4 (2016): 392–342.

Marmo, Marinella and Nerida Chazal. "The Trafficked Woman: Ideal or Blameworthy Victim?" *Advances in Sociology Research* 7, Nova Publication, Chapter 7 (2010): 125–140.

Marmot, Michael, et al. "Health Inequalities among British Civil Servants: The Whitehall II Study." *Lancet* 337, no. 8754 (June 8, 1991): 1387–1393. Doi:10.1016/0140-6736(91)93068-k.

Marmot, Michael. "Social Determinants of Health Inequalities." *Lancet* 365, no. 9464 (March 19, 2005): 1099–1104. Doi:10.1016/s0140-6736(05)74234-3.

Martinez, Omar and Guadalupe Kelle. "Sex Trafficking of LGBT Individuals." *The International Law News* 42, no. 4 (2013): 1–6. https://www.ncbi.nlm.nih.gov/pmc/articles/PMC4204396/.

Mattick, Richard P., et al. "Methadone Maintenance Therapy Versus no Opioid Replacement Therapy for Opioid Dependence." *The Cochrane Database of Systematic Reviews* 2009, no. 3 (July, 2009): CD002209. Doi:10.1002/14651858.CD002209.pub2. https://www.ncbi.nlm.nih.gov/pmc/articles/PMC7097731/.

McBride, Bronwyn, et al. "Harms of Third Party Criminalisation Under End-Demand Legislation: Undermining Sex Workers' Safety and Rights." *Culture, Health & Sexuality* 23, no. 9 (September 1, 2021): 1165–1181. Doi:10.1080/13691058.2020.1767305. https://www.ncbi.nlm.nih.gov/pmc/articles/PMC7855821/.

McDermid, Jennifer, et al. "How Client Criminalisation Under End-Demand Sex Work Laws Shapes the Occupational Health and Safety of Sex Workers in Metro Vancouver, Canada: A Qualitative Study." *BMJ Open* 12, no. 11 (November 22, 2022): e061729. Doi:10.1136/bmjopen-2022-061729. https://www.ncbi.nlm.nih.gov/pmc/articles/PMC9685237/.

McKenzie, Shamere. "Listen to Black Survivors." *Polaris* (blog). Accessed May 20, 2023. https://polarisproject.org/blog/2023/02/listen-to-black-survivors/#:~:text=Victims%3A%20The%20fact%20is%2C%20Black,most%20vulnerable%20in%20our%20communities.

McLaughlin, Michael, et al. *The Economic Burden of Incarceration in the United States*. Tallahassee: Institute for Justice Research and Development at Florida State University, 2016. https://ijrd.csw.fsu.edu/sites/g/files/upcbnu1766/files/media/images/publication_pdfs/Economic_Burden_of_Incarceration_IJRD072016_0_0.pdf

Middleton, Jennifer, et al. "Adverse Childhood Experiences (ACEs) and Homelessness: A Critical Examination of the Association between Specific ACEs and Sex Trafficking among Homeless Youth in Kentuckiana." *Journal of Human Trafficking* 10, no. 1 (2022): 121–134. Doi:10.1080/23322705.2021.2020061.

Miller, Alice M. "Sexuality, Violence Against Women, and Human Rights: Women Make Demands and Ladies Get Protection." *Health and Human Rights* 7, no. 2 (2004): 16–47.

Miller, Kevin. "LePage Says He'll Go to Jail before He Lets Maine Expand Medicaid without Funding." *Press Herald*. July 12, 2018. https://www.pressherald.com/2018/07/12/paul-lepage-says-hed-go-to-jail-before-he-expands-medicaid/.

Mitchell, Gregory. *Panics Without Borders: How Global Sporting Events Drive Myths About Sex Trafficking*. Oakland: University of California Press, 2022.

Modi, Hermangi et al., "Exploring Barriers to Mental Health Care in the U.S." AAMC Research and Action Institute, October 10, 2022. https://www.aamcresearchinstitute.org/our-work/issue-brief/exploring-barriers-mental-health-care-us.

Monazzam, Niki and Kristen M. Budd. *Incarcerated Women and Girls*. Washington, D.C.: The Sentencing Project, 2023.

Morgan, Sandie. *Human Trafficking and Public Health*. Baldwin, Susie. 2020. (podcast).

Murphy, Laura T. *Labor and Sex Trafficking among Homeless Youth: A Ten-City Study*. New Orleans: Modern Slavery Research Project, 2016.

Musto, Jennifer. *Control and Protect: Collaboration, Carceral Protection, and Domestic Sex Trafficking in the United States*. Berkeley: University of California Press, 2016.

———. "Domestic Minor Sex Trafficking and the Detention-to-Protection Pipeline." *Dialectical Anthropology* 37, no. 2 (2013): 257–276. https://doi.org/10.1007/s10624-013-9295-0.

National Center for Education Evaluation and Regional Assistance. *Do Disadvantaged Students Get Less Effective Teaching? Key Findings from Recent Institute of Education Sciences Studies.* Washington, D.C.: Institute of Education Sciences, 2014.

National Conference of State Legislatures. *Disproportionality and Race Equity in Child Welfare.* Washington, D.C. NCSL, 2021.

National Harm Reduction Coalition "Sex Work & Harm Reduction." Accessed September 28, 2023. https://harmreduction.org/issues/sex-work/harm-reduction-facts/.

National Low Income Housing Coalition. "Housing Needs by State." Accessed May 22, 2024. https://nlihc.org/housing-needs-by-state.

National Survivor Network. "End Demand Tactics Harm all People in the Sex Trades, Including Survivors of Trafficking." Press Release. Accessed September 21, 2023. https://nationalsurvivornetwork.org/enddemandstatement/.

Nembhard, Susan, Kierra B. Jones, and Jahnavi Jagannath. "Partial Decriminalization of Sex Work could Cause More Harm than Good." Urban Institute, April 15, 2021. https://www.urban.org/urban-wire/partial-decriminalization-sex-work-could-cause-more-harm-good.

Newman, Etan. *No Way to Treat a Guest: Why the H2-A Agricultural Visa Program Fails U.S. and Foreign Workers.* Washington, D.C.: Farmworker Justice, n.d.

Norman, Zara. "Maine is Leading New England in Housing Production, but It Isn't Enough." *Bangor Daily News*, February 26, 2024. http://www.bangordailynews.com/2024/02/26/state/state-housing/maine-leading-new-england-in-housing-production-joam40zk0w/.

Northridge, Mary E., Anjali Kumar, and Raghbir Kaur. "Disparities in Access to Oral Health Care." *Annual Review of Public Health* 41, no. 1 (2020): 513–535. https://doi.org/10.1146/annurev-publhealth-040119-094318.

Novak, Emily H. "Vagrants, Vixens, and Victims: Exploring the Limitations of Human Trafficking Victim Recognition Criteria in Texas." Master of Arts Thesis, Texas Woman's University, 2016.

O'Brien, Erin. *Challenging the Human Trafficking Narrative: Victims, Villains, and Heroes.* London: Routledge, 2019.

O'Connell Davidson, Julia. *Modern Slavery: The Margins of Freedom.* New York: Palgrave Macmillan, 2015.

———. *Prostitution, Power and Freedom.* Ann Arbor: University of Michigan Press, 1998.

———. "Will the Real Sex Slave Please Stand Up?" *Feminist Review* 83, no. 1 (2006): 4–22. https://doi.org/10.1057/palgrave.fr.9400278.

Office for Victims of Crime. "OVC FY 2022 Enhanced Collaborative Model Task Force to Combat Human Trafficking." Press Release. Accessed September 20, 2023. https://ovc.ojp.gov/funding/opportunities/o-ovc-2022-171264.

———. "OVC FY 2023 Enhanced Collaborative Model (ECM) Task Force to Combat Human Trafficking OVC." Accessed August 14, 2023. https://ovc.ojp.gov/funding/opportunities/o-ovc-2023-171656.

———. "The Vital Role of Case Management & Service Planning." Accessed September 14, 2023. https://www.ovcttac.gov/taskforceguide/eguide/4-supporting-victims/43-the-vital-role-of-case-management-service-planning/.

On-Ramps, Intersections, and Exit Routes: A Roadmap for Systems and Industries to Prevent and Disrupt Human Trafficking. Polaris, 2018.

"Organizations that Support the Decriminalization of Prostitution." Decriminalize Sex Work. Accessed September 21, 2023. https://decriminalizesex.work/why-decriminalization/organizations-endorsing-decriminalization/.

Oselin, Sharon S. *Leaving Prostitution: Getting Out and Staying Out of Sex Work.* New York: New York University Press, 2014.

Parrenas, Rhacel Salazar. *Servants of Globalization: Women, Migration and Domestic Work.* Stanford: Stanford University Press, 2001.

Peden, Kelsey. "After the Rescue: California's Legal Methods to Prevent Re-Trafficking," *SSRN*, December 15, 2020. https://ssrn.com/abstract=3835365

Pelto, Ashleigh. "Criminal Record Relief for Human Trafficking Survivors: Analysis of Current State Statutes and the Need for a Federal Model Statute." *Michigan Journal of Gender & Law* 27, no. 2 (2021): 473. https://repository.law.umich.edu/mjgl/vol27/iss2/6?utm_source=repository.law.umich.edu%2Fmjgl%2Fvol27%2Fiss2%2F6&utm_medium=PDF&utm_campaign=PDFCoverPages.

Perea, Juan F. "The Echoes of Slavery: Recognizing the Racist Origins of the Agricultural and Domestic Worker Exclusion from the National Labor Relations Act." *Ohio State Law Journal* 72, no. 1 (2011): 95–138.

Peters, Alicia. *Preventing Human Trafficking.* Gender Policy Report, University of Minnesota, January 25, 2023.

———. *Responding to Human Trafficking: Sex, Gender, and Culture in the Law.* Philadelphia: University of Pennsylvania Press, 2015.

Phillips, Suzannah, et al. *Clearing the Slate: Seeking Effective Remedies for Criminalized Trafficking Victims.* New York: International Women's Human Rights Clinic (IWHRC) at the City University of New York School of Law, 2014.

Pliley, Jessica. "From White Slavery to Anti-Prostitution, the Long View: Law, Policy and Sex Trafficking." In *Human Bondage and Abolition: New Histories of Past and Present Slaveries*, ed. Elizabeth Swanson and James Brewer Stuart. Cambridge: Cambridge University Press, 2018.

Polizzotti, Michael. *New Hampshire's Numbers: Resource Inequities by County and Population Group in 2014–2018.* New Hampshire Fiscal Policy Institute, 2020.

Popp, Evan. "Renewed Energy to Address Maine's 'broken' Mental Health Care System in Upcoming Session ." *Maine Morning Star*, November 15, 2023. https://mainemorningstar.com/2023/11/15/renewed-energy-to-address-maines-broken-mental-health-care-system-in-upcoming-session/.

The Power of Framing Human Trafficking as a Public Health Issue. Office on Trafficking in Person, Administration for Children & Families, U.S. Department of Health and Human Services. Last modified January 11, 2016. Accessed August 8, 2023. https://www.acf.hhs.gov/otip/report/resource/publichealthlens.

Quesada, James, Laurie Kain Hart, and Philippe Bourgois. "Structural Vulnerability and Health: Latino Migrant Laborers in the United States." *Medical Anthropology* 30, no. 4 (2011): 339–362. http://dx.doi.org/10.1080/01459740.2011.576725.

Raphael, Jody and Brenda Myers-Powell. *From Victims to Victimizers: Interviews with 25 Ex-Pimps in Chicago.* Minneapolis: DePaul College of Law, 2010.

Reid, Joan A., et al. "Human Trafficking of Minors and Childhood Adversity in Florida." *American Journal of Public Health* 107, no. 2 (February 1, 2017): 306–311. doi:10.2105/AJPH.2016.303564. https://www.ncbi.nlm.nih.gov/pmc/articles/PMC5227932/.

Ripe for Reform: Abuses of Agricultural Workers in the H-2A Visa Program. Centro de los Derechos del Migrante, Inc., 2020.

Rivera, Justice, ed. *Towards Bodily Autonomy Anthology: A Healing Justice Anthology Decolonizing Sex Work and Drug Use.* Justice Rivera, 2022.

Sanghera, Jyoti. "Unpacking the Trafficking Discourse." In *Trafficking and Prostitution Reconsidered*, ed. Kamala Kempadoo, Kamala, Jyoti Sanghera, and Bandana Pattanaik. Boulder: Paradigm Publishers, 2005.

Saulsberry, Loren, et al. "The Social Vulnerability Metric (SVM) as a New Tool for Public Health." *Health Services Research* 58, no. 4 (2023): 873–881. https://doi.org/10.1111/1475-6773.14102.

Scheper-Hughes, Nancy. "Ire in Ireland." *Ethnography* 1, no. 1 (2000): 117–140.

Schwarz, Corinne. "Theorizing Human Trafficking through Slow Violence." *Feminist Theory* 24, no. 4 (2022): 535–554. doi:10.1177/14647001211062731.

Schwarz, Corinne, et al. "The Trafficking Continuum: Service Providers' Perspectives on Vulnerability, Exploitation, and Trafficking." *Affilia* 34, no. 1 (2019): 116–132. https://doi.org/10.1177/0886109918803648.

Schwarz, Corinne, Emily J. Kennedy, and Hannah Britton. "Aligned Across Difference: Structural Injustice, Sex Work, and Human Trafficking." *Feminist Formations* 29, no. 2 (2017): 1–25. https://muse.jhu.edu/article/671715.

Selva, Jenn and Gregory Lemos. "Mom Says Southwest Airlines Thought She was Trafficking Her Biracial Daughter." *CNN*, November 7, 2021. https://www.cnn.com/2021/11/07/us/southwest-airlines-human-trafficking-accusation/index.html.

Shannon, Geordan D., et al. "¿Somos Iguales? Using a Structural Violence Framework to Understand Gender and Health Inequities from an Intersectional Perspective in the Peruvian Amazon." *Global Health Action* 10, sup. 2 (2017): 1330458. doi:10.1080/16549716.2017.1330458.

Shih, Elena. "Not in My 'Backyard Abolitionism': Vigilante Rescue Against American Sex Trafficking." *Sociological Perspectives* 59, no. 1 (2016): 66–90. http://dx.doi.org/10.1177/0731121416628551.

Shih, Elena and Joel Quirk. "Introduction: Do the Hidden Costs Outweigh the Practical Benefits of Human Trafficking Awareness Campaigns?" openDemocracy. June 20, 2019. https://www.opendemocracy.net/en/beyond-trafficking-and-slavery/introduction-do-hidden-costs-outweigh-practical-benefits-of-huma/.

Showden, Carisa Renae and Samantha Majic. *Youth Who Trade Sex in the U.S.: Intersectionality, Agency, and Vulnerability.* Philadelphia: Temple University Press, 2018.

Sigaud, Liam. "The 'Two Maines' by the Numbers." *The Maine Wire*, July 23, 2023. https://www.themainewire.com/2019/07/the-two-maines-by-the-numbers/.

Snajdr, Edward. "Beneath the Master Narrative: Human Trafficking, Myths of Sexual Slavery, and Ethnographic Realities." *Dialectical Anthropology* 37, no. 2 (2013): 229–256.

Soderlund, Gretchen. "Running from the Rescuers: New U.S. Crusades Against Sex Trafficking and the Rhetoric of Abolition." *NWSA Journal* 17, no. 3 (2005): 64–87.

Srikantiah, Jayashri. "Perfect Victims and Real Survivors: The Iconic Victim in Domestic Human Trafficking Law." *Boston University Law Review* 87, no. 157 (2007): 157–186.

Stevens, Jane. *Adding Layers to the ACEs Pyramid—what do You Think?* PACEsConnection (blog). April 7, 2015. https://www.pacesconnection.com/blog/adding-layers-to-the-aces-pyramid-what-do-you-think.

Stolz, Barbara. "Educating Policymakers and Setting the Criminal Justice Policymaking Agenda: Interest Groups and the 'Victims of Trafficking and Violence Act of 2000'." *Criminal Justice* 5, no. 4 (2005): 407–430.

Substance Abuse and Mental Health Services Administration. "Medications for Substance use Disorders." Last modified April 11, 2024. https://www.samhsa.gov/medications-substance-use-disorders.

———. "Mental Health and Substance use Disorders." Last modified June 9, 2023. https://www.samhsa.gov/find-help/disorders.

Suchland, Jennifer. *What's Wrong with the US Federal Response to "Sex Trafficking"?* Gender Policy Report, 2023. https://genderpolicyreport.umn.edu/whats-wrong-with-the-us-federal-response-to-sex-trafficking/.

Sudbury, Julia. *Global Lockdown: Race, Gender, and the Prison-Industrial Complex.* New York: Routledge, 2005.

Sue, Kimberly. *Getting Wrecked: Women, Incarceration, and the American Opioid Crisis.* Oakland: University of California Press, 2019.

"Take the Fair Chance Pledge!" Accessed September 21, 2023. https://bantheboxcampaign.org/.

Terwiel, A. "What is Carceral Feminism?" *Political Theory* 48, no. 4 (2020): 421–442. doi:10.1177/0090591719889946.

The Power of Framing Human Trafficking as a Public Health Issue. Office on Trafficking in Person, Administration for Children & Families, U.S. Department of Health and Human Services. Last modified January 11, 2016. Accessed August 8, 2023. https://www.acf.hhs.gov/otip/report/resource/publichealthlens.

Thulander, Sabrina and Caren Benjamin. *In Harm's Way: How Systems Fail Human Trafficking Survivors: Survey Results from the First National Survivor Study.* Washington, D.C.: Polaris, 2023.

Timmins, Annmarie. "'System is Broken': Mental Health Centers Seek $30 Million to Add Workers, Bolster Treatment." *New Hampshire Bulletin*, February 1, 2023. https://newhampshirebulletin.com/2023/02/01/system-is-broken-mental-health-centers-seek-30-million-to-add-workers-bolster-treatment/.

Title 17-A, §852: Aggravated Sex Trafficking, Public Law Chapter 35, (2013). https://www.mainelegislature.org/legis/statutes/17-a/title17-Asec852.html.

Title 17-A, §853: Sex Trafficking, Public Law Chapter 35, (2013). https://legislature.maine.gov/statutes/17-A/title17-Asec853.html.

Todres, Jonathan. "Moving Upstream: The Merits of a Public Health Law Approach to Human Trafficking." *North Carolina Law Review* 89, no. 2 (January, 2011): 447–506. https://papers.ssrn.com/sol3/papers.cfm?abstract_id=1742953.

Todres, Jonathan and Angela Diaz. *Preventing Child Trafficking: A Public Health Approach*. Baltimore: The Johns Hopkins University Press, 2019.

U.S. Administration for Children and Families. "Secretary Becerra Announces New HHS Task Force to Prevent Human Trafficking." Press Release. Released January 31, 2022. Accessed August 11, 2023. https://www.hhs.gov/about/news/2022/01/31/secretary-becerra-announces-new-hhs-task-force-to-prevent-human-trafficking.html.

U.S. Attorney's Office, District of Massachusetts "Dorchester Man Sentenced to 30 Years in Prison for Sex Trafficking of Minors." Press Release, May 19, 2016. Accessed July 30, 2023. https://www.justice.gov/usao-ma/pr/dorchester-man-sentenced-30-years-prison-sex-trafficking-minors.

U.S. Census Bureau. "Maine—Census Bureau Profile." Census Database. Accessed May 22, 2024. https://data.census.gov/profile/Maine?g=040XX00US23.

———. "New Hampshire—Census Bureau Profile." Census Database. Accessed May 22, 2024. https://data.census.gov/profile/New_Hampshire?g=040XX00US33#education.

———. "Race and Ethnicity in the United States: 2010 Census and 2020 Census." https://www.census.gov/library/visualizations/interactive/race-and-ethnicity-in-the-united-state-2010-and-2020-census.html.

U.S. Centers for Disease Control and Prevention. "Drug Overdose Mortality by State." Last modified March 1, 2022. https://www.cdc.gov/nchs/pressroom/sosmap/drug_poisoning_mortality/drug_poisoning.htm.

U.S. Department of Health and Human Services. "Human Trafficking Youth Prevention Education (HTYPE) Demonstration Program: Year 1 Reflections." Accessed September 20, 2023. https://www.acf.hhs.gov/opre/report/human-trafficking-youth-prevention-education-htype-demonstration-program-year-1.

U.S. Department of Health and Human Services Administration for Children & Families Children's Bureau. "Family Support Services." Accessed September 28, 2023. https://www.childwelfare.gov/topics/supporting/support-services/.

U.S. Department of Justice, District of Maine. "District of Maine Selected as Phase II Anti-Trafficking Coordination Team." Press Release, December 18, 2015. Accessed August 14, 2023. https://www.justice.gov/usao-me/pr/district-maine-selected-phase-ii-anti-trafficking-coordination-team.

U.S. Department of Justice Office of Public Affairs. "Defendant Who Exploited Opioid Addictions of Young Women Convicted of Crimes Related to Drug Trafficking and Prostitution." Press Release, March 25, 2019. Accessed July 19, 2023. https://www.justice.gov/opa/pr/defendant-who-exploited-opioid-addictions-young-women-convicted-crimes-related-drug.

U.S. Department of Justice Office of Public Affairs. "New Hampshire Man Sentenced to 21 Years in Prison for Sex Trafficking of a Minor and Other Crimes." Press Release, June 25, 2021. Accessed July 31, 2023. https://www.justice.gov/opa/pr/new-hampshire-man-sentenced-21-years-prison-sex-trafficking-minor-and-other-crimes.

U.S. Department of State. "3Ps: Prosecution, Protection, and Prevention." Accessed September 20, 2023. https://www.state.gov/3ps-prosecution-protection-and-prevention/.

U.S. Department of State Office to Monitor and Combat Trafficking in Persons. "U.S. Advisory Council on Human Trafficking." Accessed September 28, 2023. https://www.state.gov/u-s-advisory-council-on-human-trafficking/.

U.S. Federal Bureau of Investigation. "2019 Crime in the United States Table 43." Crime in the U.S. Database. Accessed June 7, 2024. https://ucr.fbi.gov/crime-in-the-u.s/2019/crime-in-the-u.s.-2019/tables/table-43.

Vance, Carole. "Innocence and Experience: Melodramatic Narratives of Sex Trafficking and their Consequences for Law and Policy." *History of the Present* 2, no. 2 (2012): 200–218.

———. "States of Contradiction: Twelve Ways to do Nothing about Trafficking while Pretending to." *Social Research* 78, no. 3 (2011): 933–948.

———. "Thinking Trafficking, Thinking Sex." *GLQ: A Journal of Lesbian and Gay Studies* 17, no. 1 (2010): 135–143.

Vasquez, Tina. "Human Trafficking or a Guest Worker Program? H-2A's Systemic Issues Result in Ratastrophic [sic] Violations." *Futuro Unidad Hinojosa, April 14, 2023.* https://futuroinvestigates.org/investigative-stories/head-down/human-trafficking-or-a-guest-worker-program-h-2as-systemic-issues-result-in-catastrophic-violations/.

Victims of Trafficking and Violence Protection Act of 2000, Public Law 106–386, 22 U.S.C. 7101 Et Seq. 2000.

Waitzkin, Howard. "One and a Half Centuries of Forgetting and Rediscovering: Virchow's Lasting Contributions to Social Medicine." *Classics in Social Medicine* 1, no. 2, (2005): 5–10. https://www.socialmedicine.info/index.php/socialmedicine/article/view/6

Walkowitz, Judith R. "The Maiden Tribute of Modern Babylon." In *City of Dreadful Delight: A Narrative of Sexual Danger in Late Victorian London.* Chicago: University of Chicago Press, 1992.

Weitzer, Ronald. "The Social Construction of Sex Trafficking: Ideology and Institutionalization of a Moral Crusade." *Politics and Society* 35, (2007): 447–475.

Wendelin, Greta. "A Rhetoric of Pornography: Private Style and Public Policy in the Maiden Tribute of Modern Babylon." *Rhetoric Society Quarterly* 42, no. 4 (2012): 375–396.

White, K. B. *Impact of Arrest and Conviction Histories on Trafficking Survivors.* Freedom Network USA, 2021.

The White House. "American Rescue Plan." Accessed September 28, 2023. https://www.whitehouse.gov/american-rescue-plan/.

———. "The National Action Plan to Combat Human Trafficking (NAP)." Accessed September 28, 2023. https://www.whitehouse.gov/wp-content/uploads/2021/12/National-Action-Plan-to-Combat-Human-Trafficking.pdf.

"Why Sex Work Should Be Decriminalized." Human Rights Watch. Accessed May 23, 2024. https://www.hrw.org/news/2019/08/07/why-sex-work-should-be-decriminalized.

Wilkinson, Richard G. and Michael Marmot. *The Solid Facts: Social Determinants of Health*. Copenhagen: WHO Regional Office for Europe, 1998.

World Health Organization. "Social Determinants of Health." Accessed May 21, 2024. https://www.who.int/health-topics/social-determinants-of-health#tab=tab_1.

Zarowsky, Christina, Slim Haddad, and Vinh-Kim Nguyen. "Beyond 'Vulnerable Groups': Contexts and Dynamics of Vulnerability." *Global Health Promotion* 20, (2012): 3–9. doi:10.1177/1757975912470062. http://ghp.sagepub.com.

Zhang, Sheldon. "Beyond the 'Natasha' Story—A Review and Critique of Current Research on Sex Trafficking." *Global Crime* 10, no. 3 (2009): 178–195.

INDEX

ACKNOWLEDGMENTS

It is overwhelming to try and convey my gratitude for all those who contributed to this book in a multitude of ways since the project's inception. There are so many people whom I cannot name for reasons of confidentiality but who were vital participants in the research that informs the book. Most important, I want to acknowledge and thank the survivors who shared their stories with me for their courage, openness, and honesty. I am inspired by their strength and grateful for the trust they put in me in hopes of stopping others from experiencing the types of situations they endured.

I also owe a multitude of thanks to the caseworkers, program directors, advocates, investigators, prosecutors, and other frontline workers who shared their experiences and insights on the trafficking response. Many also offered support and assistance with making introductions and coordinating interviews—without their help this book never would have happened. Several individuals who contributed to the research in important ways have since passed. I mourn their losses and am thankful for the valuable contributions they made to anti-trafficking work in Maine and New Hampshire. This project drew on more than my professional networks, and I am grateful to Katie Kondrat, Jason Stein, and Gary Cote for caring about the project and sharing their contacts with me.

At the University of New England, my colleagues in the College of Arts and Sciences, the School of Social and Behavioral Sciences, and the Gender, Women, and Sexuality Studies Program have been a source of support and camaraderie. Special thanks go to Julie Peterson, Jenny Stiegler-Balfour, Alex Campbell, Arthur Anderson, Sam McReynolds, Bridget Harr, Trish Long, Brian Duff, Ali Ahmeida, and Jennifer Tuttle. I am also grateful for the financial support provided by the University of New England. Two University Faculty Mini Grants and two sabbaticals made the research the book is based on and its writing possible.

Publishing with the University of Pennsylvania Press a second time has been a delightfully smooth process, and it has been a pleasure working with Walter Biggins, Mel Smith, and Noreen O'Connor-Abel as well as with Bert Lockwood, series editor of the Pennsylvania Studies in Human Rights series. I have deep appreciation for the two anonymous reviewers who provided engaged comments and valuable feedback and who made the book stronger as a result. Thank you also to Katie Van Heest for her artful editing, to Jess Herdman for her swift proofreading, and to Lisa Rivero for her always impeccable indexing skills.

Carole Vance has offered over two decades of friendship, support, and mentorship. Fifteen years after completing my dissertation, I still hear her voice and visualize the comments she might make as I write and edit. I am grateful for the carefully selected articles on pets, cooking, and strange anti-trafficking policies that she sends my way. I am also indebted to a number of other colleagues, mentors, and friends who have influenced my thinking on trafficking and forced labor over the years, including Ali Miller, Daniella Cameron, Denise Brennan, Elizabeth Bernstein, Florrie Burke, Pardis Mahdavi, Sealing Cheng, and Svati Shah.

Most of all, I am grateful to my family and friends who are my biggest source of support. I lost my father and greatest academic champion over the course of the project. My mom continues to gently ask about my writing progress and is a dedicated cheerleader. Geoff, Melissa, Ronnie, and Danny, thank you for being there. Thank you to the Cacciola family for their enthusiastic support—even Liz who continues to insist I change genres and start writing crime novels. The Wellesley "biddies"—Holly Danzeisen, Emily Krell, Meredith Gunlicks, Dawn Mechanic-Hamilton, and Rachel Wadsworth—have become my family over thirty years of friendship. I love you all. Eleanor Childs, you are a gem. Finally, Tara, Kleio, Evie, and our labradoodle, Emmylou, fill my heart with joy on a daily basis. Evie joined our family just prior to the start of this research and it's hard to remember a time before she was here smiling, giving hugs, and keeping us all entertained with her wit and charm. Kleio has grown and matured into an amazing, smart, and Taylor Swift-obsessed middle schooler since the start of the project and checks in from time to time about "that book you're writing." And, finally, my deepest thanks go to Tara, my best friend, partner, and co-parent for her endless encouragement, understanding, and dedication to good food and good times.

My name is on the cover of this book, but it is the survivors who are the true experts, and their voices are the ones most needed in discussions about how to prevent and end trafficking. I have tried to do justice to what they shared with me and hope their accounts will resonate with readers and result in a broader conception of anti-trafficking work and policy.

All royalties from this book will be donated to Freedom Network USA to support the organization's work advocating for improved access to services and legal protections for survivors and comprehensive human trafficking prevention.

www.ingramcontent.com/pod-product-compliance
Lightning Source LLC
LaVergne TN
LVHW091531200926
848483LV00002B/362

9781512827835